INTERNATIONAL LABOR STANDARDS

International Labor Standards

Globalization, Trade, and Public Policy

Edited by

ROBERT J. FLANAGAN

WILLIAM B. GOULD IV

STANFORD LAW AND POLITICS

An imprint of Stanford University Press • Stanford, California

Stanford University Press
Stanford, California
© 2003 by the Board of Trustees of the
Leland Stanford Junior University
Printed in the United States of America

Chapter 3, "Labor Law for a Global Economy: The Uneasy Case for International Labor Standards," was originally published in the *Nebraska Law Review* ©2001, Nebraska Law Review. Reprinted with permission.

Library of Congress Cataloging-in-Publication Data

International labor standards : globalization, trade, and public policy / edited by Robert J. Flanagan, William B. Gould IV.
    p.   cm.
Includes bibliographical references and index.
ISBN 0-8047-4690-7
    1. Labor laws and legislation, International.   2. International trade.
3. Globalization.   I. Flanagan, Robert J.   II. Gould, William B.

K1705 .I55   2003
341.7′63—dc21   2003012808

This book is printed on acid-free, archival-quality paper

Original printing 2004

Last figure below indicates year of this printing:
12   11   10   09   08   07   06   05   04   03

Designed and typeset at Stanford University Press in 10/13 Minion

Contents

Contributors

SARAH H. CLEVELAND is Marrs McLean Professor of Law at the University of Texas School of Law.

GARY S. FIELDS is Professor of Labor Economics and Chair of the Department of International and Comparative Labor, School of Industrial and Labor Relations, Cornell University.

ROBERT J. FLANAGAN is the Konosuke Matsushita Professor of International Labor Economics and Policy Analysis at the Graduate School of Business, Stanford University.

ENRIQUE DE LA GARZA TOLEDO is Professor of Sociology at the Metropolitan University in Mexico and a Visiting Professor at the University of California, Berkeley.

WILLIAM B. GOULD IV is the Charles A. Beardsley Emeritus Professor of Law at Stanford Law School and former Chairman of the U.S. National Labor Relations Board.

VIRGINIA A. LEARY is the Fromm Professor Emeritus of International and Comparative Law, University of California, Hastings College of the Law.

JUSTINE NOLAN is the former Director of the Workers Rights Program at the Lawyers' Committee for Human Rights in Washington, D.C.

MICHAEL POSNER is the Executive Director of the Lawyers' Committee for Human Rights and a member of the White House Apparel Industry Partnership Task Force.

INTERNATIONAL
LABOR STANDARDS

Introduction

ROBERT J. FLANAGAN

WILLIAM B. GOULD IV

For over fifty years, most countries of the world have reduced tariffs and other barriers to international commerce through a sequence of negotiations conducted under the auspices of the General Agreement on Tariffs and Trade (GATT) and its successor organization, the World Trade Organization (WTO). Over the same period, restrictions on international capital flows have also diminished substantially. The subsequent growth of trade and foreign direct investment (FDI) contributed importantly to postwar economic growth, but has also raised questions about the relationship between global economic integration and labor conditions. The conference that produced the papers in this volume invited a number of economists and legal scholars to consider the relationships between globalization and labor conditions and to assess alternative approaches to improving global labor conditions.

To provide some context, we note that the post–World War II expansion of trade and foreign investment actually represents the second major wave of globalization. Substantial increases in international trade, capital flows, and migration between 1820 and 1913 produced significant economic growth and convergence of living standards, particularly between North Atlantic nations. It is notable that international migration was the driving force: "[M]ass migration prior to the Great War probably accounted for about 70 percent of the overall real wage convergence observed in the Atlantic economy as a whole."[1] This first wave of globalization ended with increased barriers to migration in the receiving countries and large increases in tariffs during the period between the two world wars.

The GATT and WTO negotiations producing lower trade barriers did not address national restrictions on immigration, and an important difference between the two waves of globalization is the greater limitations on economically driven international migration in the more recent period. The limitations since the beginning of the twentieth century on this demonstrably powerful mechanism for narrowing differences in labor conditions between countries may have intensified concerns about the implications of global competition and/or the activities of multinational companies for labor. These same limitations on international migration may also have encouraged proposals for nonmarket approaches to improving labor conditions.

Both the free movement of labor and goods produce their own separate range of globalization victims and the political resistance that goes with each one. *The Economist* has noted that the "[g]aps in the prices of traded goods have become much smaller after many years of liberalization. Not so gaps in the wages of similarly qualified individuals in different parts of the world. So the gains from liberalizing immigration restrictions are vastly greater than those from further freeing the movement of goods or capital."[2] The U.S. Supreme Court's refusal to accord existing labor law remedies to undocumented workers within American borders heightens pressure to fill an international regulatory vacuum.[3]

International political responses to these concerns go back at least to the early years of the retreat from globalization with the establishment of the International Labor Organization (ILO) as a branch of the League of Nations in 1919 (and later the United Nations). Since then the ILO has developed over 180 "conventions," known more commonly as "labor standards," through negotiations between labor, management, and government representatives of member countries. The ILO conventions sometimes prescribed labor market outcomes (e.g., maximum hours, maternal protection) and sometimes prescribed policy "machinery" without prescribing the exact outcome (e.g., minimum wage fixing machinery, workers' compensation arrangements). Ratification of ILO conventions by member countries is voluntary and highly variable, however. (By 2002, the number of conventions actually ratified by member countries ranged from a low of 2 to a high of 128.) Uneven patterns of ratification by member countries and concerns that member countries do not always follow through by passing and enforcing domestic legislation to support ratified conventions have provoked doubts about the efficacy of the ILO approach, at least as historically constituted, however. Yet the data show a positive cross-country association between the number of ILO standards ratified and actual labor conditions.

During the 1990s, the ILO increasingly focused policy discussions on eight "core" or "fundamental" labor standards that arguably pertain to basic worker rights (freedom of association including collective bargaining, non-discrimination, bans on forced labor, and limits on child labor) rather than outcomes. Subsequently, some industrialized countries have proposed that the WTO link international labor standards to future trade policy discussions. One proposal would impose trade sanctions on countries that do not implement and enforce international labor standards. Developing countries generally oppose proposals to link discussions of trade policy and labor standards.

In organizing the conference, we sought to obtain some papers that would address issues raised by recent proposals to link trade policy and labor standards as well as papers that would consider the links between globalization and labor conditions more broadly. The proposals raise several challenging issues. Perhaps the most fundamental are: What market failures justify government regulation of labor standards? In the absence of international regulations, will countries degrade their labor conditions in order to obtain competitive advantages? Why should international standards override domestic political processes in determining a country's level of labor standards? What are the most effective forums for the development of international labor standards? What evidence is available on the comparative efficacy of increased trade and growth versus labor standards as mechanisms for improving labor conditions? Are there important alternatives to international regulation for improving labor standards? The papers in this volume are organized around these questions.

The dominant economic assertion underlying the proposals is that globalization produces a worldwide deterioration of labor conditions as countries try to compete in international markets by reducing labor costs in an effort to sell more exports or attract more FDI. This "race-to-the-bottom" view, initially addressed by two wide-ranging Organization for Economic Cooperation and Development (OECD) reports,[4] holds that good labor conditions are expensive, and each country in turn will degrade labor conditions in order to expand or maintain its share of international commerce, producing a global prisoner's dilemma.

The paper by Professor Robert J. Flanagan examines the empirical basis for this assertion. Professor Flanagan first investigates the nature of the relationship between political labor standards—ILO conventions ratified through domestic political processes—and the actual labor conditions that public policy presumably targets. While countries with superior labor conditions have on average ratified more ILO conventions than countries with poor labor conditions, the question of causality has not been explored previously. The positive correlation across countries between the number of ILO conventions ratified and the level of actual labor conditions might arise because countries that ratify the conventions then alter their domestic policies in order to improve labor conditions. Or, countries may avoid the costs of altering their domestic policies by ratifying only ILO conventions that they have already met. Which of the scenarios is true? A regression analysis of over one hundred countries at different stages of development indicates that the latter scenario explains the correlation. Perhaps more important, the analysis indicates that labor conditions (including measures of child labor, freedom of association, and health) are improved by economic growth and an open trade policy. The trade sanctions proposed to induce adoption of international labor standards would tend to worsen labor conditions. At the same time, ratifications of core and noncore labor standards have no significant effect on labor conditions.

Professor Flanagan's paper also uses the international database to assess the specifics of the race-to-the bottom argument. He finds that about 90 percent of the substantial international variation in manufacturing wages is explained by international variations in manufacturing productivity. Once productivity effects are held constant, ratifications of ILO core standards have no effect on wages in fixed effects estimation, although they do have some effect in the cross-section analyses. Flanagan argues that if poor labor standards do not lower labor costs (relative to productivity), the claim that countries with low labor standards enjoy superior export performance and attract more FDI lacks a firm basis. The last part of his paper reports additional regression analyses of the determinants of export and FDI performance. After controlling for general economic influences on these variables, the analysis reveals no influence of political labor standards, actual labor conditions, or unusually high or low wages (deviations of wages from productivity) on either export performance or FDI inflows. Taken as a whole, the empirical analysis in the Flanagan paper does not find that a race-to-the-bottom emerged during a period in which labor standards were effectively left to domestic political processes (since the costs of nonratification of ILO conventions were negligible). What then is the basis for international regulation to trump domestic political choices?

As noted earlier, proposals to link international labor standards and trade policy create divisions between some industrialized nations and most developing countries, which would prefer to let domestic political processes determine each country's level of standards. The paper by Professor Gary S. Fields assesses the concerns of the latter countries. After reviewing how the ILO has approached labor standards, Fields documents the developing country view that the policy proposals represent a type of protectionism in which rich countries try to rob poor countries of their comparative advantage. Developing countries instead argue that labor standards and conditions necessarily vary with the level of a country's development, as they have over the history of the currently industrialized nations. Professor Fields argues that the view of the developing countries is most persuasive for the noncore labor standards emphasized by the ILO earlier in its history, for many of these standards might have influenced labor market outcomes. On the other hand, Fields does not accept the view of developing countries for the core labor standards at the center of the current policy debate, since, in his view, they address basic worker rights rather than outcomes. Some of the other papers in this volume as well as some of the conference discussion questioned this distinction between rights and outcomes. Fields also notes that an alternative to using trade sanctions to impose a single set of political labor standards worldwide would be to simply require countries to enforce their own laws pertaining to labor conditions.

Professor William B. Gould IV discusses the evolution of law, both domestic and international, relating to international labor standards, as well as tariffs and other forms of protectionism. In discussing the contemporary scene, the Gould paper stresses the relationship between foreign aid, as well as international human rights and criminal jurisprudence, and the development of international labor standards.

The paper examines the rationale for international standards—whether public or private—at the international, regional, and national levels. It notes that no research, including the OECD studies that are examined in the paper, yet focuses upon China and the relationship between its policies and the "race-to-the-bottom" phenomenon. The paper examines the argument that the movement toward international standards is inherently protectionist. It also examines the way in which national policies can compensate free trade's losers, thus assuaging protectionist impulses.

The paper discusses which issues are appropriate to the regulation of international labor standards and what forum and machinery ought to be promoted. Here, the paper looks at the International Labor Organization, World Trade Organization, and regional machinery such as the North American Free Trade Agreement (NAFTA). It then discusses the fast-track debate as well as methods for resolution of such disputes, including corporate codes of conduct.

Professor Sarah H. Cleveland, in her paper, notes the trend toward increased nation-state ratification of International Labor Organization conventions and the fact that the number of countries ratifying so-called core conventions doubled between 1995 and 2002. She also notes the resurgence of the ILO through its Working Party on the Social Aspects of Globalization and the World Commission on the Social Dimension of Globalization as a follow-up to its implementation of its 1998 Declaration of Rights, as well as the ILO's aggressive stance vis-à-vis Myanmar and its policy of forced labor. Professor Cleveland then describes regional and bilateral labor standards mechanisms such as those undertaken by the European Community; the NAFTA involving the United States, Mexico, and Canada; and the Common Market of the South (MERCOSUR). She notes the attention now given to labor standards by international financial organizations such as the World Bank, International Monetary Fund, the Inter-American Development Bank, and the African Development Bank. And she notes the two-decade-old trend toward unilateral actions in both the United States and the European Union.

One of the most interesting features of the Cleveland paper is the description and analysis given of transnational litigation, which is designed to promote international labor standards in American domestic courts. It may be that such litigation, along with the corporate codes of conduct and social labeling initiatives that she describes, are the most important first or fundamental steps forward toward the promotion of international and regional machinery designed to accomplish the same objectives.

Professor Cleveland then analyses the case for international labor standards and finds that it has merit. She notes that the rationale for international labor standards is the same one as that for international human rights standards generally—that is, that a minimum standard of conduct is appropriate and that so much that has been regulated domestically is now the object of international regulation and oversight. Here she illustrates the international instruments already in place, with some reference to the emergence of the ILO itself. Additionally, Professor Cleveland sees labor standards as existing so as to prevent "the exploitation of labor as a means of gaining a trade advantage."

The Cleveland paper also discusses the linkage between labor and trade and the question of which labor standards are appropriate for regulation in a globalized economy. With regard to the latter, Professor Cleveland starts with the so-called fundamental rights but would expand coverage to include "ILO core standards plus" protection from very hazardous working conditions and subsistence wages, as well as protection for migrant workers. Since core standards will themselves impose labor costs, the principal consideration should not be whether the standard has a neutral impact on labor costs but rather whether it is "sufficiently fundamental to the life and well-being of employees to warrant status as a core labor standard." In her view, beyond a certain level, the comparative advantage for developing countries should not be tolerated. She finds that three of the four core standards—that is, freedom of association, nondiscrimination, and forced labor—are sufficiently fundamental to apply regardless of a country's level of development. Regarding child labor, she notes more flexibility and that the prohibition has less clear support in general human rights instruments. While she concedes that wage levels and health and safety are correlated with the level of a country's development, nonetheless she states that below a "relative baseline" certain practices are unacceptable. Professor Cleveland emphasizes that she is not advocating the universal minimum wage. Rather, her focus is upon a living wage, though she notes the complexity of that quest. Finally, Professor Cleveland suggests a compromise between the industrialized and developing nations constituting a quid pro quo for Western state protection of migrants and developing states accepting other core labor standards.

Professor Virginia A. Leary's paper begins by asking what form international labor standards should take and inquiring about the rationale for the ILO adoption of certain "core" labor standards as well as its Declaration. She begins by referencing the reasons for American lack of attention to the ILO: that is, (1) an antigovernment American philosophy of collective bargaining and autonomy for the parties in the process; (2) failure to ratify most ILO conventions because of deeply engrained American unilateralism; and (3) a failure on the part of the United States itself to adhere to ILO standards domestically, particularly under the National Labor Relations Act.

Professor Leary examines the question of whether treaties are the best form for labor standards and concludes that in both the labor and environmental arena they are "remarkably adaptable." She chronicles the recent ILO initiatives, which Professor Cleveland identifies as well, and she notes recent attempts to collaborate with the WTO, the World Bank, and other international institutions. She remarks that the refusal by the WTO to consider international labor standards has renewed anew the relevance of the ILO.

Professor Leary then considers the issue of linkage between labor and trade and notes that the issue of economic competitiveness emerged as early as the nineteenth century. She notes that the issue of protectionism is alive and well, and "invocation of labor standards may serve as a pretext" for it. Her paper describes the treatment of labor matters by the WTO and notes the rejection of the so-called social clause tying labor and trade liberalization together. Here Professor Leary notes the WTO *Asbestos Case* decision, concluding that France was entitled to prohibit a certain type of asbestos from Canada on the grounds of a risk to health.

Professor Leary takes note of the politics involved in the development of NAFTA and limitations in that instrument. She then goes on to discuss multinational corporations in the context of the so-called ILO Tripartite Declaration on Multinational Enterprises and Social Policy, which are devised to guide the voluntary efforts of governments, employers, and workers' organi-

zations in adopting social policies. She examines the monitoring efforts of the
ILO and subtly criticizes aspects of such initiatives as the unwillingness of a
public body like the ILO to identify parties by name when making submis-
sions to it. She notes that no independent examination of the influence and
effectiveness of the Tripartite Declaration has been made. Leary writes that
"[t]he timidity of the ILO twenty-two years ago when the Declaration was
adopted was perhaps understandable, but is less so today when the subject of
labor rights and multinational enterprises is so clearly on the international
agenda."

Professor Leary then describes the OECD Declaration on International
Investment and Multinational Enterprises. She notes that the influence of
the ILO core labor standards and the Declaration, as well as an obligation for
employers to provide information to employee representatives as needed for
meaningful negotiations and to observe standards not less favorable than
those in the host country of a multinational, are a substantial portion of the
cornerstone of the OECD guidelines. Similarly, she takes note of the provisions obliging employers to ensure occupational health and safety and to
provide reasonable notice in the event that a closure that triggers collective
dismissals is instituted.

Professor Leary concludes by noting the perceived ineffectiveness of the
ILO inside the United States and yet draws attention to areas of effectiveness
in other parts of the world. She concludes that the OECD guidelines may be
one of the most promising areas of intergovernmental approaches to business social policy, notwithstanding their nonbinding nature. Professor Leary
concludes by noting that "form *and* function are important in the development of international labor standards, but the function but not the form remains primary."

Another approach that has been proposed to mitigate the impact of
globalization on labor conditions is regulating the conduct of multinational
companies rather than nation-states. Critiques of globalization frequently include the suspicion that multinational companies may degrade, or at least do
not improve, local labor conditions in the countries in which they operate.
Such evidence that exists indicates that on average, multinational companies
pay higher wages than local (host-country) firms for a given skill of worker.
Some of the discomfort with the activities of multinationals may reflect the

fact that they accept local practices and standards that are not tolerated in home countries. While the labor practices of multinationals are not subject to direct regulation by international bodies, there have been many efforts to develop and implement voluntary codes of conduct for multinational companies, both privately and by international organizations.

The paper by Michael Posner and Justine Nolan examines the rich diversity of codes of conduct and the issues that must be addressed in developing such codes. With hundreds of companies now publicly committed to upholding basic labor standards, they find that corporate codes now include a wide variety of subjects both within and without the core standards. They note the wide variety of reasons that may be responsible for the adoption of the codes—that is, "activist pressure, brand preservation and/or recognition of their responsibility to respect basic human rights."

Regarding the scope of corporate codes, the authors note the fact that some codes explicitly require compliance on the part of the company's sub contractors or suppliers, while others are silent on this issue. While some industry or trade association groups have come together to devise common standards and reporting mechanisms, many companies devise independent codes. Both the paper and the conference discussion brought out some inherent limitations on the coverage of corporate codes of conduct. Much employment in developing countries is likely to be in the informal sector, whereas multinationals operate in the formal sector. (The coverage of subcontractors may be important here.) Even within the formal sector, companies with widely recognized brands have the strongest incentives to implement codes, for it is easiest for consumers to express their views on labor conditions with branded goods through boycotts or other activities. Finally, there is the question, raised earlier in the discussion of international regulation of labor standards, of whether corporate codes of conduct actually change corporate behavior. Codes of conduct may simply reflect pre-existing labor conditions at a company. Such codes would identify companies with superior labor practices, but would not signal a change in practices.

With regard to monitoring, the authors discuss multi-stakeholder codes that provide external monitoring initiatives as well as those that provide for direct or indirect government involvement through the OECD guidelines or the more recent UN Global Compact. The authors note that the challenge to monitoring is considerable and that the issue is critical. As they state, the question is who, how, what, and where to monitor along the supply chain. They note that there are four critical characteristics in the monitoring process: (1) applying measurable, meaningful standards; (2) independence of monitors; (3) transparency in reporting; and (4) incorporation of local non-governmental organization (NGO) and union dimensions. After examining these criteria, the authors discuss the potential interplay between public and private procedures and discuss particular cases, such as the apparel industry and the Fair Labor Association, as well as Cambodia's apparel factories and child labor in the soccer ball industry in Pakistan.

Notwithstanding the importance of general theoretical arguments and statistical findings, we wished to include an in-depth case study of how labor conditions have changed in a developing country that has pursued more open trade policies. The paper by Professor Enrique de la Garza Toledo provides a profile of changes in Mexican labor markets during a period of expanding international trade. Professor de la Garza points out that Mexico reduced trade barriers in 1986, some years before the completion of NAFTA. He then provides a portrait of a transitional dual economy, in which technology, real wages, and employment have improved in larger firms in the export sector, while labor conditions remain at best unchanged in the rest of the economy. Moreover, he argues that there has been little spillover from the gains of firms in the export sector to other firms via outsourcing and other commercial links.

Professor de la Garza argues that since the mid-1980s, more flexible labor relations, public policy efforts to link wage increases to productivity increases, and a diminished role for Mexican labor unions have accompanied the expansion in trade. This has occurred within Mexico's government-dominated corporatist institutional framework and has produced strains within the traditional labor institutions that culminated in 1997 with the secession of several large unions from the Labor Congress to form the National Workers' Union. Professor de la Garza provides an assessment of how this last development is likely to alter the traditional relationships between unions, employers, and the government in Mexico. At the same time, NAFTA may have accelerated efforts to reform Mexican labor laws to permit greater workplace flexibility, which is likely to increase tensions within labor's ranks and further challenge the viability of the traditional labor market institutions. While no reform has yet passed, the dominant proposals mainly reflect employer interests in meeting the challenges of increased international competition. Professor de la Garza's account accords little role in improving labor conditions to the ratification of ILO conventions by the Mexican government, but he argues that the Labor Side Conditions to NAFTA may have a more powerful influence.

There are three major unresolved problems for which our conference did not provide explicit treatment. The first relates to the prospect of new regional trade agreements beyond the United States–Canada–Mexico NAFTA agreement discussed by Professor de la Garza. What does the NAFTA experience portend for them? The 2002 election of Ignatio de la Silva (Lula) as president of Brazil will surely affect both free trade negotiations pertaining to all of Latin America as well as the labor provisions that are part of such instruments.

Second, the role of the International Labor Organization in the international labor standards dialogue may be affected by its new Global Commission, which is scheduled to issue a report by the end of 2003. The absence of a legal instrument to enforce the ILO 1998 Declaration of Rights could turn the ILO toward different mechanisms and new avenues.

And finally there is the note on which this introductory discussion began—that is, the immigration issue, which must be part of the globalization debate. The failure of the United States and Mexico to address this matter in the wake of September 11, 2001, as well as the European Union's impending admittance of previously Soviet bloc labor that will gravitate toward the West, means that the immigration debate will be ever more insistent. Future discussions must give it more attention.[5]

Acknowledgment

The co-editors would like to acknowledge their deep appreciation for the assistance provided by Ms. Sarah Preston during all phases of the conference preparation. Her relentless competence, sound advice, and good humor made even the most challenging tasks manageable. This volume is stronger because of her efforts.

Notes

1. Kevin H. O'Rourke and Jeffrey G. Williamson, *Globalization and History* (Cambridge: MIT Press, 1999), p. 273.

2. "Survey of Migration: A Modest Contribution," *The Economist* (London), Nov. 2–8, 2002, p. 15.

3. *Hoffman Plastic Compounds, Inc. v. NLRB*, 535 U.S. 137 (Mar. 27, 2002).

4. Organization for Economic Cooperation and Development, *Trade, Employment, and Labour Standards: A Study of Core Workers' Rights and International Trade* (1996); OECD, *International Trade and Core Labour Standards* (2000).

5. "The European Union: Eastward Ho!" *The Economist*, Dec. 7, 2002, p. 45: "The EU's current members have insisted on an interim of seven years before there is fully free movement of labour."

Labor Standards and International Competitive Advantage

ROBERT J. FLANAGAN

D o countries with low labor standards obtain inherent advantages in markets for international trade and investment? This question is at the heart of protracted debates about whether the trade benefits accorded members of the World Trade Organization (WTO) should be conditional on adherence to international labor standards developed by the International Labor Organization (ILO).

Contemporary discussions of the relationship between labor standards and trade policy reflect a conflict between two points of view. One camp sees the adoption of labor standards proposed by the ILO as an important mechanism for improving the condition of labor, particularly in developing countries, but at least implicitly acknowledges that such standards may raise production costs. This group therefore argues that countries that fail to adopt key labor standards acquire unfair international competitive advantage over countries that ratify the ILO standards and proposes WTO actions to curb purported advantages. A second camp contends that the implementation of such policies could become a form of protectionism by robbing developing countries of their comparative advantage.[1] Politically, some industrialized countries subscribe to the first position. Most developing countries subscribe to the second.

The "unfair economic advantage" view presumes that (1) national political processes fail to correct market failures producing poor labor conditions, (2) ratification of ILO labor standards leads to improved labor conditions, and (3) improved conditions raise the cost of labor sufficiently to reduce international competitiveness. Efforts to preserve international competitiveness then lead nations to degrade labor standards in a "race to the bottom," according to this view. An alternative view of the political economy of international labor standards predicts that countries are most likely to ratify standards that they have already attained, so that the symbolic act of ratification has no implications for labor costs and international competitiveness. In fact, little is known about either the interaction between the "political" labor standards formulated by the ILO and actual labor conditions or their relationship to international trade and investment patterns.

This paper addresses these important empirical issues using a panel sample of about one hundred countries at different stages of development for the period 1980 to 1999. After reviewing the nature of ILO labor standards (Section I), the paper examines the determinants of labor conditions and tests for the impact of adopting international labor standards (Section II). The estimation procedures recognize that the ratification of labor standards by a country is an endogenous political act. In particular, ratification is least costly for countries that have already attained those standards. This part of the paper finds that the adoption of international labor standards does not influence labor rights and conditions, but ratification of ILO standards is instead a function of a country's labor conditions, which improve with economic development. Contrary to claims by some opponents of globalization, the empirical analysis also finds that countries with an open trade policy or a large trade sector do not have inferior labor conditions, given their stage of development.

The empirical analysis then addresses the question of whether poor labor conditions and/or an absence of political labor standards produces low labor costs (Section III). About 90 percent of the international variation in real labor costs is associated with cross-country differences in labor productivity. To the extent that poor labor conditions contribute to low productivity, countries with poor labor conditions will be low wage countries. Yet the analysis finds neither direct nor indirect effects of ratification or other measures of labor standards on labor costs.

Section IV tests for connections between labor standards and trade and investment patterns. If ratification of ILO standards does not influence labor costs, the argument that nonratification provides a competitive advantage would seem to disappear. Nonetheless, the paper provides direct tests of the hypotheses that low labor standards produce superior export performance or attract more foreign direct investment (FDI). Consistent with the evidence for labor costs, ratification activity and other measures of labor standards are not significantly related to either exports or FDI. The analyses also find that countries with unusually low (high) wages (relative to productivity) do not have higher (lower) exports and FDI. On the other hand, free trade policies have a powerful positive influence on trade and investment flows. In summary, this analysis of a diverse cross-section of countries over the past twenty years finds no support for the key empirical propositions underlying the race-to-the-bottom arguments for tying labor standards to WTO trade policies.

I. "Political" Labor Standards

Debates over potential links between international labor standards and trade policy are remarkably brief about the interplay between a political act (the ratification of an ILO labor standard) and the actual condition of labor in a country. Indeed, the implicit assumption that the political act influences labor conditions appears unexamined. This section provides background on the "political labor standards" developed by the ILO and ratified by some member countries.[2]

Founded in 1919, the International Labor Organization is the only surviving major creation of the Treaty of Versailles, which created the League of Nations. In 1946 it became the first specialized agency of the United Nations, and it remains the only UN agency in which worker and employer representatives participate as equal partners with governments. The preamble to the ILO anticipates modern race-to-the-bottom (RTTB) arguments in stating "the failure of any nation to adopt humane conditions of labour is an obstacle in the way of other nations which desire to improve the conditions in their own countries."[3] The ILO pursues its mandate to promote "internationally recognized human and labour rights" by formulating "international labour standards in the form of Conventions and Recommendations setting minimum standards of basic labour rights."[4]

By February 2002, the ILO had formulated 184 conventions pertaining to labor conditions ranging from the very general to the very particular.[5] There are now 175 member countries, and the number of ratifications of operative conventions (existing at least ten years) ranges from a high of 160 (forced labor convention) to a low of 1 (wages, hours of work, and manning [sea] convention). The most widely ratified conventions address general issues such as equal remuneration, the right to organize and bargain collectively, and employment discrimination, while the least frequently adopted address labor conditions for narrowly defined worker groups. Conventions bind only member countries that ratify them, and even these countries may denounce previously ratified conventions after ten years from the date on which the Convention first takes effect.

The ILO, other international organizations, and several external constituencies now emphasize eight "fundamental" or "core" labor standards, which address issues of forced labor (conventions on forced labor [1930] and the abolition of forced labor [1957]), freedom of association (conventions on freedom of association and protection of right to organize [1948] and the right to organize and bargain collectively [1948]), discrimination (conventions on equal remuneration [1951] and discrimination in employment and occupation [1958]), and child labor (conventions on minimum age [1973] and worst forms of child labor [1999]). On their face, the ILO core conventions seek to establish worker rights rather than direct economic outcomes. (For example, the minimum age of employment convention leaves the determination of a specific minimum age to each country within parameters set by the convention.) That said, ratification of most core conventions would influence labor market outcomes, *if ratification altered labor market arrangements in member countries.* By reducing labor supply, for example, abolition of forced labor and minimum age requirements should raise wages of some jobs. Similarly, legislation that facilitates collective bargaining is likely to produce changes in pay and working conditions in at least some sectors. Whether these impacts are appropriate at all stages of development has been part of the ongoing debate over labor standards and trade policy.

Ratification of the core conventions varies widely among member countries. As of February 2002, about one-third of the member countries had ratified all eight core conventions (with considerable ratification activity after 1998).[6] The United States is one of four countries that have ratified only two fundamental conventions.[7] Interestingly, while the United States has ratified conventions addressing child labor and forced labor, it has not ratified the four conventions addressing freedom of association and discrimination—two areas of human rights in which the country has strong domestic legislation. This observation signals much broader interpretive issues to which we shall return in later sections.

ILO enforcement resources consist of carrots, not sticks, and the costs incurred by countries that fail to ratify ILO conventions seem low. The ILO constitution permits the ILO to ask member countries to explain why they have not ratified particular conventions (Article 19), to report on the implementation of conventions that they have ratified (Article 22), and (since 1998) to report on efforts to address the principles of core labor standards that have not been ratified. Compliance with reporting requirements is low. The ILO also provides technical and financial assistance to countries seeking to improve enforcement of ILO conventions.

Article 26 empowers the ILO to investigate noncompliance complaints. After an investigation and report of findings by a Commission of Inquiry, the ILO may only recommend changes in a member country's laws and practices. The ILO website observation that "[t]he complaints procedure has not been used often" seems well supported by the fact that there have been only twenty-five Article 26 complaints since 1960 (six during the 1990s). If countries ignore ILO recommendations, the ILO cannot impose direct sanctions, but Article 33 permits it to recommend that member countries take appropriate action.[8] These features of ILO activities condition the empirical analysis of political labor standards and labor conditions (including labor rights) in Section II.

II. Ratification and Labor Conditions

Does ratification of "political" labor standards improve labor conditions? If ratification of ILO conventions leads to the passage and enforcement of national legislation that alters working conditions, international labor standards may improve the condition of labor. As the prior section clarifies, however, nonratification of ILO conventions is virtually costless. In contrast, ratification of ILO conventions that require the passage and implementation of new domestic legislation to alter labor conditions can impose significant domestic economic and political costs on a country. Why would countries commit to potentially costly domestic actions by ratifying ILO conventions, when the costs of nonratification are low?

This political calculus implies that countries that ratify the standards are likely to be the countries for which ratification is least costly in terms of adjusting national legislation and institutions, notably member countries whose national legislation already provides protections that are at least as strong as those proposed in the ILO convention. In this scenario, the causality is reversed, with gains in human development leading and facilitating the ratification of political labor standards. Ratification is a purely symbolic act.

Any effort to determine the effects of ratifying ILO conventions on labor conditions must disentangle the opposing directions of causality in these two scenarios. The empirical work reported in the rest of this section addresses this issue by studying the determinants of (1) ratification behavior and (2) labor rights and conditions. These two relationships are summarized by the following two-equation system:

$$(1)\ \text{RATIFY} = f(\text{LABCOND, OPENNESS, X})$$
$$(2)\ \text{LABCOND} = g(\text{RATIFY, OPENNESS, Z})$$

Equation (1) summarizes the ideas that the ratification of ILO conventions depends on (a) domestic costs of ratification (i.e., the hypothesis that ratification is positively related to the current level of labor conditions, LABCOND), (b) the openness of the economy to international trade (more open economies may be more reluctant to ratify ILO conventions if they believe that ratification raises labor costs), and (c) a vector of variables, X, capturing the prevailing cultural values and norms of a country. These variables, which include measures of the dominant religion in the country and the nature of the legal system, go to the question of why different countries might choose different labor conditions for themselves.

Studies of the effect of religious institutions on economic development emphasize that the Muslim and Catholic religions were historically opposed to institutions that facilitated economic development (Landes, 1998; La Porta et al., 1999), while Protestantism fostered a strong work ethic (Weber, 1958). More important for political expressions regarding workers' rights and conditions, however, are shifts within the Catholic church that have produced papal encyclicals supportive of workers rights since at least the 1930s, as well as a general support for democratization since the 1960s (Huntington, 1968). Legal institutions, on the other hand, mediate the relative power of the state and the individual. At one extreme, socialist systems accord the state a dominant role in the ownership of property and control of resource allocation. At the other extreme, common law systems place dominant emphasis on the private rights of individuals and take a more skeptical stance toward the role of the state. Civil law systems take an intermediate position. These characterizations hint at the attractiveness of legal systems as an institutional influence on levels of economic development (La Porta et al., 1999). The influence of legal systems on labor standards is less well defined. In respecting the private rights of individuals, common law systems may weight private ownership rights highly and resist government intervention favoring labor standards (relative to other legal systems).[9] On the other hand, socialist systems are presumably reluctant to accord rights that would interfere with the state's resource allocation and rent-extraction activities.

Equation (2) summarizes the ideas that actual labor conditions in a country depend on (a) the ratification of ILO conventions (RATIFY), (b) international trade or trade policy (OPENNESS), and (c) nonpolicy determinants of labor conditions, Z. The hypothesis that the political act of ratifying ILO conventions improves actual labor rights and conditions has been discussed above and predicts a significantly positive influence of RATIFY on LABCOND. Some proponents of tying labor standards to trade policy also claim that labor conditions deteriorate with globalization. Equation (2) includes the OPENNESS variables to test this hypothesis. Addressing these policy questions requires a model that holds constant factors that determine labor conditions in the absence of international trade or labor standards. An obvious candidate for Z is the level of economic development (per capita income). Higher per capita income permits the allocation of increasing amounts of time to nonmarket activities (e.g., shifting children from employment to schooling) and also permits better diets, health care, and other activities contributing to longer life expectancy. Moreover, higher income societies can "afford" to limit workplace externalities—for example, by regulating workplace health and safety.

The regression analyses of equations (1) and (2) are conducted on data for about one hundred countries in 1980 and 1990.[10] Measures of both the num-

ber of noncore ILO conventions (NONCORE LS) and the number of core
ILO conventions (CORE LS) ratified by a country alternately appear as
measures of RATIFY. The list of variables that might be used as proxies for
labor conditions (LABCOND) is potentially large, but practically limited by
availability of data for a broad sample of countries.[11] This analysis uses measures of child labor, civil liberties, and the health of the workforce (which
should capture the consequences of alternative but less available measures of
labor conditions, such as hours of work, and workplace safety). Wage levels
are analyzed separately in the next section. The labor force participation of
children ten to fourteen years old provides a measure of the extent of child
labor (CHILDLAB) in a country, while civil liberties (CIVLIB) are measured
by an index ranging from 1 to 7, with a score of 1 indicating the most liberties.[12] These two variables appear directly relevant to the core labor standards
addressing child labor and freedom of association rights. Life expectancy at
birth (LIFEEXP) provides a measure of health status.

The regression analyses test three measures of the international openness
(OPENNESS) of an economy. EXPORT and TRADE, respectively, represent
the shares of exports and exports plus imports in GDP. OPEN is a dummy
variable taking the value 1 if a country is open and 0 if it is closed. A country
is closed if any of the following holds: nontariff barriers cover 40 percent or
more of trade, the average tariff rate equals or exceeds 40 percent, the "black
market premium" equals or exceeds 20 percent, a socialist economic system
prevails, or there is a state monopoly on major exports.[13] The remaining explanatory variables in the ratification regressions seek to capture the prevailing cultural values that would influence a country's ratification process.
Following La Porta et al. (1999) and Chau and Kanbur (2001), the analysis
tests for the effect of a country's legal system on ratifications with a set of
dummy variables for British common law (the omitted reference category in
the regressions), French civil law, German civil law, Scandinavian civil law,
and socialist law. A vector of dummy variables taking the value 1 for the religion of the majority of a country's population and 0 otherwise tests for the
effects of religious values on the ratification process.[14]

Analysis of Ratification Behavior

Tables 1 and 2 report the three-stage least squares (3SLS) results of cross-country regressions of NONCORE LS and CORE LS on the variables discussed above.[15] Two considerations govern the application of 3SLS. As discussed earlier, causality could in principle run from ratifications to labor conditions (exogenous ratifications) or from labor conditions to ratifications (endogenous ratifications). Equations (1) and (2), which capture this joint dependency, should be estimated as a simultaneous system to sort out the direction-of-influence question. Secondly, ratifications of core and noncore labor standards measure a country's *effective* legal labor standards with error. Identification of the countries that have ratified an unusually high or unusually low number of core labor standards (given their economic and social characteristics) highlights this issue. Relative to predicted numbers of ratifications, the Central African Republic, Ghana, Honduras, Niger, and Zambia have ratified the most core standards, while Botswana, El Salvador, Gambia, and the United States have ratified the fewest.[16] Some countries may ratify a labor standard but fail to pass and enforce supportive national legislation, while other countries with domestic policies that meet or exceed ILO conventions may not ratify them because of technical inconsistencies between domestic legislation and the conventions. By instrumenting the ratification variables, 3SLS estimation provides an approach to correcting the measurement error and estimating the impact of effective labor standards on labor conditions.

The first three regressions in Table 1 analyze the relationship between the three measures of labor conditions and noncore ratifications as of 1980. Each indicator of labor conditions is statistically significant, with signs supporting the view that countries ratify standards that they have already attained. (Recall that lower values of CHILDLAB and CIVLIB signify superior conditions.) Of the measures of openness to trade, trial regressions indicated that the overall TRADE measure is superior to EXPORT and OPEN. Since the (unreported) coefficient on EXPORT is measured much less precisely, the combined results imply that domestic, import-competing industries have a stronger influence than export industries on ratification policy. Nonetheless, one should not make too much of this particular result. The strongest result implies that it would take a trade-to-GDP ratio difference of 14 percentage points between countries to produce a difference of one ratification.

TABLE 1
Noncore Ratifications (3SLS Estimates)

Independent variables	1980			1990		
	(1)	(2)	(3)	(4)	(5)	(6)
CHILDLAB	−0.590 (.119)*			−0.891 (.175)*		
CIVLIB		−4.921 (1.124)*			−7.233 (1.549)*	
LIFEEXP			0.945 (.207)*			1.292 (.267)*
TRADE	−0.072 (.039)***	−0.044 (0.030)	−0.044 (0.036)	−0.100 (.041)**	−0.078 (.033)**	−0.093 (.040)**
CATHO	14.679 (6.215)**	12.313 (5.677)**	16.545 (6.479)*	16.071 (7.536)**	13.658 (6.841)**	14.908 (7.328)**
HINDU	5.847 (9.746)	2.718 (8.568)	9.161 (9.960)	7.248 (12.293)	10.331 (10.871)	8.631 (12.201)
MUSLIM	13.651 (6.397)**	8.964 (5.619)	16.891 (7.070)**	13.955 (7.791)***	9.969 (6.461)	14.832 (7.986)***
OTHERCHR	5.984 (6.303)	4.159 (5.336)	8.444 (6.636)	9.890 (7.073)	6.875 (6.710)	7.593 (7.442)
OTHER	13.284 (7.631)***	7.080 (6.556)	17.768 (8.428)**	11.687 (9.159)	6.348 (7.230)	12.763 (9.512)
FRENCHL	2.802 (3.164)	3.780 (2.682)	5.608 (3.161)***	8.214 (3.721)**	6.852 (3.192)**	10.304 (3.873)*
GERMANL	−5.013 (6.966)	−6.678 (6.304)	−3.860 (6.765)	−6.383 (7.655)	−8.519 (6.878)	−8.952 (7.472)
SCANDL	22.518 (8.762)	16.458 (8.039)**	19.878 (8.551)**	25.984 (9.725)*	16.574 (8.481)**	22.056 (9.456)**
SOCIALIST	5.079 (6.808)	2.131 (5.921)	6.048 (6.748)	6.038 (7.479)	.180 (6.527)	5.238 (7.605)
Constant	28.260	37.938	−45.010	32.528	47.959	−60.733
R^2	0.288	0.224	0.339	0.246	0.314	0.378
Root MSE	13.818	14.135	13.276	17.109	16.070	15.385
Number of obs.	101	107	102	92	95	92

SOURCES: See Appendix A.
*p-value < .01.   ** p-value < .05.   *** p-value < .10.

Turning to variables representing cultural influences on the ratification process, the results indicate that the religious makeup of a country can be an important influence on ratification. Relative to Confucian states, Muslim, Catholic, and "other" (Jewish) countries ratify significantly more labor standards, and relative to the British common law system, countries with a Scandinavian civil law system ratify more ILO conventions, ceteris paribus. Ratifications are not significantly different in countries with socialist legal systems.[17]

TABLE 2
Core Ratifications (3SLS)

Independent variables	1980			1990		
	(1)	(2)	(3)	(4)	(5)	(6)
CHILDLAB	−.034 (.013)**			−.049 (.017)*		
CIVLIB		−.151 (.138)			−.227 (.166)	
LIFEEXP			0.041 (.024)**			0.050 (.026)***
TRADE	−.005 (.004)	−.001 (.004)	−.001 (.004)	−.005 (.004)	−.003 (.004)	−.003 (.004)
CATHO	3.322 (.712)*	3.338 (.744)*	3.666 (.730)*	3.584 (.791)*	3.369 (.834)*	3.522 (.741)*
HINDU	1.427 (1.120)	.946 (1.160)	2.346 (1.052)**	1.715 (1.319)	1.986 (1.331)	2.262 (1.184)***
MUSLIM	3.591 (.734)*	3.336 (.747)*	4.406 (.790)*	3.420 (.824)*	2.907 (.796)*	3.932 (.797)*
OTHERCHR	1.967 (.731)*	2.258 (.747)*	3.044 (.721)*	2.543 (.816)*	2.558 (.830)*	3.057 (.740)*
OTHER	4.031 (.876)*	3.533 (.879)*	5.241 (.937)*	4.644 (.973)*	3.617 (.905)*	5.421 (.959)*
FRENCHL	.049 (.363)	−0.066 (.356)	.216 (.331)	.266 (.391)	.259 (.377)	.534 (.371)
GERMANL	.436 (.799)	.607 (.847)	1.297 (.714)***	.261 (.809)	.215 (.834)	1.011 (.720)
SCANDL	2.53 (1.001)*	2.296 (1.051)**	2.321 (.919)**	2.280 (1.006)**	1.866 (1.005)***	2.26 (.916)**
SOCIALIST	−.625 (.782)	−.912 (.801)	−.232 (.712)	.322 (.801)	−0.253 (.801)	.612 (.724)
Constant	2.486	2.285	−1.642	2.493	2.848	−1.909
R^2	.355	.299	.307	.342	.305	.345
Root MSQ	1.56	1.60	1.61	1.56	1.58	1.55
Number of obs.	101	107	102	92	95	92

SOURCES: See Appendix A.
*p-value < .01.   ** p-value < .05.   *** p-value < .10.

Regressions (4)–(6) apply the same specifications to noncore ratifications in 1990. The results parallel the findings for 1980, except that the negative effect of trade on noncore ratifications is consistently significant, although still modest in impact. In summary, the regression analyses in Table 1 document the endogeneity of ratification activity. Existing labor conditions in a country, as well as the size of the trade sector, the prevailing legal system, and the dominant religion, influence the ratification of ILO conventions.

Table 2 reports the results of a parallel analysis of the ratification of core labor standards. With only eight such standards, there is less variance to explain and the statistical results are somewhat less precise. Nonetheless, with the exception of the results for the civil liberties variable, the results support the endogenous labor standards view that countries ratify core standards that they have already attained. Specifically, in both 1980 and 1990, countries with less child labor, a healthier workforce and (with less statistical precision) more civil liberties on average commit to more core labor standards. Ratification of core labor standards also appears to be largely symbolic. Contrary to the results for noncore labor standards, countries with large TRADE sectors have not ratified fewer core standards. Religious and legal system variables remain influential.

Determinants of Labor Conditions

This section addresses two central empirical questions raised by proposals to tie labor standards to trade policy: (1) Does free trade worsen labor conditions? (2) Does the adoption of labor standards improve labor conditions? Tables 3 (1980) and 4 (1990) present 3SLS estimates of the following implementation of equation (2):

$$(3)\ \text{LABCOND} = c_0 + c_1\,\text{GDPCAP} + c_2\,\text{OPENNESS} + c_3\,\text{LS} + \varepsilon$$

The tables report separate results for child labor, civil liberties, and health (life expectancy). As expected, highly developed countries have superior labor conditions. (A quadratic specification of GDPCAP provides a better fit in the child labor regressions and indicates a gradually diminishing relationship between economic development and the reduction of child labor.) Economic growth is clearly a powerful force for improving the condition of labor.

Turning to the results for trade and labor standards, globalization skeptics expect $c_2 < 0$ and $c_3 > 0$ (and the reverse for the CHLAB and CIVLIB dependant variables).[18] The results for the various OPENNESS variables effectively refute the RTTB view of the effect of trade policy on labor conditions. Health conditions and civil liberties are stronger, not weaker, in economies with more open trade policies. Moreover, these countries have less child labor.[19] The size of a country's export sector relative to GDP has no statistically significant influence on labor conditions.[20] Finally, the 3SLS estimation indi-

TABLE 3
3SLS Analysis of Labor Conditions, 1980

Independent variables	Child labor		Civil liberties		Life expectancy	
	(1)	(2)	(3)	(4)	(5)	(6)
GDPCAP	−0.01026	−0.01043	−0.00028	−.00026	0.00034	0.00208
	(.00107)*	(.00129)*	(.00005)*	(.00006)*	(.00004)*	(.00032)*
GDPSQ	0.000006	0.000005				
	(.000001)*	(.000001)*				
OPEN	−4.132	−4.468	−1.150	−1.01	2.258	3.263
	(2.971)	(2.847)	(.387)*	(.338)*	(2.031)	(1.962)***
CORE LS	1.427		.016		−1.831	
	(.958)		(.136)		(.808)**	
NONCORE LS		.150		−.017		−.029
		(.159)		(.021)		(.106)
Constant	37.02	40.105	5.343	5.743	58.131	51.183
R^2	.681	.692	.561	.562	.525	.639
Root MSE	9.837	9.658	1.317	6.912	7.733	6.74
Number of obs.	101	101	107	107	102	102

SOURCES: See Appendix A.
*p-value < .01.   ** p-value < .05.   *** p-value < .10.

TABLE 4
3SLS Analysis of Labor Conditions, 1990

Independent variables	Child labor		Civil liberties		Life expectancy	
	(1)	(2)	(3)	(4)	(5)	(6)
GDPCAP	−0.00765	−0.00687	−0.00021	−0.00019	0.00148	0.00140
	(.0009)*	(.00088)*	(.00003)*	(.00003)*	(.00017)*	(.00018)*
GDPSQ	0.000004	0.000003				
	(.000001)*	(.000001)*				
OPEN	−2.643	−3.596	−1.025	−.884	5.968	5.468
	(2.625)	(2.275)	(.277)*	(.248)*	(1.780)*	(1.698)*
CORE LS	.962		−.181		−1.175	
	(.904)		(.110)***		(.727)	
NONCORE LS		.016		−.022***		.021
		(.099)		(.012)		(.068)
Constant	29.900	34.068	5.941	5.569	57.576	51.805
R^2	.624	.639	.637	.624	.568	.655
Root MSE	9.297	9.116	1.06	1.079	7.064	6.31
Number of obs.	92	92	95	95	92	92

SOURCES: See Appendix A.
*p-value < .01.   ** p-value < .05.   *** p-value < .10.

cates that with two exceptions, neither effective core nor noncore labor standards are significantly related to any of the measures of labor rights and conditions. One exception is the anomalous finding (significant in 1980 only) that life expectancy is lower in countries that ratify many core labor standards. The other exception is the finding (for 1990 only) that countries with more core or noncore labor standards have greater civil liberties.

The statistical results reported in Tables 1–4 provide little support for the proposition that effective labor standards improve labor conditions in a regime of voluntary ratification. Nevertheless, measures of freely chosen ratification behavior will not necessarily describe the impact of standards imposed by laws and regulations flowing from international agreements. Can one simulate the effects of involuntary, exogenous standards using data from a regime of voluntary standards? One proposal would use the country-specific residuals from a regression determining ratifications as a measure of such exogenous labor standards (Brown, 2000). This variable measures the extent to which a country's ratifications depart from what one would on average expect based on the country's economic and cultural characteristics. International regulations could be a source of such departures. Regressions for each of the three measures of labor conditions were estimated, alternately using residuals from regressions explaining core and noncore ratifications for the RATIFY variable. None of the residuals attained statistical significance in these (unreported) regressions.

To summarize, this section addressed the question of whether adoption of ILO labor standards produces improvements in labor conditions, as predicted by advocates of linking labor standards to trade policy, or whether labor conditions instead determine the ratification of political labor standards. The statistical analysis of ratifications and labor conditions found little evidence that the effective number of core or noncore labor standards led to improvements in the condition of labor. On the other hand, there is strong evidence that countries with open trade policies have superior labor rights and health conditions and less child labor. Those who propose imposing trade sanctions in an effort to induce adherence to ILO labor standards appear to be proposing a policy (trade sanctions) which is likely to reduce labor conditions to induce compliance with labor standards that are not demonstrably effective in improving labor conditions.

Misunderstandings of the relationship between labor standards and labor conditions appear to rest on a failure to appreciate the endogeneity of labor standards. The statistical analysis *does* support the hypothesis that countries with superior labor conditions are more likely to ratify ILO conventions. The finding that ratifications are largely symbolic, reflecting previously attained labor conditions, undermines the RTTB view that ratifications raise labor costs. And if no linkage to labor costs exists, then nonratification should not produce superior export and foreign direct investment performance. A direct examination of these issues follows.

III. Labor Cost (Compensation) Analysis

The argument that countries with low labor standards have superior trade and FDI performance rests on the proposition that adherence to labor standards will raise labor costs, placing countries at a competitive disadvantage in international markets. Yet elementary economic analysis predicts that labor productivity ultimately determines the equilibrium real compensation of workers. This section examines the extent to which cross-country productivity differentials explain international labor cost differences and tests for whether there is a further relationship between measures of labor standards and wages.

Using cross-country panel data for the manufacturing sector, the analysis relates labor costs (total compensation) per worker to value added per worker and the average price level of consumption in purchasing power parity (PPP) terms to capture cost-of-living differences not accounted for by the exchange rate conversion. The compensation measure is sufficiently broad to capture the cost of benefits required by legislation, although the effectiveness in capturing some elements of compensation may vary from country to country.[21] The independent variable captures the effects on productivity of education, training, experience, and other factors frequently specified in wage regressions on individual data, as well as unobservable influences. Data refer to workers of both sexes. The panel consists of five-year averages for 1980–84 (eighty-four countries) and 1995–99 (fifty-one countries).[22]

Table 5, which provides descriptive data for the main variables for each of the time periods, confirms that the sample includes a wide range of devel-

TABLE 5

Descriptive Statistics, Labor Cost Analysis

	Mean	Std. Dev.	Min	Max
1980–84 (N = 85)				
LABCOST	5972	5007	104	19103
PRODUCT	15,894	10,573	234	47,276
PRICE	68.6	34.8	21.7	198.2
CORE LS	4.5	2.0	0	7
NONCORE LS	27.7	17.6	0	78
1995–99 (N = 51)				
LABCOST	13,695	12,305	94	38,415
PRODUCT	34,656	25,948	228	92,582
PRICE	79.1	38.4	3.7	164.6
CORE LS	5.1	1.9	0	7
NONCORE LS	39.7	22.1	0	95

SOURCES: See Appendix A for definitions and sources.

opment experience. In the early 1980s, compensation per worker in the lowest wage country (Kenya) was 0.5 percent of compensation in the highest wage country (the United States). How can a country whose manufacturing labor costs are over 180 times manufacturing wages in another country sell its products in international markets? A clue is provided by the 1980 productivity data, which show a virtually identical difference between the least productive country (again, Kenya) and the most productive country (the United States). The data for the late 1990s show even wider (but again, virtually identical) differences between the most- and least-productive countries. Table 5 also indicates that the ratification of both total and core ILO conventions varies widely and that no country has ratified all eight of the latter.[23]

Tables 6 and 7 report for 1980–84 and 1995–99, respectively, the results of cross-section ordinary least squares (OLSQ) regressions of period averages of labor costs (compensation) per employee on labor productivity and the price level (all specified as natural logarithms), as well as several measures of ratification of ILO conventions. Regression 1 in Tables 6 and 7 shows that cross-country variations in labor productivity and price levels account for 87–88 percent of the cross-country variation in labor compensation in both periods.[24] On average, a 10 percent productivity difference between countries is associated with an 8.5–9 percent difference in compensation per worker. Lesson number one is that cross-country differences in employee compen-

TABLE 6

Labor Cost Analysis, 1980–84

(Robust standard errors in parentheses)

Variables	(1)	(2)	(3)	(4)	(5)
ln PRODUCT	.913	.908	.91	.908	.899
	(.081)*	(.082)*	(.095)*	(.088)*	(.078)*
ln PRICE	.439	.428	.408	.424	.397
	(.252)***	(.253)***	(.281)	(.280)	(0.250)
CORE LS		.019			
		(.017)			
NONCORE LS					.005
					(.002)**
C98			−.081		
			(.094)		
C105			.158		
			(.098)		
C111			−.029		
			(.098)		
C138			.069		
			(.133)		
DC98				−.001	
				(.004)	
DC105				.004	
				(.005)	
DC111				.001	
				(0.006)	
DC138				.014	
				(.038)	
Constant	−2.09	−2.08	−1.99	−2.04	−1.92
R^2	.88	.89	.89	.89	.89
Root MSE	.347	.347	.349	.354	.339
Number of obs.	84	84	84	84	84

SOURCES: See Appendix A.
   *p-value < .01.   ** p-value < .05.   *** p-value < .10.

sation are powerfully related to productivity differences.[25] Raising the relative productivity of the labor force is one reliable way to raise compensation. Lesson number two is that this relationship is quite stable over time. The relationship between labor costs, productivity, and prices, its statistical significance, and the ability of productivity variations to explain wage variations is virtually identical in the early 1980s and the late 1990s.

While productivity and price levels account for the vast majority of international wage variation, some scope remains for additional influence on

TABLE 7

Labor Cost Analysis, 1995–99

(Robust standard errors in parentheses)

Variables	(1)	(2)	(3)	(4)	(5)	Fixed effects (6)	(7)
ln PRODUCT	.859	.892	.872	.863	.88	.949	.959
	(.092)*	(.081)*	(.099)*	(.095)*	(.087)*	(.061)*	(.071)*
ln PRICE	.506	.40	.479	.453	.377	.189	.197
	(.282)**	(.255)	(.299)	(.308)	(.263)	(.091)**	(.093)**
CORE LS		.093				−.066	
		(.049)***				(.044)	
NONCORE LS					.008		−.004
					(.004)**		(.004)
C98			.094				
			(.188)				
C105			.340				
			(.236)				
C111			.135				
			(.159)				
C138			−.051				
			(.149)				
DC98				−.0001			
				(.0045)			
DC105				.0083			
				(.0069)			
DC111				.0063			
				(.0054)			
DC138				.0029			
				(.0084)			
Constant	−1.84	−2.2	−2.3	−2.01	−1.79	−1.08	−1.4
R^2	.88	.89	.89	.89	.89	.86	.85
Root MSE	.347	.347	.349	.354	.339	.007	.085
Number of obs.	51	51	51	51	51	51	51

SOURCES: See Appendix A.
  *p-value < .01.   ** p-value < .05.   *** p-value < .10.

compensation from domestic and international institutions. We now examine whether countries that fail to ratify ILO conventions have low wages
relative to productivity. The analysis reported in the previous section indicates that ratification of ILO conventions may signal information about the
condition of labor in a country not because ratification produces an improvement in the condition of labor but rather because countries with good
labor conditions incur low ratification costs. This inference implies that rati-

fication of ILO conventions should have no influence on labor costs, conditional on a country's productivity level.

Regression 2 tests for a relationship between the number of core labor standards (CORE LS) ratified by a country (as of the *beginning* of the estimation period) and compensation, conditional on productivity and the price level. Proposals to tie labor standards requirements to WTO benefits appear to rest on the proposition that this relationship is significantly positive—that is, labor costs are lower in countries that do not ratify the core conventions. In contrast, the endogenous labor standards view predicts no relationship between compensation and ratifications (conditional on productivity and prices). For the early 1980s, the regression coefficient CORE LS is positive but not statistically significant; for the late 1990s, it is positive and statistically significant at the 10 percent level. Taken at face value, the coefficient implies an average compensation difference of 9 percent per core labor standard ratified by the late 1990s. We shall return to the question of whether the result should be taken at face value.

Summary measures, such as CORE LS, place conventions addressing issues as varied as collective bargaining, discrimination, forced labor, and child labor on an equal statistical footing, which is hard to defend. Moreover, if ratification forces a country to alter its domestic policies (contrary to the endogenous labor standards hypothesis), summary measures take no account of the length of time that a country has had since ratification to bring its legislation and enforcement into compliance. Regression 3 in Tables 6 and 7 tests for an influence of individual core labor standards on compensation. Since the eight core labor standards in fact address four areas—child labor, freedom of association, forced labor, and discrimination—these regressions relate compensation to dummy variables for one convention from each of the four areas, as well as the productivity and price levels.[26] For each time period, there is no significant correlation between compensation and ratification of any of the four core standards. Similarly, regression 4 shows no evidence that ratifications of the same core conventions gradually influence compensation over time.[27]

Regression 5 tests for a relationship between the number of noncore ILO conventions (NONCORE LS) ratified by a country as of the beginning of the estimation period and compensation per worker, conditional on productivity and the price level. Taken at face value, the coefficient on ratifications is positive and statistically significant for both time periods. The coefficient implies that ratification of an additional convention is associated with higher compensation of about 0.5 (early 1980s) to 0.7 percent (late 1990s).[28] Consistent with the RTTB hypothesis, in the cross-section analysis labor costs are positively correlated with total ratifications in both periods and with core ratifications in 1994–99. But can the cross-section results be accepted at face value?

There are two potential problems with the OLSQ analysis. First, cross-section analysis may not disentangle the question of whether ratification leads to higher wages or vice versa. The potential endogeneity of ratifications should be mitigated by the fact that the standards variables are defined as of the beginning of the estimation periods. If a problem remains, two stage least squares (2SLS) estimation can address it, but if ratifications are exogenous in the wage equation, OLSQ estimation is more efficient. To determine whether 2SLS is necessary, the Hausman (1978) test for endogeneity of independent variables was applied.[29] The Hausman test did not reject the hypothesis that coefficients obtained by the two estimation methods are the same. That is, by rejecting the endogeneity of CORE LS and NONCORE LS, the test supports the use of OLSQ over 2SLS.[30]

Second, if unobserved country-specific factors are correlated with both wages and ratifications, the cross-section estimates of the relationship between ratifications and wages will be biased. The presence of unions or extensive domestic labor market regulation might produce both more ratifications and higher labor cost, for example. Fixed effect estimation effectively eliminates this potential source of bias by "differencing out" the country-specific effects that do not change over time. Moreover, fixed-effects estimation will remove fixed, country-specific differences in the measurement and coverage of the compensation data. We therefore use the panel feature of the database to estimate a fixed effects model.[31]

Regressions 6 and 7 in Table 7 provide fixed effects estimates of the relationship between compensation and ratifications. The fixed effects estimates confirm the significant relationships between productivity, price levels, and compensation, but find no significant relationship between compensation and ratification measures.[32] For this panel of fifty-one countries for which data are available for both time periods, there is no significant relationship between changes in the ratification of core or total labor standards and changes in compensation between the early 1980s and the late 1990s.[33]

In summary, the statistical analyses reported in this section find a powerful relationship between a country's real labor costs and its productivity level in manufacturing. After holding the influence of productivity constant, however, the data reveal no significant relationship between ratification of either core or total ILO conventions, after addressing the issues of causality and potential bias through fixed effects estimation. This "nonresult" is consistent with the view that countries tend to adopt labor standards that their domestic politics and policies have already met. Notwithstanding this conclusion, the remaining analyses incorporate the possibility that ratifications or measures of actual labor rights and conditions in a country may influence wages. Subsequent sections also include tests for the effects of unusually high or low wages (relative to productivity) on export and FDI performance.

IV. Do Labor Standards Suppress Exports and Foreign Direct Investment?

The previous sections have demonstrated that (1) the ratification of ILO conventions (political labor standards) is endogenous, with ratifications most likely in countries were the costs of ratification are lowest; (2) free trade is associated with higher, not lower, labor conditions and rights; (3) political labor standards are at best weakly related to labor conditions in a country; and (4) political labor standards do not influence labor costs. Result (4) would seem to undermine RTTB arguments that countries that do not ratify ILO conventions enjoy better export performance and attract more foreign direct investment, since this argument assumes that relatively low labor costs accompany nonratification. Nonetheless, this section tests for links between labor standards and subsequent export and FDI performance. After establishing baseline models that explain international differences in export and FDI performance, we add measures of labor standards to determine their effect in the context of the model.[34]

Exports and Labor Standards

Whether grouped by stage of development or region, countries showed little change in their shares of world exports over the 1980–99 period (UNCTAD 2000a, Table 1.9). Looking across countries, however, the ratio of exports to GDP ranges from 1.4 percent (Bangladesh) to 66 percent (Belgium) in the sample of about 80 countries that have data on all of the variables. These countries represent a sufficiently wide spread of development experience to offer a fair test of the RTTB hypothesis that ratification of ILO conventions puts countries at a competitive disadvantage in international trade.[35]

The baseline model for explaining exports assumes that demand for a country's exports depends on the relative price of its exports, its sources of comparative advantage, and the costs of conducting trade (mainly transportation costs and the costs imposed by trade barriers). We estimate variants of the following regression model on the cross-country database.

$$\text{EXPORT} = a_0 + a_1 \text{ TOT} + a_2 \text{ LABLAND} + a_3 \text{ HUMANK} + a_4 \text{ TRCOST} + a_5 \text{ OPEN} + e$$

The dependent variable, EXPORT, is the ratio of exports to GDP in current international prices averaged over 1980–84 (Summers and Heston, 1993). TOT is the merchandise terms of trade shock defined as the difference in the growth rates of merchandise export and import prices over 1980–84 and is expected to have a negative influence on EXPORT.[36] We include two measures of comparative advantage. LABLAND, the population of a country divided by its area, provides a measure of labor intensity. HUMANK, the average schooling years in the population over age twenty-five in 1980, provides a measure of the quality of the labor force. These are expected to be positively related to exports.

Proxies for transport costs (TRCOST) and measures of trade barriers represent trade costs. In the former category, the independent variables include DISTANCE, the average distance (in thousands of kilometers) to the capitals of the world's twenty major exporters weighted by value of bilateral imports, a 0–1 dummy variable for whether a country is an ISLAND, and a dummy (LANDLOCK) taking the value 1 for landlocked countries. Trade policy is captured by the dummy variable OPEN (defined in Section II).[37] Since more

TABLE 8

Ratifications and Export/GDP Ratio, 1980–84

(Robust standard errors in parentheses)

Independent variables	(1)	(2)	(3)	(4)	(5)	(6)
TOT	−1.217 (.528)**	−1.19 (.538)**	−1.097 (.526)**	−1.10 (.530)**	−1.424 (.307)*	−1.506 (.326)*
LABLAND	.00008 (.000006)*	.00008 (.000007)*	.00006 (0.0001)	.00008 (.000009)*	.0001 (.00001)*	.00009 (.00001)*
HUMANK	.022 (.004)*		.023 (.004)*	.023 (.005)*	.018 (.004)*	.021 (.005)*
DISTANCE	−.023 (.004)*	−.021 (.005)*	−.023 (.004)*	−.024 (.004)*	−.019 (.004)*	−.022 (.004)*
ISLAND	.013 (.028)	.019 (.030)	.019 (.030)	.017 (.031)	.053 (.027)***	.042 (.030)***
LANDLOCK	.032 (.024)	.007 (.025)	.039 (.027)	.038 (.026)	.056 (.027)**	.041 (.033)
OPEN	.016 (.022)	.095 (.028)*	.018 (.023)	.018 (.022)	.008 (.022)	−.0009 (.023)
CORE PR			−.00006 (.008)			
NONCORE PR				−.0001 (.0009)		
CORE RES					.016 (.011)	
NONCORES						−.0003 (.0016)
Constant	.180	.175	.178	.182	.091	.182
R²	.63	.51	.60	.60	.66	.66
Root MSE	.093	.104	.091	.091	.082	.083
Number of obs.	80	87	78	78	65	65

SOURCES: See Appendix A.
*p-value < .01.   ** p-value < .05.   *** p-value < .10.

open countries should have more trade, we expect a positive coefficient on this variable.

Table 8 reports the regression results for 1980–84. The variables discussed above account for 63 percent of the international variance in export performance among the eighty sample countries (regression 1) and generally have the expected signs.[38] Increases in the terms of trade and larger distances from major markets reduce exports, while labor intensity and human capital investments raise exports. The coefficient on OPEN supports the idea that free trade raises exports, but is not statistically significant. As it happens, the performance of the trade policy variable is quite sensitive to the inclusion of HUMANK in the regression (regression 2). Countries with highly educated workers tend to have open trade policies and to export more. When the educational attainment variable is omitted, OPEN becomes statistically significant and indicates that the export/GDP ratio is 9.5 points higher in countries with free trade policies.

The next regressions add alternative measures of political labor standards to the baseline specification to test for an influence on subsequent export performance. The RTTB hypothesis predicts a significant inverse relationship between ratifications and export performance. Regressions 3 and 4, respectively, add the number of ratifications of core (CORE LS) and noncore (NONCORE LS) ILO conventions as of the beginning of the estimation period to the baseline specification. Although each has a negative coefficient, the results are neither economically nor statistically significant.[39] Indeed, they are the weakest variables in their respective regressions.

As the earlier discussion emphasized, ratifications of ILO core and noncore conventions measure a country's effective labor standards with error, so that the ratification variables may not capture the relationship between effective labor standards and export performance. But the errors go in both directions; for a variety of reasons, ratifications may exceed or fall short of effective labor standards in a country. The remaining regressions examine the effects of alternative measurements of labor standards and labor conditions on export performance. The first approach removes the measurement error "noise" that results from using actual ratifications to measure effective labor standards by recognizing that effective labor standards will vary with the cultural and social norms of different countries and using predictions of core (COREPR) and noncore (NONCOREPR) ratifications based on those factors as estimates of effective labor standards.[40] The coefficients on these variables are also not statistically significant.

Next, we tested for the effects of actual labor conditions—child labor, civil liberties, and life expectancy—on exports. According to the RTTB argument, countries with more child labor, fewer civil liberties (including freedom of association), and shorter life expectancy should have superior export performance. Substituting these variables for the measures of ratifications reported in Table 8 produces little change in the overall structure of the export equation, and none of the coefficients on the labor conditions variables are statistically significant.[41]

Finally, we examine the effects of low labor costs on exports. The analysis in the previous section demonstrated that international real labor cost differentials mainly reflect international productivity differences. Nevertheless, country-specific factors can raise or lower labor costs relative to productivity, raising the question of whether countries with low (high) wages relative to productivity experience superior (inferior) export performance. The final analysis of export performance addresses this question by substituting a variable for actual minus predicted labor costs in manufacturing for the measures of ratifications and other labor conditions discussed earlier. (A country's labor costs per employee are predicted on the basis of its labor productivity and price level.) This variable is marginally significant (coefficient [robust standard error] is .0638 [.0349]), but the sign is the *opposite* of the RTTB hypothesis. Countries in which labor costs per worker are high relative to labor productivity and prices have a higher share of GDP in exports.

In summary, the regression analyses of international differences in export performance offer scant support for the RTTB hypothesis that poor labor standards enhance a country's export performance. In fact, the share of exports in GDP bears no reliable statistical relationship to a country's (1) ratification of ILO core and noncore conventions, (2) level of effective labor standards, (3) wage levels or (4) extent of child labor and civil liberties. One regression shows weak statistical evidence that low life expectancy may be associated with higher export shares, but there is much stronger evidence that investments in schooling have a powerful positive effect on exports. Overall, the evidence is not consistent with the hypothesis that poor labor conditions facilitate exports. Instead, export patterns are influenced by factors determining comparative advantage and the costs of conducting trade.

Foreign Direct Investment

International capital flows increased through the late nineteenth century to the beginning of World War I. During this period, capital flows were dominantly unilateral, from capital-rich creditor countries, such as Great Britain, France, and Germany, to less developed countries where capital was scarce and its marginal product was high. The interwar period saw a great diminution in global economic relationships, including a dramatic decline in capital flows. With post–World War II reductions in trade barriers, the return to flexible exchange rates in much of the world following the demise of the Bretton Woods system in 1972, and a subsequent relaxation of capital controls, international capital flows increased and during the 1990s regained the levels attained at the peak of the earlier period of globalization.

In modern times, the destination for international capital flows changed markedly. Capital-poor developing countries, which had received disproportionately large shares of global investment flows at the beginning of the twentieth century, now receive disproportionately small shares. Paradoxically, most capital no longer flows toward the least developed nations where scarce capital presumably has a relatively high marginal product. Instead, "capital transactions seem to be mostly a rich-rich affair, a process of 'diversification finance' rather than 'development finance'" (Obstfeld and Taylor, 2001, p. 00).

International capital flows include both portfolio investment and FDI.[42] Portfolio investment flows are more important, but since 1970 when the International Monetary Fund began to publish regular comprehensive estimates of international capital flows, the share of FDI in world capital flows has increased from about 6 percent to over 30 percent in the last half of the 1990s (Lipsey, 2001).[43]

RTTB arguments hold that countries that fail to ratify political labor standards may gain abnormally large shares of world FDI. One difficulty faced by this argument is that most FDI flows, like total international capital flows, now occur *between* industrialized countries, which most frequently have superior labor standards and conditions (Table 9). During the 1990s, roughly 70 percent of gross FDI flows went to the developed countries, which were also the sources of almost 90 percent of gross FDI flows.[44] Developing countries increased their share of world FDI during the 1990s, but never received more than a third of FDI inflows. Clearly, efforts to evade international labor standards cannot be the primary factor governing the international distribution of FDI.[45]

A second difficulty with the argument that FDI is attracted to countries with poor labor conditions follows from the analysis in section III: Poor labor conditions signal low skills as well as low wages, and not all investments

TABLE 9

FDI Inflows & Outflows, 1982–99

(Percent)

Countries	Share of world FDI inflows			Share of gross fixed K form	
	1982–87	1988–93	1994–99	1988–93	1994–99
World	100.0	100.0	100.0	100.0	100.0
Developed	74.6	73.5	65.8	89.3	89.2
Developing	25.3	24.6	31.1	10.6	10.5
Central and East. Europe	0.03	1.9	3.1	.1	.3

SOURCE: UNCTAD, *World Investment 1992, 2000* (New York; United Nations, 1992, 2000). Annex table B.5.

thrive in a low-skill environment. Perhaps even more important is the fact that countries with low labor standards tend to be countries in which direct risks to investment are high. Cross-country correlations indicate that the risks of expropriation and repudiation of contracts are highest in countries with few civil liberties and considerable child labor. Testing for a relationship between standards and FDI therefore requires a baseline empirical model of FDI to which measures of political labor standards and actual labor conditions may be added. The absence of a generally accepted model of FDI complicates this approach.[46] The empirical work below considers the following potential influences on a country's share of world FDI (FDISHARE).[47]

Expected return on capital. As shown in Table 9, capital flows have shifted away from the K-scarce countries. Moreover, including the capital-labor ratio as a regressor would leave a very small sample of countries. As a result, this variable is not used in the analysis. The expected return on capital can also be influenced by various risk factors associated with the political and social climate. The regression analysis includes measures of government repudiation of contracts (REPUD), risk of expropriation (EXPROP), and corruption (CORRUP), all defined as of the beginning of the estimation period. Higher values of each of these measures imply lower risk and hence higher values of FDISHARE. The ratio of real government "consumption" expenditure to real GDP (GOVSHARE) is included to capture the degree of government intervention in the economy with high values expected to discourage FDI.

Market size. Larger markets attract horizontal FDI, which more or less replicates home-country production facilities in a foreign host-country.

Population in thousands (POP) proxies the number of potential consumers and per capita (GDP/POP) captures their wealth or potential purchasing power. AREA proxies the potential size of a country's resource base.

Trade costs. Horizontal foreign investment becomes more attractive when transportation costs or barriers to trade with a country are relatively high. The proxies for these factors are again DIST, LANDLOCK, and OPEN. Unfortunately, FDI data do not discriminate between horizontal investment and investments to establish global vertical integration. Trade costs and barriers that encourage horizontal FDI tend to discourage vertical FDI by raising the costs of moving items between different stages of the global production chain. There is no clear prediction on the signs of the coefficients.

Labor force quality and price. We have seen that economic advantages attributed to low labor costs tend to be offset by low productivity. Implicitly, the RTTB view implies that a low productivity workforce attracts FDI. An alternative view holds that high-productivity labor is complementary with FDI. The regressions include HUMANK to test for complementarities between FDI and work force quality. In testing for an effect of wages on FDI, we measure wages relative to productivity (WAGERES).

We examine the determinants of a country's share of world FDI inflows on a sample of about 70 countries at various stages of development. (The wealthiest country in the sample [the United States] has a per capita GDP that is twenty-nine times that of the poorest country [Tanzania].) Given the somewhat volatile behavior of annual FDI flows, Tables 10 and 11 present cross-section estimates for 1980–85 and 1986–1991 averages, respectively. The FDI share (dependent variable), per capita GDP, and population variables are in natural logs.

Regression 1 in each table excludes trade policy variables. For each period, the model explains about three-quarters of the cross-country variation in the log of the share of world FDI inflows. There is considerable consistency across the two periods in the signs and statistical significance of the explanatory variables. A relatively high risk of expropriation reduces a country's FDI share.[48] Countries with relatively large shares of government consumption in GDP (a proxy for general government intervention in markets) also have relatively low shares of world FDI. (Actual shares of government consumption in this sample range from six percent [Hong Kong] to 37 per-

TABLE 10

Ratifications and FDI Shares, 1980–85

(Robust standard errors in parentheses)

Independent variables	(1)	(2)	(3)	(4)	(5)	(6)
EXPROP	.329 (.117)*	.30 (.128)**	.294 (.133)**	.272 (.131)**	.297 (.135)**	.313 (.132)**
GOVSHARE	−7.702 (3.131)**	−7.249 (3.321)**	−7.864 (3.330)**	−8.278 (3.268)**	−7.504 (4.282)***	−8.139 (4.122)**
LNPOP	.187 (.124)	.202 (.128)	.214 (.145)	.133 (.135)	.114 (.150)	.126 (.154)
LNGDPCAP	.812 (.377)**	.767 (.385)**	.613 (.384)	.482 (.402)	.660 (.480)	.577 (.463)
AREA	.0003 (.00007)*	.0003 (.00006)*	.0003 (.00007)*	.0003 (.00007)*	.0004 (.00008)*	.00035 (.00008)*
DISTANCE	−.095 (.067)	−.116 (.072)	−.092 (.071)	−.088 (.067)	−.211 (.114)***	−.188 (.109)***
LANDLOCK	−.824 (.680)	−.801 (.666)	−.799 (.653)	−.863 (.646)	−.946 (.897)	−.884 (.932)
HUMANK	−.043 (.091)	−.023 (.096)	−.009 (.100)	−.013 (.098)	.021 (.105)	.016 (.107)
OPEN		.183 (.398)	.287 (.400)	.425 (.396)	−.059 (.626)	.061 (.574)
CORE LS			.093 (.080)			
NONCORE LS				.016 (.007)**		
COREPR					−.205 (.228)	
NONCOREPR						−.009 (.021)
Constant	−10.46	−10.17	−9.55	−7.67	−7.03	−7.22
R^2	0.74	0.75	0.75	0.76	0.76	0.75
Root MSQ	1.19	1.19	1.2	1.17	1.27	1.27
Number of obs.	74	70	67	68	56	56

SOURCES: See Appendix A.
*p-value < .01.   ** p-value < .05.   *** p-value < .10.

cent [Zambia].) FDI shares increase with population, the wealth (purchasing power) of the population, and the potential size of a country's resource base. Higher trade costs (associated with longer transportation distances and lack of access to sea transport) are not significantly related to FDI shares, reflecting a rough standoff between the effects on horizontal and vertical FDI discussed earlier.

Regressions 2 in Tables 10 and 11 add a trade policy variable to the base

TABLE 11

Ratifications and FDI Shares, 1986–91

(Robust standard errors in parentheses)

Independent variables	(1)	(2)	(3)	(4)	(5)	(6)
EXPROP	.428	.327	.326	.324	.341	.337
	(.109)*	(.114)*	(.115)*	(.121)*	(.117)*	(.115)*
GOVSHARE	−7.582	−7.641	−7.782	−7.692	−7.712	−7.58
	(2.101)*	(2.184)*	(2.220)*	(2.250)*	(2.315)*	(2.180)*
LNPOP	.383	.436	.425	.430	.449	.437
	(.141)*	(.129)*	(.133)*	(.138)*	(.127)*	(.129)*
LNGDPCAP	.770	.780	.782	.761	.680	.710
	(.380)**	(.380)**	(.382)**	(.405)***	(.444)	(.302)**
AREA	.00004	.00005	.00005	.00005	.00004	.00004
	(.00007)	(.00007)	(.00007)	(.00008)	(.00007)	(.00007)
DISTANCE	.048	.046	.025	.05	.064	.069
	(.064)	(.063)	(.065)	(.061)	(.060)	(.062)
LANDLOCK	−.205	.025	−.009	.024	.036	.049
	(.464)	(.421)	(.446)	(.423)	(.436)	(.436)
HUMANK	.002	−.0005	.001	−.0003	.012	−.014
	(.098)	(.097)	(.097)	(.099)	(.110)	(.099)
OPEN		.760	.711	.780	.798	.851
		(.352)**	(.355)**	(.373)**	(.371)**	(.344)**
CORE LS			−.067			
			(.070)			
NONCORE LS				−.002		
				(.007)		
COREPR					.105	
					(.149)	
NONCOREPR						.012
						(.010)
Constant	−13.9	−14.22	−13.64	−14.07	−14.31	−14.26
R²	.78	.83	.82	.82	.82	.83
Root MSQ	1.13	1.04	1.06	1.06	1.06	1.05
Number of obs.	73	71	69	70	69	70

SOURCES: See Appendix A.

*p-value < .01.   ** p-value < .05.   *** p-value < .10.

specification. Neither the OPEN dummy variable (defined in Section II) nor alternative indicators of trade policy were significantly related to FDI share in the 1980–85 period.[49] This may reflect the fact that trade barriers will tend to have opposing influence on horizontal and vertical investment flows. In the later period, however, countries with open trade policies had significantly higher FDI shares, suggesting that trade policy had a stronger influence on vertical than horizontal FDI flows.

The next two regressions address a key RTTB argument by examining the cross-country relationship between ratification of ILO conventions and FDI share. Regressions 3 and 4, respectively, add variables for the number of core (CORE LS) and noncore (NONCORE LS) conventions ratified. Core labor standard ratifications are not significantly related to FDI share. On the other hand, FDI share *increases* with the number of noncore ILO conventions ratified in 1980–85 (but not the later period)—exactly the *opposite* of the RTTB view.

As developed earlier, ratifications of ILO conventions provide a very noisy measure of actual labor conditions in a country. Therefore, the remaining regressions extend the analysis by examining the effects of alternative measurements of labor standards and labor conditions on a country's share of foreign direct investment. As in the analysis of export performance, we first test for a relationship between FDI and effective national labor standards by substituting predictions of core (COREPR) and noncore (NONCOREPR) ratifications for actual ratifications in the regressions. (This approach statistically removes the measurement error that limits the usefulness of actual ratifications as a measure of effective standards.) These variables are also not significant.

According to the RTTB argument, countries with more child labor, fewer civil liberties (including freedom of association), and shorter life expectancy should attract more FDI. To check this claim, measures of child labor, civil liberties, and health (life expectancy) were substituted for the ratification variables. In the earlier period, only the child labor variable is marginally statistically significant (p-value = .082), but its sign is inconsistent with the RTTB hypothesis. Countries with *lower* labor force participation by 10- to 14-year-olds attract more FDI, ceteris paribus. This result is consistent with the view that FDI and skilled labor are complements, and high child labor participation signals an unskilled labor force.[50] None of the measures of labor conditions are significantly related to a country's FDI share in the analysis for the late 1980s.[51] Finally, we examine the hypothesis that FDI is attracted to countries where labor costs are low (relative to productivity and prices) by adding the WAGERES variable discussed in the previous section as a regressor.[52] The regression coefficients (robust standard errors) on WAGERES are -.731 (.599) for 1980–85 and -.054 (.701) for 1986–91. While the negative coefficients are consistent with the RTTB hypothesis, neither result is statistically significant. Cross-country differences in labor costs relative to productivity fail to explain differences in FDI shares.

In summary, the data show no reliable evidence that high labor standards reduce a country's share of FDI. Given the earlier evidence that ratification is not associated with higher labor costs, this result should not be surprising. Indeed, discussions of the potential costs of labor standards often turn attention from the possibility that some labor standards may raise the productivity of investment by improving the quality of human capital. Ratification of ILO conventions is only one of many potential government influences on FDI. Within the framework of this study, it is clear that government actions to reduce risks associated with expropriation and uncertain contract status and to reduce its own presence in the economy will have a much more powerful effect on FDI shares. Other factors that could not be examined in this study (e.g., tax policies) are also likely to have a more powerful influence on FDI.

V. Conclusions

The question of how international economic and regulatory policies influence the condition of labor motivates this study. The focus is the specific hypothesis that free trade suppresses labor conditions through a mechanism in which countries (1) refuse to ratify ILO conventions so that (2) they can degrade labor conditions allowing them to (3) reduce labor costs in order to (4) raise exports and (5) attract foreign direct investment seeking cheap labor. This study tests this hypothesis with data from a period in which such regulation was more form than substance—seemingly an ideal setting for observing the mechanisms believed to be driving such a "race to the bottom," but the empirical analysis of a large sample of countries representing a wide range of economic and political development provides little support for any step in this chain of reasoning.

Consider first the linkage between trade and the political act of ratification. The results are consistent with the view that ratification is driven by a country's dominant social values and pre-existing levels of labor rights and conditions. Once these factors are accounted for, neither the size of a country's trade sector nor its trade policy stance appears to influence ratifications of the *core* ILO conventions that are the focus of policy discussions. That is, ratification signals existing levels of labor conditions. There is a significant relationship between the size of the trade sector and ratifications of *noncore* ILO conventions, however, and the evidence indicates that this is driven more by the interests of import-competing industries than exporters.

Consider next the link between the political act of ratification and actual labor conditions. The empirical analysis finds no significant relationship between ratifications of either core or noncore ILO conventions and measures of labor rights or conditions. Ratifications do not seem to produce subsequent changes in domestic policies that affect labor conditions. Moreover, the significant link found between trade and total ratifications does not translate into improved labor rights and working conditions. Of course, free trade could also influence labor conditions directly, rather than through political action over ratifications. Some race-to-the-bottom scenarios in fact assert that open international markets produce a degradation of labor conditions. The direct tests of the effect of free trade on labor conditions reveal just the opposite, however. Free trade policies are associated with better, not worse, labor rights and conditions.

With no evidence of a link between the ratification of ILO conventions and actual labor conditions, it seems unlikely that a country's ratification choice would influence its labor costs. Nonetheless, the paper presents both cross-section and fixed effects estimates of several measures of core labor standards. In both the cross-section and fixed-effect estimates, international differences in productivity drive international differences in real labor costs (compensation). With productivity held constant, neither the ratification of specific core conventions nor the length of time since ratification is significantly related to labor costs in either cross-section or fixed-effects estimation. Labor costs are positively related to total ratifications of noncore and (for the late 1990s) core labor standards in the cross-section, but not the fixed-effects estimates, indicating that the cross-section estimate is biased by unobserved country-specific factors correlated with both ratifications and labor costs. Of course, improvements in actual labor conditions may raise productivity and hence compensation, but the analysis finds no evidence that adoption of international labor standards has produced such improvements.

The last step in the RTTB hypothesis alleges that low labor standards raise exports and attract FDI. The assessment of this hypothesis considered the effects of several measures of labor standards (including ratifications of ILO conventions, a measure of effective labor standards, and measures of labor rights and conditions) on exports and FDI inflows. Contrary to the RTTB hypothesis, the analyses did not find significant linkages between export performance or FDI inflows and the measures of labor standards. In sum, the paper finds no evidence that countries with low labor standards gain competitive advantage in international markets. Poor labor conditions often signal low productivity or are one element of a package of nation characteristics that discourage FDI inflows or inhibit export performance.

Appendix A: Variable Names, Definitions and Data Sources

Variable	Definition	Source
BMP	Black market premium (ratio of black market to official exchange rate minus 1)	Wacziarg (2001)
BRITISHL	British common law dummy	World Bank website
C98	Dummy var.= 1 if country has ratified ILO Conv. #98 (right to organize and bargain)	Constructed from ILO website
C105	Dummy var. = 1 if country has ratified ILO Conv. #105 (abolition of forced labor)	Constructed from ILO website
C111	Dummy var. = 1 if country has ratified ILO Conv. #111 (nondiscrimination)	Constructed from ILO website
C138	Dummy var. = 1 if country has ratified ILO Conv. #138 (minimum age of employment)	Constructed from ILO website
CATHO	Dummy var. = 1 if majority religion is Catholic	*Encyclopedia Britannica*
CIVLIB	Index of civil liberties. Range: 1 (most freedom) to 7	Freedom House
CONFU	Dummy var. = 1 if majority religion is Confucian-Buddhist-Zen	*Encyclopedia Britannica*
CORE LS	Number of core labor standards ratified	ILO website
COREPR	Predicted core ratifications	See text
CORRUPT	Corruption (0–10)	Int'l Country Risk Guide
DC98	Number of years since country ratified C98	ILO website
DC105	Number of years since country ratified C105	ILO website
DC111	Number of years since country ratified C111	ILO website
DC138	Number of years since country ratified C138	ILO website
DEMOC	Index of democracy. Range: 0 (authoritarian) to 1 (democracy)	(Freedom in the World Reports)
DISTANCE	Average distance to capitals of 20 majority exporters weighted by value of bilateral imports (1,000 km.)	Lee
EXPORT	Ratio of export to GDP	Summers-Heston, v. 5.0
EXPROP	Risk of expropriation (0–10)	Int'l Country Risk Guide
FDISHARE	Share of world inward FDI	UNCTAD (1992, 2000b)
FRENCHL	French civil law dummy	World Bank website

GDPCAPITA	Real per capita GDP	Summers-Heston, v. 5.6
GERMANL	German civil law dummy	World Bank website
GOVSHARE	Ratio of real govt. consumption expenditure to real GDP	Summers-Heston, v. 5.5
HINDU	Dummy var. = 1 if majority religion is Hindu	*Encyclopedia Britannica*
HUMANK	Average school years population over twenty-five years of age	Barro-Lee
ISLAND	Dummy var. = 1 if country is island	World Bank
LABCOST	Labor cost per worker in manufacturing	World Bank (2001)
LABLAND	Population/area	
LANDLOCK	Dummy var. = 1 if country is landlocked	World Bank
LIFEEXP	Life expectancy at age 0	World Bank (2001)
LNGDPCAP	Natural logarithm of GDPCAP	
LNLABCOST	Natural logarithm of LABCOST	
LNPOP	Natural logarithm of POP	
LNPRODUCT	Natural logarithm of PRODUCT	
MUSLIM	Dummy var. = 1 if majority religion is Muslim	*Encyclopedia Britannica*
NONCORE LS	Total number of labor standards ratified	ILO website
NONCOREPR	Predicted noncore ratifications	See text
OPEN	Trade policy dummy var. (see text for full description)	Wacziarg (2001)
POP	Population	
PRICE	Price level of consumption	Summers-Heston, 5.0
PRODUCT	Value added per worker in manufacturing	World Bank (2001)
PUPILTEACH	Pupil/teacher ratio in secondary school	UNESCO
REPUD	Govt. repudiation of contracts (0–10)	Int'l Country Risk Guide
SCANDL	Scandin. civil law dummy	World Bank website
TOT	Terms of trade	Wacziarg (2001)
TRADE	Exports plus imports as share of GDP	Summers-Heston, v.5.0
WAGERES	Actual minus predicted LNLABCOST	

Appendix B: List of Sample Countries

| Country | Labor conditions | Labor costs | | Exports | FDI | |
		1980s	1990s		1980–85	1986–91
Algeria	X	X		X	X	X
Argentina	X	X	X	X	X	X
Australia	X	X	X	X	X	X
Austria	X	X	X	X	X	X
Bangladesh	X	X	X	X		X
Barbados	X			X		
Belgium	X	X	X	X	X	X
Benin	X			X		
Bolivia	X	X	X	X	X	X
Botswana	X	X				
Brazil	X	X	X	X	X	X
Burkina Faso	X	X				
Burundi	X					
Cameroon	X			X	X	
Canada	X	X	X	X		X
Central African Republic	X			X		

Country	Labor conditions	Labor costs		Exports	FDI	
		1980s	1990s		1980–85	1986–91
Chad	X					
Chile	X	X	X	X	X	X
China	X	X				
Colombia	X	X		X	X	X
Congo	X			X		X
Costa Rica	X	X		X	X	X
Côte d'Ivoire	X	X				
Cyprus	X			X		X
Denmark		X	X		X	
Dominican Republic	X	X		X	X	X
Ecuador	X	X	X	X	X	X
Egypt	X	X	X			
El Salvador	X	X		X	X	X
Ethiopia	X					
Finland	X	X	X	X	X	X
France	X	X		X	X	X
Gabon	X					
Gambia	X					
Germany	X	X	X	X	X	X
Ghana	X	X		X	X	X
Greece	X	X	X	X	X	X
Guatemala	X	X		X	X	X
Guinea	X					
Guinea-Bissau	X					
Guyana	X			X	X	X
Haiti	X			X	X	X
Honduras	X	X		X	X	X
Hungary	X	X	X			
India	X	X		X	X	X
Indonesia	X	X	X	X	X	X
Iran	X	X	X			
Iraq	X	X			X	X
Ireland	X	X	X	X	X	X
Israel	X	X	X	X	X	X
Italy	X	X	X	X	X	X
Jamaica	X	X	X	X		X
Japan	X	X	X	X	X	X
Jordan	X	X	X	X	X	
Kenya	X	X	X	X	X	X
Korea	X	X	X	X	X	X
Kuwait		X				
Lesotho		X				
Liberia		X			X	
Luxembourg	X					
Madagascar	X	X				
Malawi	X			X	X	X
Malaysia	X	X		X	X	X
Mali	X	X				
Mauritius		X	X	X		
Mexico	X	X	X	X	X	X
Morocco	X	X	X			
Mozambique	X				X	X

Country	Labor conditions	Labor costs		Exports	FDI	
		1980s	1990s		1980–85	1986–91
Myanmar	X					
Nepal	X	X		X		
Netherlands	X	X	X	X	X	X
New Zealand	X	X	X	X	X	X
Nicaragua	X			X		
Niger	X	X		X		X
Nigeria	X	X				
Norway	X	X	X	X	X	X
Oman			X			
Pakistan	X	X		X	X	X
Panama		X	X		X	
Papua New Guinea	X	X		X	X	X
Paraguay	X			X	X	X
Peru	X	X		X	X	X
Philippines	X	X	X	X	X	X
Poland	X	X	X			
Portugal	X	X	X	X	X	X
Rwanda	X	X		X		
Senegal	X	X		X	X	X
Sierra Leone	X	X		X		
Singapore	X	X	X		X	X
Somalia	X					
South Africa	X	X		X	X	
Spain	X	X	X	X	X	X
Sri Lanka	X	X	X	X	X	X
Sudan					X	
Sweden	X	X		X	X	X
Switzerland	X			X	X	X
Syria	X	X	X	X	X	X
Tanzania	X	X		X	X	
Thailand	X	X	X	X	X	X
Togo	X					
Trinidad and Tobago	X			X	X	X
Tunisia	X	X		X	X	X
Turkey	X	X	X	X	X	X
Uganda	X			X	X	
United Arab Emirates		X				
United Kingdom	X	X	X	X	X	X
U.S.A.	X	X	X	X	X	X
Uruguay	X	X	X	X	X	X
Venezuela	X	X	X	X	X	X
Yemen	X	X	X	X	X	X
Yugoslavia	X					
Zambia	X	X	X	X	X	X
Zimbabwe	X	X	X	X	X	X

Notes

The author thanks the Stanford Graduate School of Business for financial support, Romain Wacziarg for valuable discussions and for sharing a large international database, and Steve Beckman, Gary Fields, Bill Gould, Joop Hartog, David Kucera, John Martin, Mel Reder, Werner Sengenberger, Arvind Subramanian, and Ken Swinnerton for comments on earlier drafts.

1. For insightful perspectives on the conceptual issues, see Bhagwati and Hudec (1996), Brown (2000), Fields (1995), Maskus (2000), OECD (1996), Srinivasan (1996), and Stern (1996).

2. Henceforth, references to "labor standards" pertain to the "political" standards (conventions) developed by the International Labor Organization.

3. http://www.ilo.org/public/english/about/mandate.htm.

4. Ibid. The ILO also provides technical assistance and other services to employers' and workers' organizations.

5. In the former category are conventions on hours of work, workers' compensation, forced labor, etc. Other conventions focus more narrowly on conditions in particular occupations and industries, such as seafarers, dockworkers, fishermen, and agriculture.

6. This group includes several Eastern and Western European countries, as well as Botswana, the Central African Republic, Indonesia, Senegal, and Yemen.

7. The other countries in this category are Armenia, China, and Myanmar.

8. Article 33 was invoked only once—against Burma in March of 2000, regarding the use of forced labor. Six months after final approval of the action, no member countries had taken action against Burma. See Elliot (2001) and http://www.ilo.org/public/english/sitemap.htm (the ILO website) for more details on compliance issues.

9. The common law doctrine of employment at will provides an example.

10. Exact sample sizes vary with the availability of data for different variables. Sources and descriptions for all variables in the study appear in Appendix A. Appendix B lists the countries in the estimation samples.

11. Information on weekly hours of work is available for only a small number of mostly industrialized countries, for example.

12. The source is http://www.freedomhouse.org/ratings/index.htm. In determining the value of CIVLIB for each country, Freedom House evaluates the strength of most rights addressed in the ILO core conventions, including the presence of free trade unions and effective collective bargaining, freedom of choice of employment, equality of opportunity, and gender equality. The index also reflects evaluations of the freedom of press, religious freedom, independence of the judiciary, etc. The index is based on actual practice rather than constitutional guarantees.

13. Romain Wacziarg (2001) constructed this variable from liberalization dates

in Sachs and Warner (1995). The black market premium is defined as the difference between the black market exchange rate and the official exchange rate, divided by the official rate.

14. The reference category in the analysis is Confucian/Buddhist/Zen.

15. All tables of regression results report heteroskedasticity-robust standard errors estimated using the Huber/White estimator of the variance.

16. Technically, the two sets of countries respectively have the highest and lowest residuals from regression 2 in Table 2.

17. An index of democracy also did not produce a significant correlation.

18. For quite different views of the potential effects of international labor standards on labor conditions, see Basu (2000) and Maskus (2000).

19. This finding is consistent with the results of a recent study of the effects of trade liberalization on child labor in Vietnam. Trade liberalization was followed by increases in the price of rice and other exports, which in turn were followed by a decline in child labor force participation and an increase in school enrollments among students of secondary school age. The authors conclude: "Overall, rice price increases can account for almost half of the decline in child labor that occurs in Vietnam in the 1990s" (Edmonds and Pavcnik, 2002).

20. Unreported regressions found the same result after substituting TRADE for EXPORT.

21. Total compensation "includes direct wages, salaries, and other remuneration paid directly by employers plus all contributions by employers to social security programs on behalf of their employees." Both the compensation and productivity data are from surveys of relatively large establishments in the formal sector. "The data are converted into U.S. dollars using the average exchange rate for each year" (World Bank, 2001, Table 2.5). The fixed effects estimation discussed below removes country-specific anomalies in the measurement of compensation.

22. Appendix B lists the countries in the sample.

23. Interestingly, Kenya had ratified four core labor standards and thirty-six ILO conventions overall by 1980, while the United States had not ratified any core standards and only five conventions. As noted in the preceding section, ratifications of ILO conventions measure effective labor standards with error.

24. The regression survives a specification test—the Ramsey RESET test does not reject the hypothesis that the regression model has no omitted variables—for 1980–84, but not for the later period. Subsequent regressions pass this test unless otherwise noted.

25. Golub (1997) and Rodrik (1996, 1999) obtain similar results from smaller samples of countries and different time periods.

26. The four conventions are C98 (right to organize and bargain collectively),

C111 (discrimination in equality of opportunity or conditions of employment on the basis of race, religion, gender, political opinion, or social origin), C105 (abolition of forced labor), and C138 (minimum age of employment). The dummy variables take the value 1 if a country had ratified a convention by the *beginning* of the estimation period and zero otherwise.

27. The variables, DC98, DC105, DC111, and DC138, specify the number of years between the ratification of the four core standards and the beginning of the period for which compensation and productivity are measured.

28. Substituting actual minus predicted ratifications in an effort to capture the effect of involuntary ratifications did not produce statistically significant results.

29. This test effectively tests for statistically significant differences between the OLSQ and 2SLS estimates. Drawing on the analysis in the previous section, the instruments for CORE LS were dummy variables for (1) the majority religion and (2) the legal system of each country.

30. In a further check on the potential endogeneity of labor standards in the wage equation, separate regressions of *changes* in the number of core ILO conventions and total conventions ratified between 1980 and 1990 on the *levels* of the compensation and productivity variables in the 1980–84 period found no significant correlations.

31. On the other hand, random effects estimation seems inappropriate, because it is likely that the unobserved, country-specific fixed effects are correlated with explanatory variables. The possible endogeneity of labor standards implies that countries with unobservable (e.g., unspecified institutional) factors producing higher (lower) wages are more likely to ratify ILO conventions, for example. A similar argument may be made with respect to the productivity variable.

32. Notwithstanding the doubts expressed earlier, unreported random effect models were also computed. However, a specification test suggested by Hausman (1978) indicates that the random country-specific effects are correlated with the regressors, producing biased estimates of the latter.

33. Fixed effects rest on accurately measured changes in the policy variable over time. Since the official ILO website provides the ratifications data, mismeasurement seems unlikely. Between 1980 and 1995, 107 countries ratified at least one ILO convention, and 37 countries ratified at least one core convention. The sample range is from zero to thirty-three ratifications.

34. Earlier empirical studies of links between labor standards, exports, and FDI (OECD [1996]; Raynauld and Vidal [1998]) generally neglect the crucial role of other determinants. The study by Rodrik (1996) on a smaller sample of countries is an important exception.

35. Trade theory suggests an alternative mechanism, which (contrary to the

RTTB view) rationalizes a positive correlation between labor standards and trade. Free trade leads a country to specialize in sectors of comparative advantage, a process that induces labor and other resources to move into sectors in which they are relatively productive internationally. The movement into relatively productive (higher wage) sectors should improve the condition of labor, thereby reducing the cost of ratifying ILO conventions.

36. Romain Wacziarg (2001) calculated this variable from World Bank data.

37. Unreported export regressions included alternative trade policy measures, such as tariff rates and import duties as a percentage of total imports, but these variables were available for a much smaller set of countries.

38. The Ramsey RESET test rejects the hypothesis that these regression models have no omitted variables, however.

39. When the ratification variables are added to the specification in regression (2) of Table 8, the (unreported) regression coefficients are positive (contrary to the RTTB hypothesis) but not significant.

40. This is a standard approach to addressing measurement error in independent variables.

41. The coefficients (robust standard errors) for the three variables are $-.0006$ ($.0015$) for CHLAB, $.0057$ ($.0099$) for CIVLIB, and $-.0032$ ($.0025$) for LIFEEXP. When the variables are entered individually, the result for life expectancy is marginally significant—$.0036$ ($.0021$).

42. In the FDI statistics reported in International Monetary Fund (2000) and UNCTAD (2000b) foreign direct investment is defined as investment "involving a long-term relationship and reflecting a lasting interest and control of a resident entity in one economy (foreign direct investor or parent enterprise) in an enterprise resident of a different economy (FDI enterprise or affiliate enterprise or foreign affiliate)." In ordinary language, "[c]apital used by a firm in one country to establish a plant in another is labeled foreign direct investment, as are large purchases of equities that imply a lasting interest in an enterprise" (U.S. President, 2002, p. 262). FDI consists of equity capital, reinvested earnings, and intracompany loans and debt transactions. Negative FDI inflows (disinvestments) arise when "at least one of the three components of FDI . . . is negative and not offset by positive amounts of the remaining components" (UNCTAD, 2000b, p. 268).

43. Froot (1991) points out that FDI really represents a cross-country spread of corporate control that may not involve actual capital flows or investment in capacity.

44. Although industrialized countries as a group are net exporters and developing countries are net importers of capital, there were four years during the 1990s in which the United States was a net importer of capital.

45. On a related point, a recent OECD study concluded that "the evidence does not clearly point to any inexorable tendency toward global 'bidding wars' among governments in their competition to attract FDI," but it warned of a "permanent danger of such 'wars.'" (Oman, 2000, p. 10).

46. A newer micro approach rests on Dunning's observation that firms that engage in multinational activity must (1) have some specific product or productivity advantage over host country firms, (2) find the foreign location advantageous over home-country production, and (3) prefer ownership of a foreign subsidiary over alternative contracting arrangements (Dunning, 1988 ; Markusen, 2002). (With regard to point (3), several prominent companies in the global footwear industry contracted with local producers as an alternative to investing in production facilities in developing countries. This is a case in which low wages did not attract foreign investment.)

47. By the late 1980s, the largest shares of world FDI inflows were in the United States (30.8 percent), the United Kingdom (13.1), France (5.8), Spain (5.2), the Netherlands (4.0), and Australia (3.9). The smallest shares were in Iran, Surinam, and Panama. The shares for China and Myanmar, two countries frequently cited for human rights abuses, were 1.9 and 0.04 percent, respectively.

48. Expropriation is only one source of investment risk. Countries in which measures of contract repudiation and corruption are relatively high also have lower FDI shares, ceteris paribus, but these measures are too intercorrelated to determine the separate contribution of each risk factor.

49. The following measures of trade policy were tested as alternatives to OPEN: tariff rates, import duties as a percentage of total imports, and the black market premium.

50. Kucera finds that child labor and literacy are negatively related across countries and also finds that the relationship between FDI and child labor is generally negative.

51. The coefficients (robust standard errors) for the early 1980s are: −.0430 (.0242) for CHLAB, −.1781 (.1169) for CIVLIB, and .0178 (.0364) for LIFEEXP. For the late 1980s: .0214 (.0268) for CHLAB, −.0592 (.1220) for CIVLIB, and .0529 (.0345) for LIFEEXP.

52. Labor costs are predicted on the basis of productivity and price level.

References

Basu, Kaushik. 2000. "The Intriguing Relation between the Adult Minimum Wage and Child Labour." *Economic Journal* 110 (March): C50–C61.

Bhagwati, Jagdish, and Robert E. Hudec, eds. 1996. *Fair Trade and Harmonization: Prerequisites for Free Trade?* Cambridge: MIT Press.

Brown, Drusilla K. 2000. "International Trade and Core Labour Standards: A Survey of the Recent Literature." OECD Labour Market and Social Policy Occasional Paper No. 43, DEELSA/ELSA/WD(2000)4, October.

Chau, Nancy H., and Ravi Kanbur. 2001. "The Adoption of International Labor Standards Conventions: Who, When and Why?" Working Paper, Cornell University, July.

Dunning, John. 1988. *Multinationals, Technology and Competitiveness.* London: Unwin Hyman.

Edmonds, Eric, and Nina Pavcnik. 2002. "Does Globalization Increase Child Labor? Evidence from Vietnam." NBER Working Paper No. 8760, February.

Elliott, Kimberly Ann. 2001. "The ILO and Enforcement of Core Labor Standards." International Economics Policy Brief No. PB00–6. Washington, D.C.: Institute for International Economics, April.

Fields, Gary S. 1995. *Trade and Labor Standards: A Review of the Issues.* Paris: OECD.

Freedom House. *Freedom in the World* (various issues).

Froot, Kenneth A. 1991. "Japanese Foreign Direct Investment." NBER Working Paper No. 3737, June.

Golub, Stephen. 1997. "Are International Labor Standards Needed to Prevent Social Dumping?" *Finance and Development,* December.

Hausman, Jerry. 1978. "Specification Tests in Econometrics." *Econometrica* 46: 1251–71.

Huntington, Samuel. 1968. *Political Order in Changing Societies.* New Haven: Yale University Press.

International Monetary Fund. 2000. *Balance of Payments Statistics.* Washington, D.C.: International Monetary Fund.

Kucera, David. 2001. "The Effects of Core Workers Rights on Labour Costs and Foreign Direct Investment: Evaluating the Conventional Wisdom." Discussion Paper 130, International Institute for Labour Studies, Geneva.

La Porta, R., F. Lopez-de-Silanes, A. Shleifer, and R. W. Vishny. 1999. "The Quality of Government." *Journal of Law, Economics and Organization* 12: 1074–78.

Landes, David. 1998. *The Wealth and Poverty of Nations.* New York: W. W. Norton.

Lee, Jong-Wha. 1993. "International Trade, Distortions and Long-Run Economic Growth." *IMF Staff Papers* 40 (June): 204–22.

Lim, Ewe-Ghee. 2001. "Determinants of and the Relationship between Foreign Direct Investment and Growth: A Summary of the Recent Literature." IMF Working Paper No. WP/01/175, November.

Lipsey, Robert E. 2001. "Foreign Direct Investment and the Operations of Multinational Firms: Concepts, History and Data." NBER Working Paper No. 8665. Reprinted in James Harrigan, ed., *Handbook of International Economics*. London: Blackwell, 2002.

Markusen, J. R. 2002. *Multinational Firms and the Theory of International Trade*. Cambridge: MIT Press.

Maskus, Keith E. 2000. "Should Core Labor Standards Be Imposed through International Trade Policy?" Working Paper, World Bank.

Obstfeld, Maurice, and Allan M. Taylor. 2001. "Globalization and Capital Markets." Working Paper, NBER.

OECD. 1996. *Trade, Employment and Labour Standards: A Study of Core Worker's Rights and International Trade*. Paris: OECD.

———. 2000. *International Trade and Core Labour Standards*. Paris: OECD.

Oman, Charles. 2000. *Policy Competition for Foreign Direct Investment*. Paris: OECD.

Raynauld, Andre, and Jean-Pierre Vidal. 1998. *Labour Standards and International Competitiveness*. Northampton, MA: Edward Elgar.

Rodrik, Dani. 1996. "Labor Standards in International Trade: Do They Matter and What Do We Do about Them?" In R. Z. Lawrence, D. Rodrik, and J. Whalley, eds., *Emerging Agenda for Global Trade: High Stakes for Developing Countries*. Policy Essay No. 20. Washington, D.C.: Overseas Development Council.

———. 1999. "Democracies Pay Higher Wages." *Quarterly Journal of Economics* 114, no. 3 (August): 707–38.

Rogers, Carol Ann, and Kenneth A. Swinnerton. 2001. "Inequality, Productivity and Child Labor: Theory and Evidence." Working Paper, Department of Economics, Georgetown University, Washington, D.C.

Sachs, J. D., and A. Warner. 1995. "Economic Reform and the Process of Global Integration." *Brookings Papers on Economic Activity*, No. 1.

Srinivasan, T. N. 1996. "Trade and Human Rights." Discussion Paper No. 765. Economic Growth Center, Yale University.

Stern, Robert M. 1996. "Issues of Trade and International Labor Standards in the WTO System." Discussion Paper No. 387. School of Public Policy, University of Michigan.

Summers, Robert, and Alan Heston. 1993. "Penn World Tables, Version 5.5," available on diskette from the National Bureau of Economic Research, Cambridge, Mass.

UNCTAD. 2000a. *Handbook of Statistics*. New York: United Nations.

———. 1992, 2000b. *World Investment Report*. New York: United Nations.

UNIDO (United Nations Industrial Development Organization). 1998. *International Yearbook of Industrial Statistics*. New York: United Nations.

U.S. President. 2002. *Economic Report of the President*. Washington, D.C.: U.S. Government Printing Office.

Wacziarg, Romain. 2001. "Measuring the Dynamic Gains from Trade." *World Bank Economic Review* 15, no. 3 (October): 393–429.

Weber, Max. 1958. *The Protestant Ethic and the Spirit of Capitalism*. New York: Charles Scribner's Sons.

World Bank. 2001. *World Development Indicators*. Washington, D.C.

International Labor Standards and Decent Work: Perspectives from the Developing World

GARY S. FIELDS

I. Introduction

Billions of people in the world live in appalling conditions. The World Bank and the United Nations reckon that three billion people—nearly half of humanity—subsist on less than U.S.$2.00 per person per day (after adjusting for differences in monetary units using Purchasing Power Parity adjustments). The challenges of economic development are enormous.

The theme of this conference, international labor standards, is one approach that is being taken to try to meet these development challenges.[1] I am and have been a strong supporter of those international labor standards that represent basic human rights in the workplace, not because of the economic effects that they would have (which, by the way, I think are positive) but simply because I believe they are right and that concerned world citizens should try to help the less fortunate among us (Fields, 1990, 1995, 2000).[2] Some kinds of work (slavery, indentured servitude, forced labor, the worst forms of child labor) are an outrage wherever in the world they occur, and they should be prohibited. Certain basic human rights in the workplace should, in my view, be guaranteed to workers—in particular, the right to freedom of association and collective bargaining. Like most other economists, I do not think that it is possible to pass laws or set standards to assure other important and sought-after conditions of work—most important, jobs themselves, earnings levels, and other conditions of employment. These, I believe, can best be achieved through rapid, broad-based economic growth, on which I have written elsewhere (Fields, 2001b).

It is a very positive development that the world community has now reached agreement on four core labor standards, described further below. The moral force of this agreement will help slow and possibly even reverse the infamous "race to the bottom"—for example, child labor in the carpet industries of India undermining Nepal's efforts to keep its carpet industry free of child labor (Hensman, 2000).

Ironically, some of the loudest and most strident voices against international labor standards come from the poorest parts of the world. My thesis in this chapter is that while *some* of the arguments being voiced against international labor standards have merit, others do not, and so I attempt to differentiate the good from the less good positions.

The paper proceeds as follows. Section II discusses international labor standards as they were and Section III international labor standards as they are. Section IV reviews the positions of developing countries with regard to international labor standards. The conclusions are summed up in Section V.

II. International Labor Standards: How It Was

Responsibility for international labor standards has traditionally rested with the International Labour Organization (ILO). The ILO, founded in 1919, is the specialized agency of the United Nations which seeks to promote social justice and internationally recognized human and labor rights, thereby improving the situation of human beings in the world of work (Report of the Director General, 1999, p. 5). The ILO's historical approach to improving workplace standards has been to promote conventions and recommendations for ratification by member countries. These conventions and recommendations cover a wide range of labor standards, including respect of fundamental human rights, protection of wages, employment security, working conditions, labor market and social policies, and industrial relations. At present, there are 184 conventions, 195 recommendations, and 175 member states.

Ratification of labor standards is central to the ILO's work program. A past Director-General, Michel Hansenne, stated: "One of our major responsibilities, therefore, is to ensure that, once adopted, standards are widely ratified by States which solemnly pledge to apply them. We would be falling far short of our claim to universality if we were to insist on the universality of standards as a matter of principle without taking the same trouble to make sure that they were universally implemented" (ILO, 1994, pp. 29–30). Similarly, the current Director-General, Juan Somavía, has called for renewing the organization's work on labor standards by reinvigorating international labor standards, enhancing the ILO's work on standards, re-evaluating standard-setting, choosing suitable subjects for standards, and reassessing existing conventions (ILO, 1999).

U.S. trade law has for many years maintained the importance of the following internationally recognized workers' rights:[3]

Freedom of association

The right to organize and bargain collectively

Prohibition of forced or compulsory labor

A minimum age for the employment of children

Guarantee of acceptable working conditions (possibly including maximum hours of work per week, a weekly rest period, limits to work by young persons, a minimum wage, minimum workplace safety and health standards, and elimination of employment discrimination)

Labor conditionality clauses are now attached to the Caribbean Basin Economic Recovery Act (1983), the GSP (Generalized System of Preferences) program (1984), the Overseas Private Investment Corporation (1985), the Multilateral Investment Guarantee Agency (1987), Section 301 of the Omnibus Trade and Competitiveness Act (1988), the Andean Trade Preference Act (1991), and Section 599 of the Foreign Operations Appropriations Act (1992). In the case of the GSP program, the President is authorized to withhold recognition of a country that "has not taken or is not taking steps to afford internationally recognized worker rights to workers in the country (including any designated zone in that country)."[4] In a dozen cases, GSP benefits have been withdrawn or suspended (USGAO, 1994; Van Liemt, 1989; Tsogas, 2001).

Turning to other parts of the world, the Social Charter of the European Union, approved by all member nations except for Britain, specifies an even broader list of worker "rights":

Freedom of movement

The right to employment and remuneration

The improvement of living and working conditions

The right to social protection

The right to freedom of association and collective bargaining

The right to vocational training

The right of men and women to equal treatment

The right of information, consultation, and participation

The right to health and safety in the workplace

The protection of children and adolescents in employment

The protection of elderly persons

The protection of persons with disabilities

How well did these far-reaching attempts work? Not at all. Most countries could and did adopt what they wished and ignored what they didn't want. Take the United States as an example. Of the eight conventions that have been designated as fundamental, the United States has ratified precisely two. This does not mean that the United States is hostile to these standards or indifferent to them, but rather that it has found other ways to achieve its desired labor standards. Indeed, in his chapter in this volume, Robert Flanagan presents detailed econometric evidence for the 1980s and 1990s showing that ratifications of labor standards made no statistically significant difference to labor rights and conditions, because these latter are improved by free trade policies and economic growth.

III. International Labor Standards: How It Is

In the mid-1990s, a sea change took place: the "try everything" approach to international labor standards was supplanted by a new, more focused position at the ILO, the Organisation for Economic Co-operation and Development (OECD), and other international agencies.[5] The World Summit on Social Development held in 1995 in Copenhagen defined core labor standards as including the prohibition of forced labor and child labor, freedom of association and the right to organize and bargain collectively, equal remuneration for men and women for work of equal value, and nondiscrimination in employment. What was important about the World Social Summit was not so much what was included but what wasn't: minimum wages, mandated fringe benefits, maximum hours of work, and the like.

Another major milestone was a 1996 OECD study on international trade, employment, and labor standards (OECD, 1996). Two branches of the OECD that had often been working in conflict with each other—the Employment, Labour and Social Affairs Committee and the Trade Committee— agreed upon a set of core labor standards (freedom of association and the right to collective bargaining, elimination of exploitative forms of child labor, the prohibition of forced labor, and nondiscrimination in employment) along with mechanisms to promote those standards worldwide.[6]

The next important event was the December 1996 Singapore ministerial meeting of the World Trade Organization. The member states reiterated their commitment to internationally recognized core labor standards, supported collaboration between the WTO and ILO secretariats, rejected the use of labor standards for protectionist purposes, and recognized the ILO as the competent body for dealing with this issue.

A truly defining moment for international labor standards was the June 1998 International Labor Conference of the ILO, which approved the Declaration on Fundamental Principles and Rights at Work. Because this document is so important to present-day international labor standards, it is reproduced in the appendix to this chapter. The declaration affirmed that all of the member states of the ILO have the responsibility to "promote and to realize, in good faith and in accordance with the Constitution [of the ILO], the principles concerning the fundamental rights," which include:

Freedom of association and effective recognition of the right to collective bargaining
The elimination of all forms of forced or compulsory labor
The effective abolition of child labor
The elimination of discrimination in respect of employment and occupation

What was so important was that these core labor standards did not have to be ratified; they were binding on the member countries of the ILO by virtue of the very fact of their membership in the organization.

Since that time, these four core labor standards have been reaffirmed in a variety of fora. In 1999, U.N. Secretary-General Kofi Annan integrated these four core labor standards into a nine-point Global Compact of shared values and principles that has been endorsed by a wide range of business groups, individual companies, organized labor, and nongovernmental organizations. Then, in August 2000, the member nations of the OECD incorporated these core labor standards into revised *Guidelines for Multinational Enterprises*. In its November 2001 Ministerial meeting at Doha, the WTO reaffirmed its support for core labor standards as laid out in the 1996 Singapore Ministerial. At that time, it also dropped all labor-related issues from its agenda, leaving those to the ILO.

Alas, the international financial institutions—in particular, the World Bank and the International Monetary Fund but also the Asian Development Bank, the Inter-American Development Bank, the African Development Bank, and the European Bank for Reconstruction and Development—have not endorsed or worked actively to support these core labor standards (OECD, 2000, pp. 57–59).[7] The main reason for their reticence, apparently, is opposition to freedom of association and collective bargaining, because of the possible harmful effects that the exercise of these rights might have. These worries can, I submit, be largely overcome by setting up industrial relations systems in ways that prescribe and proscribe what employers and unions must do, may do, and may not do. John Pencavel has written thoughtfully on this (Pencavel, 1997). The failure of the international financial institutions to back core labor standards is a real pity, both because of the implications of their nonsupport for workers in the developing world and because it opens up these organizations to criticism and protests, many of which could be avoided.

Today, the ILO continues to advance core labor standards as a central part of its work program, which has now been reoriented toward the mission of "Decent Work for All." Under Director-General Juan Somavía, Decent Work aims not just to create jobs for women and men everywhere but also to create jobs of acceptable quality. The ILO aims to redress the so-called Decent Work Deficit by pursuing four strategic objectives: full employment, improved levels of socioeconomic security, universal respect for fundamental principles and rights at work, and the strengthening of social dialogue (ILO, 1999, 2001). Core labor standards fall under the "universal respect for fundamental principles and rights at work." The ILO's work program gives priority to these core standards over all others.

I regard Decent Work as a new and welcome redirection of the ILO's efforts and have written more on this in Fields (2001a). Jobs in which core labor standards are not honored cannot be regarded as decent. This is how I define indecent work: work under conditions so odious or harmful that it would be better for people not to work at all than to work under such damaging conditions. In opposing indecent work defined in this way and seeking its elimination, I recognize that the alternative may not be pretty. What would happen to those who are displaced cannot be ignored. If they move into the so-called informal sector and engage in street-vending, petty services, family farming, or microenterprises, it is one thing. But if the alternative is prostitution, picking through garbage dumps, or worse, it is quite another. These fallback options vary from place to place; what they are must be recognized.

Decent Work shifts the focus of the ILO to workplace outcomes: once core labor standards are satisfied, attention shifts to how much work there is, how remunerative and secure is the work, and under what conditions that work is carried out. These criteria raise a genuine development challenge: finding ways to increase employment and wages and pull labor market conditions up through economic growth in order to improve the economic well-being of people around the world and lessen poverty in the world. I urge the ILO, the World Bank, and other national and international development institutions to form a genuine partnership centered on these objectives.

IV. Developing Country Views on International Labor Standards: Perceptions and Reality

If international labor standards might in fact lead to increased employment, higher earnings levels, and better workplace conditions for the working people of the world, it would be expected that many of the stakeholders in the developing countries—the labor unions, unorganized workers, nongovernmental organizations, and government agencies—and their friends in the developed world would be enthusiastic supporters of standards. Indeed, there are many, many voices in both the developed and developing worlds that are supportive of international labor standards. It goes without saying that labor groups and human rights groups like the International Confederation of Free

Trade Unions, the International Labor Rights Fund, and the OECD's Trade Union Advisory Council support these standards. So too do some labor economists, a very visible and vocal example being Harvard's Richard Freeman (1997). Then there are the former number two officials at the World Bank, Joseph Stiglitz (2000), and the International Monetary Fund, Stanley Fischer (2000). The list of supporters could go on at great length.

The fact that international labor standards are favored by organized labor in the developed countries is often decried as "disguised protectionism" and not very well disguised protectionism at that. In the case of those labor unions and labor ministries in the rich countries that aim to protect their interests against those of developing country workers, the claim of protectionism is a believable one. Sometimes, the protectionist motive is made explicit, as in the suggestion to "raise the cost of doing business in other nations through international organizing, international labor standards, and multinational bargaining campaigns" (Hecker and Hallock, 1991, p. 5) or as in the call by the President of the U.S. labor union UNITE (the Union of Needletrades, Industrial, and Textile Employees), Bruce Raynor, to "protect good union jobs in this country" (Raynor, 2001). Yet, it would surely be unfair to label all those who favor international labor standards (myself among them) as protectionist. In Richard Freeman's words, "Most advocates of standards want what they say they want: to guarantee as far as possible certain basic rights to workers around the world."

There are, however, many opponents of international labor standards. The opposition takes two forms. Some oppose international labor standards per se. Others oppose linking labor standards to international trade.

Let us start with the line of argument about standards per se. Many companies believe that standards will hamper their ability to pursue business objectives. Their opposition to international labor standards comes as no surprise.

Perhaps more surprising is that while most developing countries are on the record as supporting core labor standards, not all do. Here is a vivid and articulate statement of opposition to labor standards coming from Malaysia's Prime Minister:

> Western governments openly propose to eliminate the competitive edge of East Asia. The recent proposal for a world-wide minimum wage is a blatant example.

Westerners know that this is the sole comparative advantage of the developing countries. All other comparative advantages (technology, capital, rich domestic markets, legal frameworks, management and marketing networks) are with the developed states. It is obvious that professed concern about workers' welfare is motivated by selfish interest. Sanctimonious pronouncements on humanitarian, democratic and environmental issues are likely to be motivated by a similar selfish desire to put as many obstacles as possible in the way of anyone attempting to catch up and compete with the West. (Mahathir, 1994)

And another by India's Commerce and Industry Minister, Murasoli Maran:

The Western world, the industrialized world, wants to take away our comparative advantage. It is a pernicious way of robbing our comparative advantage. The developing countries consider it as a maneuver by wealthy nations to force our wages up, to undermine our competitiveness. This is the secret. (*New York Times*, December 17, 1999)

In both these cases, the argument concerns the *effect* of standards—in particular, the higher labor costs that they would engender.

In essence, this is a stages-of-development argument. Many developing countries contend that poor labor standards are more a symptom of their lower level of economic development than any deliberate intent or design on their part. An example is a statement by Mr. Supachai Panitchpakdi of Thailand, the Director-General Designate of the WTO, who said: "Sanctions against bad labor practices will almost automatically hit smaller developing nations because they have had bad labor records due to poverty" (*International Herald Tribune*, December 8, 1999). This argument makes sense if the "bad labor records" in question concern workers' earnings or other employment benefits. It makes much less sense in terms of internationally agreed *core* labor standards. As an Indian labor activist, Sujata Gothoskar of Bombay, stated: "With this argument, every struggle by the workers for a better life may be argued as eroding the competitive advantage of our country. Does this not negate the rationale and existence of the trade unions themselves?" (cited in Hensman, 2000).

The stages-of-development argument comes up in another form. Some developing countries argue that given their lower stage of economic development, the rapid economic transformations many are currently undergoing, and the high degree of informality in their labor markets, it would not be appropriate to apply such aspects of labor rights as are found in Europe—in particular, union representation on boards and other aspects of the European model of labor relations (Salazar-Xirinachs, 1999). Here too, we have an objection that is based on something other than *core* labor standards: the core labor standards concerning freedom of association and collective bargaining do not provide for union membership on boards of companies, works councils, or anything else.

Moving from standards to ways of achieving them, we come to the question of the linkage of trade and labor standards—in particular, the question of trade sanctions for countries that do not abide by internationally agreed labor standards. Many developing country governments fear that if such a linkage is established, their access to world markets may be jeopardized, which, it might be said, is protectionist in its own way. Among the consistent critics of such linkages are the governments of such leading developing countries as India, China, Malaysia, South Africa, Brazil, and Mexico, and the member states of the Association of South-East Asian Nations, the South Asian trade ministers, an association of African nations, the Rio Group of Latin American Nations, and the Organization of American States. For example, India "has all along maintained that it is not against core labor standards in itself, but opposed to its abuse for trade purposes to deny market access to exports from developing countries" ("EU Backtracks," 2000).

At the WTO ministerial meeting in Seattle in 1999, more than one hundred WTO members from the developing world opposed international labor standards, saying that they can't afford them. As the *New York Times* noted editorially at the time (December 3, 1999), "There is no easy resolution of this issue, because member nations do not agree on what labor rights provisions should be set." Since then, the so-called G-15 of developing countries has been formed (members include Algeria, Argentina, Brazil, Chile, Egypt, India, Indonesia, Kenya, Jamaica, Malaysia, Mexico, Nigeria, Peru, Senegal, Sri Lanka, Venezuela, and Zimbabwe). This organization has come out strongly against linking core labor standards (and also environmental standards) to global trade.

On this issue of trade sanctions, the debate is strong on both sides.[8] In my judgment, there is a valid reason to worry about trade sanctions and a valid reason not to. The valid reason *to* worry is that U.S. law still carries the possibility of *unilateral* trade sanctions against countries that are judged (by the United States) to have engaged in an unfair trade practice (against the United States). A reason *not* to worry is that *multilateral* trade sanctions are effectively off the table. Let me say a bit about each.

First, on *unilateral* trade sanctions, U.S. law contains a provision known popularly as "Super 301," after the section of the U.S. Trade Code to which it refers. Since 1988, "denial of internationally recognized worker rights" has been included among the list of unfair trade practices. For this purpose, the "internationally recognized worker rights" include a "guarantee of acceptable working conditions" including minimum wages, hours of work, and the like. Developing countries are right to be concerned. After all, if tariffs can be imposed unilaterally on imported steel under Section 203 of the Trade Act, as they just were in recent months, what is to prevent the United States from withdrawing GSP benefits from developing countries or imposing other penalties on them under Section 301 of the same act? Jagdish Bhagwati (1995, 1998), Arvind Panagariya (2000), and T. N. Srinivasan (1998) are among the highly vocal critics of the possibility of trade sanctions in U.S. law.

On the other hand, on the issue of *multilateral* trade sanctions, the developing countries need not worry. The simple fact is that labor standards are not now subject to the rules and disciplines imposed by the world's trading organization, the WTO, and are not likely to be. Although some nations in Europe and North America favor such a linkage, most other countries do not (including, it might be added, the European Union itself).[9] The WTO's official website sums up the present situation thus:

> Most developing countries and many developed nations believe the issue of core labour standards does not belong in the WTO. These member governments see the issue of trade and labour standards as a guise for protectionism in developed-country markets. Developing-country officials have said that efforts to bring labour standards into the WTO represent a smokescreen for undermining the comparative advantage of lower-wage developing countries. Many officials in developing countries argue that better working conditions and improved labour rights arise through economic growth. They say that if the issue of core labour standards became enforceable under WTO rules, any sanctions imposed against countries with lower labour standards would merely perpetuate poverty and delay improvements in workplace standards. (WTO, 2002)

The WTO has not budged from the position it took when it was first created in 1996: that matters of labor standards are best left to the ILO and are outside the purview of the WTO.

Developing countries complain that linking labor standards to trade may be a slippery slope, leading only to further demands from developed countries in the future. Many developing countries, such as India and Brazil, oppose even discussing labor standards within the WTO, because it would be a step toward empowering the WTO to impose sanctions against countries that do not enforce prescribed labor standards. These countries worry that by bringing labor standards and other issues such as environment into the WTO, the organization may be overloaded, thereby being rendered incapable of concentrating on its core mission of liberalizing the world trading system, from which these countries hope to benefit through increased market access.

Returning to the concern of developed countries to get developing countries to do what *we* want *them* to do in the area of labor standards, a more practical approach would be to tie trade agreements with us to the commitment by developing countries to enforce *their own* labor laws. This was done in the case of the recently concluded trade treaty between the United States and Jordan and applies to pending agreements with Chile and Singapore. In other situations, the problem of low labor standards in developing countries is in part one of institutional deficiency rather than any lack of desire to see the standards implemented. Enforcement is itself costly, both in terms of scarce administrative capabilities and in terms of scarce financial resources. It is worth noting in this context that under some interpretations of international law, abridgement of rights including labor rights is acceptable if satisfying the right is too expensive. We can and should be more generous with foreign aid to help bring about such improvements.

V. Conclusion

First, the old approach to international labor standards involved setting some 184 standards, which the ILO encouraged its 175 member countries around the world to adopt. The United States itself has tried to impose labor standards on its trading partners by threatening trade sanctions against those trading partners who failed to adhere to the prescribed standards. These measures were viewed, justifiably, as protectionist by developing and developed countries alike.

Second, after a long debate, world opinion has coalesced around the need for and desirability of core labor standards in four areas: freedom of association and effective recognition of the right to collective bargaining, the elimination of all forms of forced or compulsory labor, the effective abolition of child labor, and the elimination of discrimination in respect of employment and occupation. Employer, worker, and government representatives in the ILO have issued a Declaration on Fundamental Principles and Rights at Work, according to which acceptance of these standards is binding on the countries of the world by virtue of their membership in the ILO with no ratifications or further action being required. With these core labor standards as base, the ILO has launched a "Decent Work" agenda aimed at securing decent work for women and men everywhere.

Third, many developing countries continue to oppose international labor standards. Their principal points of opposition include losing their comparative advantage, losing the benefits of free trade, and the inappropriateness of imposing demanding standards at their current stage of development. While some of their concerns are warranted, other of these arguments fail to stand up to scrutiny, either because the arguments themselves are not well reasoned or because they reflect a misunderstanding of what core labor standards they are now being asked to abide by. It would appear, therefore, that to an important degree, developing countries' opposition to international labor standards comes more from what *was* being proposed than from what *is now* on the table. Those in the international community who support more widespread labor standards would do well to avoid such shorthands as "internationally recognized labor standards," "worker rights," and the like and instead discuss "the four core labor standards" in general or one of the four in particular.

In conclusion, then, should the developing countries have labor standards that are different from Western or international standards? My answer is, yes and no. The *core* labor standards discussed in this paper—including freedom of association and collective bargaining, the elimination of all forms of forced or compulsory labor, the effective abolition of child labor, and the

elimination of discrimination in respect of employment and occupation—
are fundamental human rights in the workplace. They should be honored in
the developing countries the same as elsewhere. On the other hand, as a
practical matter, certain important labor standards—in particular, earnings
levels but also minimum wages, maximum hours of work, mandated fringe
benefits, occupational safety and health regulations, and the like—must be
allowed to *differ* across countries. These latter standards should be determined within countries and not by international mandate.

The developing countries are right in opposing the imposition of standards regarding earnings, hours, benefits, or safety and health before labor
market conditions warrant. But such mandates have all but disappeared
from serious policy discussion at present, and therefore many arguments
now being voiced against labor standards are simply irrelevant. What *is* relevant is the appallingly high rates of unemployment and underemployment,
low levels of earnings, high rates of poverty, and appalling standards of living
of literally billions of people in the world. How to achieve economic growth
of a type that will remedy these conditions is a matter of great international
urgency.

Appendix: ILO Declaration on Fundamental Principles and Rights at Work

86th Session, Geneva, June 1998

Whereas the ILO was founded in the conviction that social justice is essential to
universal and lasting peace;

Whereas economic growth is essential but not sufficient to ensure equity, social
progress and the eradication of poverty, confirming the need for the ILO to promote
strong social policies, justice and democratic institutions;

Whereas the ILO should, now more than ever, draw upon all its standard-setting,
technical cooperation and research resources in all its areas of competence, in particular employment, vocational training and working conditions, to ensure that, in
the context of a global strategy for economic and social development, economic and
social policies are mutually reinforcing components in order to create broad-based
sustainable development;

Whereas the ILO should give special attention to the problems of persons with
special social needs, particularly the unemployed and migrant workers, and mobilize

and encourage international, regional and national efforts aimed at resolving their problems, and promote effective policies aimed at job creation;

Whereas, in seeking to maintain the link between social progress and economic growth, the guarantee of Fundamental Principles and Rights at Work is of particular significance in that it enables the persons concerned, to claim freely and on the basis of equality of opportunity, their fair share of the wealth which they have helped to generate, and to achieve fully their human potential;

Whereas the ILO is the constitutionally mandated international organization and the competent body to set and deal with international labour standards, and enjoys universal support and acknowledgement in promoting Fundamental Rights at Work as the expression of its constitutional principles;

Whereas it is urgent, in a situation of growing economic interdependence, to re-affirm the immutable nature of the Fundamental Principles and Rights embodied in the Constitution of the Organization and to promote their universal application;

The International Labour Conference

1. Recalls:

(a) that in freely joining the ILO, all Members have endorsed the principles and rights set out in its Constitution and in the Declaration of Philadelphia, and have undertaken to work towards attaining the overall objectives of the Organization to the best of their resources and fully in line with their specific circumstances;

(b) that these principles and rights have been expressed and developed in the form of specific rights and obligations in Conventions recognized as fundamental both inside and outside the Organization.

2. Declares that all Members, even if they have not ratified the Conventions in question, have an obligation arising from the very fact of membership in the Organization to respect, to promote and to realize, in good faith and in accordance with the Constitution, the principles concerning the fundamental rights which are the subject of those Conventions, namely:

(a) freedom of association and the effective recognition of the right to collective bargaining;

(b) the elimination of all forms of forced or compulsory labour;

(c) the effective abolition of child labour; and

(d) the elimination of discrimination in respect of employment and occupation.

3. Recognizes the obligation on the Organization to assist its Members, in response to their established and expressed needs, in order to attain these objectives by making full use of its constitutional, operational and budgetary resources, including, by the mobilization of external resources and support, as well as by encouraging other international organizations with which the ILO has established relations, pursuant to article 12 of its Constitution, to support these efforts:

(a) by offering technical cooperation and advisory services to promote the ratification and implementation of the fundamental Conventions;

(b) by assisting those Members not yet in a position to ratify some or all of these Conventions in their efforts to respect, to promote and to realize the principles concerning fundamental rights which are the subject of these Conventions; and

(c) by helping the Members in their efforts to create a climate for economic and social development.

4. Decides that, to give full effect to this Declaration, a promotional follow-up, which is meaningful and effective, shall be implemented in accordance with the measures specified in the annex hereto, which shall be considered as an integral part of this Declaration.

5. Stresses that labour standards should not be used for protectionist trade purposes, and that nothing in this Declaration and its follow-up shall be invoked or otherwise used for such purposes; in addition, the comparative advantage of any country should in no way be called into question by this Declaration and its follow-up.

Notes

An earlier version of this paper was presented at the Conference on International Labor Standards, Stanford Law School, May 2002. I am very pleased to acknowledge the helpful contributions of Puja Gupta and Dhushyanth Raju to this paper, as well as insightful comments by Robert Flanagan, William Gould, Arvind Subramanian, and Kenneth Swinnerton.

1. Another approach is broad-based economic growth, on which I have also been working for a long time. For a summary, see Fields (2001b).

2. See also the discussions by Leary (1996) and Swinnerton (1997).

3. See, for example, Lyle (1991), Reich (1994), and Tsogas (2001).

4. At the time that this paper is being written, that particular provision has lapsed, but it is likely to be renewed shortly.

5. Many in the trade union movement and their supporters regard this as a dangerous basket to put all one's eggs in (Turner, Katz, and Hurd, 2001; Compa, 2002).

6. Trade sanctions were mentioned but were neither approved nor disapproved.

7. The World Bank, for instance, states: "There is a case for international concern over core standards"—hardly a ringing endorsement (World Bank, 1995, p. 6).

8. For an eloquent statement in favor of linkage, see Hensman (2000). For an eloquent statement opposed, see Bhagwati (2001).

9. According to Pascal Lamy, the European Commissioner for Trade, "We do not want sanctions. I repeat we do not want sanctions here. We differ from the USA on the issue of core labor standards" (*The Statesman*, Mar. 6, 2000).

References

Bhagwati, Jagdish. 1995. "Trade Liberalization and Fair Trade Demands: Addressing the Environmental and Labour Standards Issues." *World Economy* 18 (November): 745–59.

———. 1998. *A Stream of Windows*. Cambridge: MIT Press.

———. "Free Trade and Labour." *Financial Times*, August 29, 2001.

Compa, Lance. 2002. "Promise and Peril: Core Labor Standards in Global Trade and Investment." In George Andreopoulos, ed., *International Human Rights a Half Century after the Universal Declaration*. New York: Peter Lang.

Compa, Lance, et al. 2001. *Workers in the Global Economy*. Ithaca, N.Y.: Cornell University School of Industrial and Labor Relations.

"EU Backtracks on Core Labour Standards." *The Statesman* (India), March 6, 2000.

Fields, Gary S. 1990. "Labor Standards, Economic Development, and International Trade." In Stephen Herzenberg and Jorge F. Pérez-López, eds., *Labor Standards and Development in the Global Economy*. Washington: U.S. Department of Labor.

———. 1995. *Trade and Labour Standards: A Review of the Issues*. Paris: OECD.

———. 2000. "The Role of Labor Standards in U.S. Trade Policies." In Alan V. Deardorff and Robert M. Stern, eds., *Social Dimensions of U.S. Trade Policy*. Ann Arbor: University of Michigan Press.

———. 2001a. "'Decent Work' and Development Policies." Cornell University, School of Industrial and Labor Relations, Working Paper, September.

———. 2001b. *Distribution and Development: A New Look at the Developing World*. Cambridge: MIT Press and the Russell Sage Foundation.

Fischer, Stanley. 2000. "Globalization: Valid Concerns?" Speech presented to the Federal Reserve Bank of Kansas City Economic Symposium, Jackson Hole, Wyoming, August 26.

Freeman, Richard. 1997. "International Labor Standards and World Trade: Friends or Foes?" In Jeffrey J. Schott, ed., *The World Trading System: Challenges Ahead*. Washington: Institute for International Economics.

Hecker, S., and M. Hallock. 1991. *Labor in a Global Economy: Perspectives from the U.S. and Canada*. Eugene: University of Oregon Press.

Hensman, Rohini. 2000. "World Trade and Workers' Rights: To Link or Not to Link?" *Economic and Political Weekly*, April 8.

———. 2001. "World Trade and Workers' Rights: In Search of an Internationalist Position." *Antipode* 33: 3, Special Issue, Bombay, India.

ILO. 1994. *Defending Values, Promoting Change*. Geneva: ILO.

———. 1999. *Report of the Director-General: Decent Work*. Report presented at the 87th Session of the International Labour Conference, Geneva, June.

————. 2001. *Report of the Director-General: Reducing the Decent Work Deficit—A Global Challenge*. Report presented at the 89th Session of the International Labor Conference, Geneva, Switzerland, June.

International Confederation of Free Trade Unions and World Confederation of Labour. 2002. "Beyond the Monterrey Consensus: A Trade Union Agenda for the Governance of Globalization," March.

International Herald Tribune. 1999. "Seattle Not a Waste, Thai Says." December 8.

Leary, Virginia A. 1996. "Workers' Rights and International Trade: The Social Clause (GATT, ILO, NAFTA, U.S. Laws)." In Jagdish Bhagwati and Robert Hudec, eds., *Fair Trade and Harmonization: Prerequisites for Free Trade? Volume 2*. Cambridge: MIT Press.

Lyle, Faye. 1991. "Worker Rights in U.S. Policy." In *Foreign Labor Trends*, pp. 91–154. Washington: Bureau of International Labor Affairs.

Mahathir, Mohammed. 1994. "East Asia Will Find Its Own Roads to Democracy." *International Herald Tribune*, May 17.

OECD. 1996. *Trade, Employment, and Labour Standards*. Paris: OECD.

————. 2000. *International Trade and Core Labour Standards*. Paris: OECD.

Panagariya, Arvind. 2000. "Trade-Labour Link: A Post-Seattle Analysis." In Zdenek Drabek, ed., *Globalization Under Threat*. Cheltenham, U.K.: Edward Elgar.

Pencavel, John. 1997. "The Legal Framework for Collective Bargaining in Developing Countries." In Sebastian Edwards and Nora Claudia Lustig, eds., *Labor Markets in Latin America*, pp. 27–61. Washington: Brookings Institution.

Raynor, Bruce. 2001. "Global Sweatshops and the Worldwide Labor Movement." Speech at Cornell University, August 30.

Reich, Robert. 1994. "Keynote Address." In U.S. Department of Labor, *International Labor Standards and Global Economic Integration*. Washington: Bureau of International Labor Affairs.

Salazar-Xirinachs, José M. 1999. "The Trade-Labor Nexus: Developing Countries' Perspectives." Speech given at the ODC/Friedrich Ebert Stiftung Conference on Trade, Labor Standards, and the WTO. Washington, DC, November 15.

Srinivasan, T. N. 1998. "Trade and Human Rights." In Alan Deardorff and Robert Stern, eds., *Representation of Constituent Interests in the Design and Implementation of U.S. Trade Policies*. Ann Arbor: University of Michigan Press.

Stiglitz, Joseph E. 2000. "Democratic Development as the Fruits of Labor." Keynote Address to the Industrial Relations Research Association, Boston, January 8.

Swinnerton, Kenneth A. 1997. "An Essay on Economic Efficiency and Core Labor Standards." *The World Economy* 20, no. 1 (January): 73–86.

Tsogas, George. 2001. *Labor Regulation in a Global Economy*. London: M. E. Sharpe.

Turner, Lowell, Harry Katz, and Richard Hurd, eds. 2001. *Rekindling the Movement:*

Labor's Quest for Relevance in the 21st Century. Ithaca, NY: Cornell University Press.

U.S. General Accounting Office. 1994. *International Trade Assessment of the Generalized System of Preferences Program*. Washington, DC: Government Printing Office.

Van Liemt, Gijsbert. 1989. "Minimum Labour Standards and International Trade: Would a Social Clause Work?" *International Labour Review* 128, no. 4: 433–48.

"Why India and Others See U.S. as Villain in Trade." *New York Times*, December 17, 1999.

World Bank. 1995. *World Development Report*. New York: Oxford University Press.

World Trade Organization. 2002. "Trade and Labour Standards: Subject of Intense Debate." http://www.wto.org/english/thewto_e/minist_e/min99_e/english/about_e/18lab_e.htm.

Labor Law for a Global Economy: The Uneasy Case for International Labor Standards

WILLIAM B. GOULD IV

> [O]pen trade is not contrary to the interest of working people. Competition and integration lead to stronger growth, more and better jobs, more widely shared gains. Renewed protectionism in any of our nations would lead to a spiral of retaliation that would diminish the standard of living for working people everywhere.[1]
>
> —President Bill Clinton

I. Introduction

In many respects the current debate about international labor standards is a mirror image of the tension between labor law and antitrust policies in the American domestic arena. From a labor policy perspective, a substantial portion of the dynamics relates to the attempt to improve working conditions so as to promote the dignity of labor and, in so doing, an environment of enhanced living standards. The Clayton Antitrust Act of 1914 in this country states that labor is not an article of commerce and is thus a cost of production that is genuinely unique.[2] This is the direct link to the international human rights campaign that has received more prominence in the United States over the past three decades and its connection to the employment relationship.

But at the same time, unimpeded trade is designed to promote competition, which benefits the consuming public through more efficient processes and thus lower prices. The unprecedented prosperity of the past five and a half decades is undoubtedly attributable, in substantial part, to the rejection of the Smoot-Hawley Act,[3] sponsoring protectionism, and the adoption of the Reciprocal Trade Agreement Act of 1934,[4] which led to the decline in average world tariffs from approximately 40 percent in 1947 to less than 5 percent at the beginning of the last decade.[5]

The Organisation for Economic Co-operation and Development (OECD) has noted that in the post–World War II period, the worldwide increase in trade between the industrialized world and low-wage developing countries is generally associated with a major contribution to economic growth.[6] As has been noted:

> While living standards in developing countries generally lag behind those of the developed world, some developing countries are catching up—namely, those that are open to trade. Indeed, the more open developing countries are to trade, the faster their standards of living converge with those of the developed world. For instance, thirty years ago, South Korea was as poor as Ghana. Today, in large part because of trade liberalization, South Korea is as wealthy as Portugal, with a per capita gross domestic product (GDP) exceeding $12,000. Countries as diverse as Nicaragua, Poland, and New Zealand have also benefited enormously from trade liberalization.[7]

American antitrust law has trumped labor law in the domestic arena when unions, particularly with the aid of employers who have their own concerns about product competitiveness and the product market, build walls around themselves so as to shelter themselves from competition, thus injuring the public interest.[8] The ongoing conundrum lies in the fact that labor unions and thus the policies that support them proceed from the assumption that competition between workers in the same facilities, companies, and industries is at odds with their collective interests. The idea of trade unionism and the collective bargaining process is thus working at cross-purposes with antitrust policy, which promotes competitiveness and, historically, deemed attempts to invoke a unity of interest as collusion or unlawful restraint of trade.[9] Now the debate about international labor standards has put this policy conflict into the global arena.

These competing policies are further dramatized by the fact that the labor movement's drive toward better employment conditions has its roots in both moral and economic concerns.[10] Again, the idea of dignity is what makes some of this subject matter similar to human rights issues throughout the world. And the focus is egalitarian, an attempt to distribute more fairly the balance of power between workers and employers—to "level the playing field," in modern parlance. Yet simultaneously, the attempt to improve conditions necessarily speaks in terms of comparisons and comparability and thus cuts across more than the work station—that is, the plant, company, and industry as a basis for raising employees up from demeaning circumstances and warring against unfair competition between workers.

The idea of international labor standards first gained momentum in early nineteenth-century Great Britain with Robert Owen as their proponent—and it was catalyzed by the expansion of the antislavery movement. Advocacy for this idea found strength in France, Switzerland, and Germany, and proponents claimed that basic human rights were involved inasmuch as the benefits had their source in morality. But then as now, an argument for uniformity across nations, which can override the nation state's sovereignty, was put forward on the grounds that nations providing improved wages and benefits would otherwise lose their competitive position. Thus, advocacy flourished, and continues to flourish, in the richer countries. Yet it is an argument that arises in the context of advanced countries competing among themselves when the question of comparative advantage enjoyed by developing countries, existing at a different economic state of development, is unknown.

The first of major organized meetings was organized by the Swiss government in 1881, and dealt with international legislation on factories. After a failure to attract sympathetic recruits, Switzerland tried again with a conference planned for Berne in 1889—but it was not held, though four other countries accepted invitations. In 1890, Germany organized a conference in Berlin that fourteen states attended. This conference lasted ten days, but produced no policy conclusions. Subsequent meetings were held in Brussels (the United States participated in this one, along with twelve European countries), Paris, Basel, Cologne, and, once again, Berne.[11]

Between 1904 and 1915 there were more than twenty bilateral agreements on labor issues between various European countries and in one case even the United States. Italy, France, and Germany were the most frequently involved. Most often these agreements related to issues that have clear transnational implications—that is, insurance compensation for accidents involving citizens of one country while working in another. Little more developed. Indeed, in the domestic arena in countries like the United States, both policy and constitutional hurdles were placed in the way of social and economic regulation of even child labor,[12] though the "Brandeis Brief" produced a Supreme Court decision upholding the constitutionality of protective legislation for women.[13]

At the conclusion of World War I, President Woodrow Wilson's sponsorship of international democratic rights was seen as a way to avoid future conflicts. The Treaty of Versailles created the League of Nations as an instrument to obtain this objective but the United States did not ratify it, largely at the urging of Senator Henry Cabot Lodge of Massachusetts. Thus the United States joined neither the League nor its new entity designed to promote international labor standards, the International Labor Organization, which was created as a part of the League in 1919.[14] The League failed when Axis aggression went unremedied, but the ILO survived the League's demise.

In part this is attributable to the fact that President Franklin D. Roosevelt's administration decided to opt for U.S. membership in the ILO in 1934,[15] giving it a measure of support that the League never had. Moreover, the ILO was never directly tarnished by the 1930's military aggression, as was the League itself, and was thus better positioned to survive. At the end of World War II it became an agency of the United Nations.

Simultaneously, the idea that the repression of labor, most dramatically through forced labor as well as other antidemocratic policies in Germany, Italy, and Japan, was a substantial factor in international discord, prompted the Allies to feature labor policy as part of the occupations of both Germany and Japan. The MacArthur Occupation in Japan created a policy in which explicit constitutional rights for labor, unknown in the United States, were promulgated.[16]

In its early years, the ILO was concerned with minimum conditions of employment such as hours of work and night work and the like. But in the midst of World War II it promoted the Philadelphia Conference, which led to the key Conventions promoting the right of workers both to organize (Convention 87)[17] and to engage in the collective bargaining process (Convention 98).[18] The preamble to the ILO Constitution reflects the dual objectives for international labor standards, which first emerged in the nineteenth century, shortly before the agency's creation in 1919. The idea of international labor standards has always presented two faces as the result of these dual objectives.

The preamble states that "universal and lasting peace can be established only if it is based upon social justice."[19] Moreover, the preamble also states that the "failure of any nation to adopt humane conditions of labor is an obstacle in the way of other nations which desire to improve the conditions in their own countries."[20] This is the idea of unfair competition, an idea that had found a receptive audience in Europe much earlier.[21] It is also reflected in portions of the preamble of the National Labor Relations Act (NLRA), enacted to promote freedom of association and collective bargaining in the United States,[22] shortly after the United States joined the ILO. This aspect of international labor standards and the fact that the richer nations continue to sponsor them has plagued the movement from its inception through the turn of this new century. It figures substantially in the debate known as the "the race to the bottom," which, some contend, emerged because of the absence of some kind of international regulation.[23]

A final factor in the equation relates to global poverty—a theme addressed by the first portion of the ILO preamble. There has been a dramatic decline in foreign assistance provided by the industrialized nations to the developing countries. Whatever the virtues of free trade—and they are obviously considerable—their spread and application have been uneven, leaving African and Muslim countries disproportionately beyond their beneficence.[24] Even the Bush administration, its proposals hobbled with inadequacy,[25] appears to have accepted the maxim that global poverty can be diminished only with aid and trade operating in tandem.

Despite being the wealthiest nation in the world, the United States has done surprisingly little to help developing countries. The decline is particularly dramatic in the United States when one realizes that 3.21 percent of GDP was provided in foreign aid in 1949.[26] Admittedly, this statistic is somewhat distorted because the United States was providing so much to war-torn Europe through the Marshall Plan so as to get that continent on its feet. Yet, even in the 1960s foreign assistance fell below 1 percent of GDP. Now the United States expends 0.08 percent on foreign assistance,[27] and has balked at the UN target of 0.7 percent, established so as to halve world poverty by 2015.

The United States not only failed to keep up with its own past performance in the foreign aid arena—it is also currently failing to keep up with the
Joneses in the international community. Although foreign aid expenditures
dropped nearly across the board in the 1990s,[28] the United States has led this
race to the bottom. In the late 1980s, Japan dethroned the U.S. as the world's
number one provider of foreign aid.[29] Today the United States ranks dead
last among Western developed nations in percentage of GDP devoted to foreign aid.[30] Scandinavian countries have consistently met the UN's foreign aid
expenditure goal of 0.7 percent of GDP.[31] The expenditures of other Western
industrialized countries have also dwarfed those of the United States in recent years. Denmark is currently setting the pace, spending a full 1 percent of
its GDP on foreign aid.[32] France has managed to devote 0.6 percent of its
GDP to foreign aid,[33] and the EU average stands at about 0.3 percent.[34] The
OECD average is also 0.3 percent, almost four times that of the United
States.[35] Italy and Greece are the only Western countries that devote 0.2 percent of their GDP to aid. At the other end of the continuum is Denmark with
1.06 percent, The Netherlands at 0.84 percent, and Sweden at 0.8 percent.[36]

Moreover, in responding to the UN initiative, the United States was "careful to avoid any language that could have weakened the mandate of the [In-
ternational Monetary Fund and World Bank] or . . . increased the say of the
UN General Assembly, where every country holds an equal vote."[37] The 2002
Bush administration proposals for foreign aid increases leave the United
States lagging behind European generosity and good policy. The Bush administration appears to continue to denigrate the significance of foreign aid
to the well-being of developing countries and, notwithstanding the fact that
country to country aid is provided in the Middle East, for instance, without
scrutiny of the reforms undertaken by the recipient countries, it insists that
the 80 percent success rate of the World Bank and IMF is "not enough" for
today's occupants of the White House.[38] As John Cassidy has noted: "Between 1970 and 1993, developing countries with good economic policies but
low aid payments grew at an annual rate of 2.2 per cent per capita, whereas
developing countries with good economic policies and high aid payments
grew almost twice as fast, at an annual rate of 3.7 per cent."[39]

My judgment is that these two issues, aid and trade, are deeply con-
nected.[40] The lowering of tariff barriers in the rich countries is important for

the poor nations.[41] Moreover, the issue of aid directly affects the implementation feasibility of some of the international labor standards, most particularly child labor which requires financial aid to families who will lose income as the result of effective child labor prohibitions. Finally, it seems clear that the threat posed to the West by those whom globalization has overlooked has been made dramatically manifest by the events of September 11, 2001. Global poverty and discontent are best challenged through practical standards, domestic policies that are designed to address the concerns of workers dislocated as the result of free trade, and dramatically increased foreign assistance to the developing countries of the world.

II. The Policy Debate about International Labor Standards Today

The idea of international human rights, of course, has gained momentum through other post–World War II instruments such as the Universal Declaration of Human Rights,[42] the International Covenant on Civil and Political Rights (ICCPR),[43] and the International Covenant on Economic, Social, and Cultural Rights (ICESCR).[44] All of these agreements label the right to freedom of association as a fundamental right. In this country, these policies began to flourish in the 1970s through the Carter administration's adoption of an international human rights program.[45]

And the past decade has witnessed the emergence of Yugoslavian and Rwandan war crimes tribunals, as well as the threatened criminal prosecution of General Augusto Pinochet in Great Britain, and thus, for the first time since the Nuremberg trials, an attempt to apply criminal prosecutions internationally. The European Court of Human Rights has focused attention on principles that transcend and supersede national law of the Member States of the Council of Europe.[46]

But the more recent debate about international labor standards has found its focus in two phenomena. The first is the growing income and wage inequality in the United States[47] and, in some measure, Great Britain. It is contended this trend has its roots in unprecedented globalization and unfair trade by countries that undercut the labor standards in the industrialized world.

The same argument is put forward, perhaps with slightly less intensity, with regard to developments in Europe. There, an inefficient and inflexible labor market has at least been partially responsible for double-digit unemployment. However, in Europe this unemployment exists amid a strong social safety net—a stark difference from the American scene,[48] where there are now prospects for an even further weakened welfare system.[49] In short, the difficulty in America is poverty and inequality and in Europe, unemployment and lack of jobs,[50] and the contention by some is that globalization has produced these phenomena.[51]

Is a "race to the bottom" fueled by free trade policies responsible for these difficulties? The issue is dramatized not only by the increasing Third World imports in certain labor intensive industries where the work has been done here by unskilled workers but also, as the most favored nations legislative debate in the United States in 2000 testifies,[52] by China's emergence as a major player on the international scene. Its accession to the World Trade Organization demonstrates this problem vividly.

How can the United States and the industrialized world, it is asked, possibly compete when countries like China with lower labor standards and minuscule wages are in competition for the same markets? The difficulty here is that there is not much evidence to support the proposition that there is a "race to the bottom" with nations in competition with one another across national boundaries.[53] Thus "there is little empirical support for a link between increased world trade and a decline in labor conditions."[54] One of the features of this phenomenon is a comparative disadvantage in technological innovation and labor productivity in nations that have a comparative advantage in wages and other benefits.

Professor Robert Flanagan of the Stanford Graduate School of Business cites the example of Kenya and the United States in the early 1980s, when American wages were 183 times as high as those of Kenya. Ironically, the productivity of an American worker was exactly 183 times greater.[55] As nations and companies become more prosperous, productivity gains through technological innovations allow workers to become richer.

For instance, in less than a decade, Korean wages rose from one-tenth of American wages to two-fifths. As Professor Gary Fields has noted:

In the early stages of Korean economic growth, labor market conditions improved via reduction in unemployment with real wages holding essentially constant. . . . Labor earnings and per capita growth proceeded apace of one another thereafter. These gains led to marked improvements in standards of living, leading Korea to a place at or near the top of middle-income countries in such dimensions as life expectancy, infant mortality, access to safe water, adult literacy, and school enrollment rates. . . . The growing richness of the Korean economy permitted the country to introduce new social programs while improving and expanding the existing ones. Minimum wages were introduced, employment insurance systems instituted, and social protections systems created.

At the same time, not every aspect of Korea's social situation was rosy. Labor unions were suppressed openly in Korea until 1987; the labor movement has only recently won some but not all of the battles in the struggle for free collective bargaining and freedom of association at the enterprise and federation levels. Wages were repressed, because of worries that increases in wages would undercut comparative advantage and threaten economic growth. (In my view, these worries were misplaced, as indeed is borne out by the continuation of very rapid economic growth in Korea throughout the 1980s and most of the 1990s.) The gap in earnings and job opportunities between men and women remains large, with discrimination against women playing an important role . . .

Notwithstanding these problems, Korea succeeded in dramatically improving the material well-being of working people. Real wages (adjusted for inflation) grew in Korea at the same rate that per capita Gross National Product did. This was achieved not by being forced under international pressure to adhere to externally-set labor standards and not by setting an ambitious domestic labor code with which companies had to comply. Nor were their successes brought about by cracking down on unions, placing limits on wages, or disempowering women in the labor market. The lives of working people in Korea were improved because of economic growth, which tightened the labor market to the point where full employment was achieved and maintained and wages and working conditions were pulled up by the rapidly-growing demand for labor. Employers raised wages not because the government told them to, but because the *market* told them to.

Korea's labor market success story is one that has been duplicated in kind in the other rapidly-growing economies of East and Southeast Asia . . . The achievement of full employment, rapidly-rising real wages, improvements in the types of jobs that people are in, falling rates of poverty—all of these have happened because of the success of the East Asian types of growth models.[56]

The tendency for wages and income to increase alongside productivity makes it less likely that the natural tendency of the developing countries to catch up with technological innovations from the industrialized world will destroy the economic balance between the two worlds of countries. States one writer:

> The great fear of the race-to-the-bottom crowd—that U.S. multinationals will locate production facilities in developing countries, exploit local resources, and re-export back to the United States—has not materialized. In fact, that type of activity characterizes less than 4 percent of total U.S. investment abroad. The oft-cited cases of garment facilities based in poor nations and geared to consumers in advanced countries are the exception not the rule. This exception is largely due to the low capital investment and importance of labor costs in the textiles sector.[57]

The same writer notes that similar patterns have emerged with regard to environmental standards. "Mexico has enhanced its environmental protection efforts while trying to attract investment. The result? Foreign direct investment around Mexico has exploded, while the air quality has actually improved."[58]

Two important studies by the Organisation for Economic Co-operation and Development issued in 1996 and 2000 are instructive. These reports publicize a series of findings that are closely related to the race to the bottom argument. For if in fact there is a race to the bottom through which the developing countries will enjoy a comparative advantage, just as the more affluent countries will advocate international labor standards, the developing countries will resist them because of a feared impact upon their own ability to compete in world markets.

The OECD has examined the question of whether the adherence to basic labor standards interferes with their development and places them at a competitive disadvantage. As the studies indicate, the very first question that must be answered preliminarily is how one defines international labor standards at issue.[59] There is a consensus about the identity of a small set of "core" standards, though there is some dispute about this at the margin.[60]

These standards, in substantial part, are procedural and do not directly affect the substance of the employment relationship—that is, freedom of association, the right to organize and bargain collectively, nondiscrimination in employment, the prohibition of forced labor.[61] The issue of child labor and its elimination is usually considered among the so-called core principles, though such policies carry special problems with them.[62]

These standards, notes the OECD, are the most important because they "embody basic human rights," in contrast to standards relating to working time arrangements and minimum wage laws.[63] In this and related economic areas, different states of development of nation-states and, equally important, the views of democratic institutions in those countries about this matter, will be harmed by uniformity. And a view that these standards are procedural in nature leads to the idea that they establish a framework for other labor standards that may be either voluntarily negotiated by labor and management or devised through government policy.

The OECD emphasizes its concern about uniformity by its distinction between core labor standards and other labor standards. The OECD finds this distinction to be "crucial" inasmuch as working time and minimum wages can affect "patterns of comparative advantage, e.g., higher minimum wages are likely to affect trade performance negatively. But core labor standards, unlike minimum wages, will not necessarily affect comparative advantage negatively, and indeed may have a positive effect."[64]

Finally, the Declaration on Fundamental Principles and Rights at Work unanimously adopted by the ILO in 1998, which expresses support on behalf of all members for the core standards, is acknowledgement of the fact that they are viewed to be of a fundamental nature and at the center of a democratic society.[65] The same holds true of the ILO Declaration of Philadelphia of 1944, which established special support for the principles of freedom of association and collective bargaining.[66]

The OECD found that there was no empirical evidence that low core standards could be correlated with low real wage growth or that raising core standards would imply a pattern of higher real wage growth.[67] In some countries where there is little or no freedom of association there is no indication that real wages have grown faster than productivity.[68] Thus there appears to be no gain for developing countries that attempt to repress workers' rights in any of these areas and thus involve such countries in an attempt to facilitate a "race to the bottom."

Moreover, the 1996 OECD report found that a country's amount of total country exports was not altered by improvement in the freedom of association area.[69] Further, a U.S. International Trade Commission report cited by the OECD supported the view that exporting sectors in the developing countries have higher labor standards than nonexporting sectors.[70] Nonetheless, in five countries—Bangladesh, Jamaica, Sri Lanka, Pakistan, and Turkey—workers' rights have been repressed in exporting zones in a way that was not the case in the country generally.[71]

Of course, all that is reflected in the OECD report is a tendency—a tendency which, while constituting the preponderance of evidence, is by no means uniform. Nonetheless, the 1996 OECD report contains this conclusion:

> The "race to the bottom" view which argues that low standard countries will enjoy gains in export market shares to the detriment of high standards countries appears to lack solid empirical support. Countries can only succeed in repressing real wages and working conditions for a limited period of time. Thereafter, market forces will be such that wages will catch-up, thus wiping out previous competitive gains. More generally, there is evidence that, as expected, low per capita income countries have recorded significant improvements in export market shares, suggesting market forces work in the aggregate.[72]

What about foreign direct investment in developing countries? Will it not go to countries in which labor standards are inferior and thus promote a "race to the bottom" in a less dramatic and more drawn out fashion? Here again, the OECD is of the view that there is no support for low core standards as a factor in trade and investment decisions.[73] This is because there is no evidence that low core standards are associated with low labor costs that are, in fact, principal considerations in trade and investment. And, there is no evidence that the ability to attract investment or even stimulate exports in areas where labor standards are low means that the long-term growth of the country will be promoted. In essence, the OECD is of the view that the enforcement of core standards may strengthen the economic performance of developing countries.[74]

Other findings of the OECD relate to the interplay between trade liberalization and labor and the development of labor standards, particularly core standards. No single pattern of sequencing in terms of trade liberalization and better compliance with Conventions 87 and 98 is demonstrated through OECD examination. That is to say, there is no single pattern that determines whether free trade is likely to produce core labor standards or whether core labor standards as part of a democratic system induce free trade.

But the OECD notes that freedom of association rights tended to improve at least three years after the start of trade reforms in fifteen countries and that in nine countries such rates preceded trade reforms by at least three years.[75] In eight countries the two processes begin at the same time, and in six countries there has been no improvement in association rights.[76] Thus, the OECD concludes that, on balance, there is a "positive two-way relationship between these processes. Indeed, a comprehensive policy and institutional reforms have been implemented simultaneously in most of the liberalizing countries."[77]

Again, these conclusions do not seem to be consistent with the race to the bottom idea. In no case was a worsening of freedom of association rights found where trade reforms were instituted. And in no case did the promotion of freedom of association and bargaining rights impede trade liberalization.

Finally, in its 2000 report the OECD concluded that there was no "robust evidence" that firms were directing investment to "no standards" countries.[78] The OECD was of the view that countries in which core labor standards were not respected received a very small share of global investment. However, it was careful to note that there was a "significant exception" to this conclusion in China.[79]

It is still too early to say whether China's accession to the WTO will alter this picture. China's proudly proclaimed resistance to the development of independent unions in that country,[80] as well as its forced labor violations, induces us to approach that country's experience and potential for altering what has been described above with some caution. That, in itself, is an argument—or a portion of an argument—for some form of regulation.

Second, it is unclear what impact globalization has on health and safety issues. It is interesting to note that neither the OECD nor the ILO includes health and safety matters within the so-called core principles. In a sense, this absence is justifiable because of the difficulties invariably involved with defining the content. Yet the importance of health and safety and its ability to be understood across national boundaries means that it ought to get some kind of international regulatory attention.[81] Moreover, "morality *sans* borders" cannot avert its gaze from admittedly complex and vexatious issues like child labor about which there appears to be considerable consensus.[82] The Woodrow Wilson–Jimmy Carter approach to international human rights provides much of the justification for international regulation. The fact that some matters are difficult to resolve does not argue against international regulation.

Third, the burden of competition appears to fall disproportionately upon the unionized sector of the industrially advanced economies. The difficulties in the United States in terms of both low wages and unemployment have disproportionately affected the bastions of union strength like manufacturing and textiles. The causes are far more complex than globalization. Yet the decline of trade unionism is a worrisome phenomenon that a democratic pluralistic society can ill afford. Again, this erosion of the important elements of the democratic state argues for international regulation of some kind.

III. What Should Be Done?

Of course, many argue that the answer to this question is absolutely nothing. Professor Jagdish Bhagwati and others champion this view[83]—at least when it comes to linkage between trade and labor.[84] Their first argument lies in their contentions that there is no causal link between globalization and inequality and unemployment. Their view is that if imports were undercutting the unionized sector, we would see a resulting decrease in prices of such goods. Yet this phenomenon has not occurred. The response put forward by, for instance, Adrian Wood is that the decimation of entire industries like textiles[85] has emerged and that, in any event, technology—the other major culprit in this story—is in part promoted by trade.[86] Technology, it is argued, is a response to trade and is often introduced through foreign competition itself, Japan being a vivid illustration.

In any event, the argument of Bhagwati and others is that the idea of international labor standards is essentially protectionist and thus akin to other straightforward protectionist arguments proffered on behalf of industries that are harmed by foreign competition and globalization. This argument will gain strength in the wake of the Bush administration's tariff increases in the steel industry which, rather than protect the most vulnerable workers, are designed to diminish peril for uncompetitive industry.[87] Even before the steel debacle the same administration sacrificed free trade at the altar of the textile industry in order to get the Trade Promotion Act—supposedly a free trade measure—through the House of Representatives.[88]

From this analogy, the Bhagwati group concludes that international labor standards with teeth must be rejected. If, runs the argument, the industrialized countries were truly concerned about the plight of foreign workers and seeking to have them benefit through the development of such standards, they would provide more adequate foreign assistance. Yet, as we have seen, foreign assistance has diminished, particularly in the United States, reflecting a lack of genuine concern for foreign workers.

Second, it is argued that the fact that immigrant workers are routinely denied visas is another example of protectionism. If the United States truly desires to benefit foreign workers, the argument goes, then why not allow them entry to the United States so that they can enjoy the labor standards of this country? The large influx of illegal or undocumented workers is indicative of both the employers' demand for labor and the employees' demand for jobs. The exploitation of undocumented workers is unremedied by inadequate labor law coverage[89]—a point dramatized by the Supreme Court's 5–4 decision to deny undocumented workers back pay remedies under the National Labor Relations Act.[90] This ruling which creates an incentive for American employers to employ workers to whom labor law protection is denied constitutes a compelling argument in favor of the proposition that the West, and particularly the United States, is not concerned with the plight of vulnerable immigrant workers who hail from the poor nations but rather the interests of entrepreneurs within our own borders.[91]

Third, opponents of international labor standards note that the United States has not ratified any of the core conventions except for the Worst Forms of Child Labor Convention of 1999 as well as Convention 105 on the Abolition of Forced Labor, ratified belatedly in 1991.[92] Even the fundamental Conventions providing the principles and standards of freedom of association and collective bargaining have not been ratified by the United States, in part because of the argument that it is a federalist country where our national government would have difficultly committing itself to such standards. (Yet there is something more involved in this story since federalist countries other than the United States have a demonstrably superior record in ratifying ILO Conventions.)[93] At the same time, it can be argued that this policy constitutes indifference to *all* workers by American governments, Americans as well as foreigners, and that therefore job protectionism is not present.[94]

And fourth, the opponents of standards note that the United States has done a poor job of protecting the oppressed within its own borders. For instance, agricultural workers are beyond the protections of the National Labor Relations Act.[95] This policy is the mirror image of American treatment of undocumented workers. Thus in many instances protection is not afforded to the most vulnerable among us here. The United States has been resistant to the idea that international human rights–labor standards ought to be used to raise up workers who are oppressed in the United States.[96] Again, however, the evidence thus far seems to support policies that are indifferent to workers both in the United States and abroad.

What policies should be pursued within our own borders to address and assuage the concerns and difficulties of American workers and, in so doing, to diminish protectionist instincts such as those that have emerged in the steel industry in 2002? Little attention has been given to this problem.

The fact of the matter is that trade is a game of winners and losers, and the United States has done little to help the losers. In 2000, Senator Bill Bradley advocated protection for workers displaced by trade agreements through a new earnings insurance program that would give them time to learn new skills and develop new careers. Such a program would allow employees to take a job at a lower salary and the government would reimburse half the lost wages for the next three years. This would not extend or constitute unemployment compensation but would provide workers with time to develop new skills that would allow them to advance their new job and new career.[97] Senator Bradley was not elected, and the legislation was not enacted. It seems clear that at this point there is no political will to provide substantial tax money for this important policy objective. Even more modest Democratic Party attempts to expand adjustment assistance to workers secondarily affected by trade has met with Bush White House resistance.[98]

The 2002 steel industry debate resulted in increased tariffs—but not governmental assistance to protect workers' pensions and health care, which were threatened by dislocation. National labor policy must focus upon protecting workers in transition who are in industries that lack a comparative advantage and who will lose income, health benefits, and pensions—not industries that cannot compete in the world market. Thus I enthusiastically concur with the following view:

> [W]ith the wealth generated by free trade, society can provide transfers to people with less income, including those for whom trade provides no advantage or even a net disadvantage. For example, instead of pressuring the Japanese automobile industry to adopt voluntary export restraints in the 1980s, the United States could have paid cash compensation to American autoworkers. This strategy would have cost far less than the $3 billion that American consumers ultimately spent in higher car prices.[99]

Since the consumers win from free trade, it is appropriate that part of their winnings go to the free trade losers. Additionally, there will be ongoing debate about whether the trade adjustment assistance program—which has promoted assistance including benefits, relocation expenses, and training—should be strengthened so as to facilitate eligibility for benefits.[100]

In any event, that debate about legislation relates to a law that provides benefits alone and not, as advocated by Senator Bradley, benefits alongside of new jobs. A central element of the industrialized world's policies must be to provide income assistance along with jobs. As the London *Economist* has noted in criticizing the steel tariff:

> [T]he principle should be "protect the worker, not the industry." The government should improve its assistance programmes for workers who lose their health-care benefits and pensions when firms fail, and it should look at new and more generous ways of helping workers find new jobs. These policies cost money, of course—but so does shutting out imports, and far more so, the only other difference being that the effect is disguised.[101]

Beyond this approach, former Secretary of Labor Robert Reich has advocated reforming the National Labor Relations Act as a way to move toward the acceptance of trade and a form of labor standards in our own country.[102] The idea is that unions which have a fair shot of organizing new employees in industries that grow as a result of free trade will find less to resist in globalization itself. But even before the intensified debate about international labor standards, it was clear that enactment of any revisions of the National Labor

Relations Act had no chance whatsoever, even with a Democratic Congress (let alone with a Republican-controlled House, which has been the case since 1994).

Even if the needy rich have laid first claim on the United States Treasury and thus the realization of proposals propounded by Senator Bradley and labor law reform are not even remotely possible, the question still arises as to whether some of the problems at which an international framework is aimed could be remedied by existing national labor law in a sovereign state like the United States. Solidarity between unions across bargaining units and other arbitrary boundary lines is unusual—particularly in the form of secondary boycotts—and the law allowing for international secondary activity in the United States is murky.[103] Similarly, the duty to bargain with unions about corporate relocations across boundaries affords little basis for American unions to ascertain the actual grounds on which management's decision has been taken.[104] Employer decisions to relocate because of union activity are unlawful, but the applicability of this proposition is limited by the need to prove actual antiunion animus[105] or to get the National Labor Relations Board to use expedited procedures available under Section 10(j) of the Act.[106]

As the Court of Appeals for the Second Circuit in *Labor Union of Pico Korea, Ltd. v. Pico Products, Inc.* has made clear,[107] it will be difficult for American courts to exercise jurisdiction over labor disputes beyond our borders.[108] My dissenting opinion in *International Longshoremen's Association*[109] would have expanded jurisdiction under the National Labor Relations Act—but at this point it is just that, a dissent! If answers to the question of whether and what international labor standards should be promoted are to be found, one must look beyond national labor law in the United States and, in all probability, throughout the industrialized world.

What then should or needs to be done beyond efforts to cushion the blows of trade for domestic workers inside America's borders? The fact that there are outlier countries in which the "race to the bottom" does take place and that there is so little known about what will constitute China's response to free trade, that the race may well affect aspects of health and safety, along with the intrinsic value of international labor standards or rights as a matter of both decency and dignity and as an important factor in democracy and

world peace, all could argue for some form of protection that is not protectionism.

Freedom of association and collective bargaining are the bedrock of international labor standards as human rights. Beyond the concerns expressed
previously relating to trade, these rights are part of the so-called public goods
that workers are unlikely to obtain on an individual basis but can do so collectively through trade union representation.[110] Second, it seems apparent
that unions are part of the democratic pluralist society in which workers are
able to voice their views alongside of business interests. True, the United
States and, to a lesser extent, the West are sometimes inconsistent in their
promotion of such policies within the industrialized world. But they must be
pursued throughout the world.

Third, antidiscrimination principles, particularly where the question of
equal pay for equally valued work is skirted—it remains a thorny problem in
the United States itself[111]—are the second obvious candidate. Just as they do
with substantive conditions of employment like minimum wage and overtime, developing countries may maintain that freedom of association and
collective bargaining are inappropriate to them at their stage of economic
development. Is it possible to make the same claim in connection with discrimination on the basis of, for instance, sex or race or some other arbitrary
consideration? My sense is that a broad consensus cutting across national
boundaries answers this question in the negative.[112]

But beyond freedom of association, collective bargaining, and antidiscrimination, the list becomes more complicated. Forced labor is surely the
next obvious candidate. The forced labor prohibitions are very much akin to
antislavery policies.[113] It is difficult to quarrel with the idea that these kinds of
standards, whether the race to the bottom is involved or not, can be tolerated
in civilized societies in the twenty-first century.

Yet problems arise in United States in connection with prison labor.
Some states in this country allow prison work to be subcontracted to private
companies.[114] That practice appears to run afoul of the relevant ILO convention and makes consensus more difficult.[115]

But the most troublesome of all of the core labor standards and that
which appears to be most heinous and attracts consequent unfavorable pub-

licity for American and other Western multinationals is child labor itself. As the OECD has said with regard to the law and child labor:

> [It] is unlikely that the low legal provisions are the main factor behind child labour. Instead, it is the lack of enforcement of the existing provisions (however low) which poses the major problem. Enforcement is typically weak in the informal sector. In several countries, the under-provision of schools makes enforcement of child labour laws problematic. This is especially the case in rural areas of Brazil, India and Turkey. More generally, in the face of very low living standards, child labour provides an important source of income to their families.[116]

This means that attempts to remedy child labor and the way in which it stunts educational growth and opportunity lie in more assistance to affected people rather than in flat prohibitions. Income decline visited upon impoverished families places them in desperate circumstances.[117] They must be recompensed for the loss involved. The institution reviewing child labor disputes must be able to order or effectively promote assistance as a necessary complement to any prohibition.

Again, the richest countries will be required to provide the assistance. The imposition of child labor requirements without assistance will simply push children away from export industries, for instance, and into the area of pornography and sexual exploitation.

In 1999 the ILO members unanimously adopted the Worst Forms of Child Labor Convention, Convention 182. Even the United States ratified this one. Convention 182 specifically bans all forms of slavery or practices akin to slavery, forced or compulsory labor, sexual exploitation, illicit activities and other forms of work relating to children that will harm their health, safety, and morals. It would be a mistake for anyone to believe that this broadly accepted convention addresses the more fundamental problem of child labor—nor does the ILO Convention, which prohibits the employment of minors below a particular age.[118] Again, the broader problem can be addressed only with financial assistance that compensates families that are on the edge of economic devastation.

IV. The Appropriate Forum

But if there are standards that should exist internationally, the question is how to bring about adherence or enforcement. As noted above, the International Labor Organization has been the principal forum historically. The ILO utilizes a variety of means to monitor application or observance of its conventions. The first is the regular system of supervision based on the ratification of conventions by ILO member countries. The ILO, tripartite in organization, allows for any employer or workers' organization to seek an examination of a government's alleged failure to apply a convention that it has ratified. Governments may also bring complaints or concerns against other governments, and special machinery is established to address freedom of association complaints from workers' organizations or employers against governments that have not ratified Conventions 87 and 98 relating to freedom of association, the right to organize, and collective bargaining. And special machinery may be established for reporting purposes relating to labor standards issues—a good illustration of this is the special machinery established to report on apartheid in South Africa. Attempts to extend the freedom of association machinery to other core conventions such as forced labor and nondiscrimination have been rejected because those conventions are not embedded in the ILO Constitution as is true of Conventions 87 and 98. The problem here is to assure applicability of the machinery to nonratifying countries.

As noted above, the ILO Declaration on Fundamental Principles and Rights at Work, promulgated in 1998, attempts to promote observance of the core standards for countries that are members of the organization, whether the convention has been ratified by the country in question or not.[119] Yet, despite the potential of a resort to the International Court of Justice in The Hague pursuant to ILO Article 33, the fact of the matter is that it has not been tried even in the more notorious cases of South Africa, when apartheid prevailed, or Myanmar, where there were numerous problems with forced labor violations. Although it is an exaggeration to characterize the ILO as a debating society, it has at its disposal no meaningful remedies and sanctions beyond the potential for the offending country to be castigated and chastised in the court of international public opinion.[120]

Nonetheless Professor Bhagwati, and much of the business community, believe that the ILO is the best agency. States Bhagwati:

> So the common argument that ILO has no teeth, that is, no trade sanctions, is wrong. I would argue that God gave just not teeth but also a tongue; and a good tongue-lashing, based on evaluations that are credible, impartial and unbiased, can push a country into better policies through shame, guilt and the activities of NGOs that act on such findings.[121]

This view appears to be predicated upon two general considerations. The first is that the ILO possesses the expertise and has more staff than comparable organizations like the World Trade Organization, which possesses trade sanctions remedies. The ILO is the appropriate agency, though its "staff and structure need improvement."[122] Bhagwati points out that only 5 percent of the output produced by children enters foreign markets and that a broad prohibition against child labor could push children into prostitution. But it is unclear why the ILO or any other agency that possessed effective remedies could not address these issues. Similarly, his point that the United States is not itself in compliance with the fundamental core standards does not seem to undercut the idea that firm remedies should be applied against *both* industrialized and developing countries.

Admittedly, Bhagwati's point about the ILO possessing the expertise and experience is well taken. But this begs the issue of whether any agency should have strong sanctions or remedies. The attractiveness of the ILO appears to lie in the fact that it possesses not only expertise but also a tongue rather than a tooth.

The ILO has experience with the promotion of anti–child labor policies coupled with financial assistance to affected families.[123] Its restructuring must give it the authority of a world tribunal,[124] with meaningful remedies including the potential for sanctions as a last resort.[125]

A second potential forum for this issue is the World Trade Organization, whose 1999 meeting in Seattle prompted protests by various groups and organizations. The WTO's dispute resolution machinery can culminate in sanctions for violations of GATT. But, generally speaking, its jurisdiction does not attach to labor matters. Only where prison labor is involved does any provision of GATT become applicable to the WTO and its jurisdiction.[126]

As the Seattle fracas demonstrated, when President Clinton spoke of labor standards or workers' rights in the context of trade sanctions and the United States renewed proposals for an ILO-WTO working party on the subject, there is rigid resistance on the part of the developing countries to bringing this matter within the WTO's jurisdiction.[127] Those who hold this view frequently note that the ILO is the expert agency in the area of core standards and other labor issues. But, as noted, the conundrum is that the ILO has no sanctions and that, while the WTO does, there is no consensus supporting the view that the WTO should move in a direction that applies its mechanisms to unfair labor practices or trade practices that involve labor components. Indeed, in Seattle the idea of establishing working groups involving the ILO and the WTO or other international agencies reviewing the relationship between labor standards and a trading system was rejected. In Doha in 2001 the labor issue was not even on the table at the most recent WTO meeting.[128]

Are there other more suitable fora for resolving such matters? This is the most fruitful arena for the establishment and promotion of international labor standards. At the front line of activity are regional agreements or treaties, unilateral government actions and litigation involving such, as well as corporate codes of conduct.

Regional treaties have seen a great deal of activity, and it may be that this is where most of the developments will take place. As has been noted:

> Because the citizens of nation in a particular region are more likely to have similar preferences, resources, political values, and economic systems, it may be easier for them to reach effective and enforceable regional agreements. After nations have already formed such smaller compacts, it may be easier for them to move to a global agreement.[129]

These more limited first steps may make it possible to take into account the idiosyncratic expectations of different nation-states.[130] Notwithstanding the fact that such instruments create trade barriers for nonsignatories, they may constitute the first step toward international labor standards contained in legal agreements. At least in the short run, full-blown international instruments relating to labor are perhaps excessively ambitious.

The most widely discussed regional agreement is the North American Free Trade Agreement (NAFTA), which promotes enforcement of existing labor laws between the three member countries: the United States, Canada, and Mexico. The problem with NAFTA is that only existing standards are protected, and then, in the case of core standards, no remedy beyond ministerial consultations exists.

The first effort in this arena was enacted in 1993, effective January 1, 1994. President Clinton had campaigned in 1992 against the NAFTA proposed by the Bush administration on the grounds that it did not include a labor accord or labor provisions that would take into account worker rights. The NAFTA that became effective contained the first ever labor side agreement attached to a trade agreement.[131]

NAFTA creates three categories of worker rights, one category that is enforceable through the dispute resolution mechanism, culminating in sanctions, and the others not.[132] The provisions that are ultimately enforceable by sanctions are those that prohibit child labor, establish minimum employment standards pertaining to minimum wages, and promote the prevention of occupational injuries and illnesses. Core standards are remitted to a different mechanism. In the case of freedom of association, the right to organize and bargain collectively, and the right to strike, all such matters are heard by National Administrative Offices established in each country; the final step in the process is ministerial discussion between the U.S. Secretary of Labor and the Ministers of Labor in Canada and Mexico.

Other core standards, such as the prohibition of forced labor and the elimination of employment discrimination, as well as equal pay for men and women, are handled by an Evaluation Committee of Experts, and as is the case with the other core standards, no sanctions apply.

NAFTA obliges all three signatory nations to enforce their own domestic laws. But, as the American experience itself demonstrates,[133] domestic law is frequently inadequate or lacking in promoting the broad principles that are set forth in NAFTA itself. And even where the National Labor Relations Board finds violations of the Act, the Courts of Appeals may reverse the finding through its own interpretation of both fact and law. This happened in the celebrated Sprint case,[134] in which complaints were filed by the Mexican government.[135] Moreover, the NAFTA procedures themselves have been convoluted, and, as noted, there are no sanctions at the end of the road.[136]

Nonetheless, a number of accomplishments are associated with NAFTA.

First, as noted above, it is the first trade agreement to provide for labor rights. Just as the National Labor Relations Act contains a bill of rights for workers that has existed ever since 1935, an important principle has been established, notwithstanding the ineffectiveness of remedies.

Second, it seems clear that Mexico has become more democratic since NAFTA has been in existence. Indeed the Supreme Court of Mexico has held Mexican labor law, which reserves representation in a firm to one union, to be unconstitutional in that country. New and more democratic unions seem to have been set in place as the result of this process.

Third, the dispute resolution procedures of NAFTA are open and, in contrast to the WTO, the sunshine seems to have enhanced reforms. All three countries seem to have become more aware of their respective labor laws as the result of NAFTA.

But the most important feature of NAFTA was that its labor accord, notwithstanding its imperfection, might serve as a basis for a better mechanism in the future. Already the dialogue has progressed substantially beyond that which transpired in the early 1990s at the time of the major NAFTA debate.

Now the debate about whether labor should be part of the trade equation has emerged dramatically within the context of legislation designed to extend or revive the president's authority to negotiate such treaties on a so-called fast-track basis. This authority expired with the expiration of the Omnibus Trade and Competitiveness Act of 1988. The theory has been that the United States would be at a disadvantage in negotiating foreign trade agreements with other countries if those countries believed that Congress could later interfere with a negotiated agreement. The result would be either no deal at all or a deal that would more likely reflect something short of the other country's final or best offer.

Both the 104th and the 105th Congresses considered, but failed to enact, renewed fast-track authority for the president that would prohibit congressional amendments of a negotiated trade agreement and provide for limited debate. The fall of 1997 was to see this issue at an impasse, with the congressional Democrats unwilling to support President Clinton's sought after fast-track authority,[137] though a substantial number of Republicans were perfectly delighted to harm the Clinton presidency.

Thomas Friedman summed up the debate well when he said that a kind of four party system had emerged on this matter. It could be said that integrationists promoting globalization, noted Friedman, were on one side of an east-west line and that separatists who believed that neither free trade nor technological integration was good or inevitable were on the other side. But Friedman noted that another line from north to south was relevant to the globalization debate. This was the so-called distribution line that was concerned with cushioning workers from social, economic, and environmental impacts of globalization. Some like the "Integrationist-Social-Safety-Netters" were concerned with assisting the know-nots and have-nots who lacked the skills to take advantage of the new economy and were unemployed and driven into poor jobs as a result. At the other end of this distribution line were the "Let-Them-Eat-Cakers," or those who like Speaker Newt Gingrich and the Republican right wing in the Congress believed in a "winner-take-all, loser-take-care-of-yourself" economy. Said Friedman:

> You have to build a real politics of Integrationist-Social-Safety-Nettism—a politics that shows people the power and potential of global integration, while taking seriously their needs for safety nets to protect them along the way. Build it and they will come.[138]

Notwithstanding the expiration of fast-track authority and President Clinton's inability to obtain approval from the Republican Congresses with which fate consigned him to deal, the administration negotiated a U.S.-Jordan Free Trade Agreement.[139] This Agreement, rather than simply constituting an accord or side agreement as was the case with NAFTA, contained labor provisions in the body of the Agreement itself, occupying one page of the text. Moreover, the labor laws that were to be respected were not only each country's own—enforcement being required through a dispute resolution mechanism—but also "internationally recognized worker rights" and "core labor standards" as defined by the International Labor Organization. This time, in contrast to the NAFTA, the dispute resolution procedures obliged parties to take "appropriate and commensurate" measures at the process's culmination. The Jordan Agreement provided a kind of backdrop for debate about the renewal of fast-track or, as it came to be called during the Bush administration in 2001 and 2002, trade promotion authority.

Now the debate has become more complex. The Bush administration proposed a so-called toolbox of actions that could be taken in trade negotiations, one of which would relate to the protection of children and adherence to core labor standards in connection with international trade.

Some of the New Democrats, led by Congressman Cal Dooley of California, lauded Bush but expressed a concern that no appropriate mechanisms for the enforcement of trade agreements were provided by the Bush proposals.[140] The overwhelming number of Old and New Democrats opposed the Bush initiative. In a widely discussed and heralded vote in late 2001, the House of Representatives passed a Republican bill supported by a handful of Democrats such as Dooley, Jefferson, and Tanner by a vote of 215 to 214. Yet the major defect in this bill, HR 3005, relates to the vagueness of the content of future trade agreements as they relate to labor issues. The president is directed to further "certain priorities," most of which are related to labor and environmental objectives. All that the bill does is to direct the president to seek greater cooperation between the World Trade Organization and the International Labor Organization.

At the other end of the continuum is HR 3019 sponsored by Congressmen Charles Rangel of New York and Sander Levin of Michigan, which gives more direction to negotiators to achieve labor and environmental goals. Specific objectives for agreements must be undertaken. Congressional trade advisors are provided for by statute, and the bill would allow withdrawal from any fast-track procedure before the start of negotiations, during the negotiations, and before the president enters into an agreement if congressional advisors do not concur with the president on the issue of whether the agreement "substantially achieves the principal negotiating objectives."[141]

Meanwhile, the Senate passed its own 2002 trade bill, taking up the Bradley idea and providing both wage insurance and health insurance to displaced workers.[142] Much of 2002 was consumed with an impasse between the Democratic Senate and Republican House on this subject.[143]

In August 2002 the Congress enacted and President Bush signed the Trade Bill with most Republicans supporting it, House Democrats opposed, the Senate Democrats divided.[144] The new law makes labor and environmental goals "principal negotiating objectives"—but adherence to no particular standards is required. Senator Max Baucus has emphasized the assistance provided by the law to dislocated workers:[145] (1) coverage of so-called secondary workers who are eligible for benefits and workers "affected" by shifts in production if the company moves to a nation with which the United States has a free trade agreement or preferential trade agreement and where no such agreement exists, benefits ought to be provided if imports are "likely to increase" as the result of the shift; (2) such older displaced workers provided wage insurance to supplement lower paying jobs as well as health insurance; (3) income support for workers undergoing training extended from 52 to 78 weeks; (4) 65 percent health insurance reimbursement through tax credits.

The significance of health insurance may be to revive the call for comprehensive health insurance reform promoted by both President Harry Truman and President Bill Clinton. As the *Washington Post* has noted:

> Among the new benefits such workers will receive is federal tax credit to help cover the cost of health insurance. Since almost no one argues that workers who lose their jobs to foreign competition deserve better treatment than those who become unemployed for other reasons, some believe the bill could create impetus for extending similar benefits to millions more of the unemployed than it already covers. That hope, in fact, has been one of the Senate Democrats' main—albeit unspoken—motives.[146]

Lurking in the background of these debates are the strengths and deficiencies of the ILO and the WTO, two institutions with contrasting traditions, attitudes, and authority. We have already noted the problems with the ILO mechanisms for enforcement and how they contrast with WTO sanctions. One central problem with the WTO relates to its confidentiality provisions, which apply, understandably, to conciliation and mediation[147] in dispute resolution,[148] but also to adjudication itself, which would appear to be appropriately public. There is a lack of transparency and a secrecy in the WTO procedures.[149] Though the WTO appears not to have provided any justification for this aspect of its procedures, unceasing criticism has moved it toward the consideration of reforms in this area.[150]

Yet the difficulties in obtaining consensus, which is a prerequisite for WTO action, and the resistance of developing countries to the use of trade sanctions would seem to make even the use of fines rather than trade sanctions unacceptable through such a mechanism in the short run.[151] The ILO is the best forum—but a stronger ILO with remedies at its disposal.

In the near future, therefore, it seems that most of the action, while borrowing from the institutional resources and standards of both the ILO and the WTO, will constitute new institutions or dispute resolution procedures established through country to country or regional treaties. Perhaps the one with the most fruitful potential is that designed by Congressman Sander Levin as part of the 2000 China trade bill. The Levin amendment creates a congressional Executive Commission on China[152] that holds hearings (probably not in China) and produces an annual report on the rule of law and human rights. Its jurisdiction includes labor, and, if it does its job, it will surely clash with the trade union system in China.

Another area in which international labor standards can flourish is domestic trade laws such as the Generalized System of Preferences (GSP), which was established by the 1974 Trade Act,[153] and then amended in 1984. This initiative, and others,[154] such as the Caribbean Basin Initiative,[155] provide for sanctions. But they contain a number of problems. The first is that changing political winds will alter the willingness of the executive branch to enforce the laws. But the second is that they exist at the level of the nation-state and smack of unilateralism, a tendency with which this Bush administration has come to be frequently associated. Even the United States–Cambodia textile agreement undertaken outside of the WTO mechanism, which established a direct linkage between imports and adherence to labor standards, allows for unilateral determinations,[156] which may be fundamentally protectionist.[157]

Professor Sarah Cleveland has advocated the use of the Alien Tort Claims Act as a vehicle for enforcing international labor standards through labor litigation.[158] As she points out, other theories pursued by private litigants have thus far been remarkably unsuccessful.[159]

Finally, there is the world of corporate codes of conduct. Again, the OECD has provided the most substantial inventory of these voluntary initiatives undertaken by multinational companies operating away from their home base.[160]

These codes may look to laws, both local and internationally recognized instruments—although international standards such as ILO Conventions or UN Declarations are explicitly cited in only 18 percent of the codes. In the critical area of enforcement, it is important to note that a majority of the codes rely exclusively on internal monitoring. It would seem that codes are most effective where they provide for some kind of outside review, preferably with the use of qualified local people who possess not only the ability and the language but also knowledge about the community and local work practices. Moreover, one other feature of the monitoring process should allow for unannounced visits and onsite reviews of the employment relationship. This is critical because, while many codes address such matters as the level of wages and the amount of overtime that can be addressed through reviewing the records of corporations and can be performed by accounting firms, questions relating to freedom of association, nondiscrimination, and particularly allegations of sexual harassment can only be resolved through observation of the workplace and direct interviews and contact of some form with the parties involved.

A central concern that many of the codes address is relationships with subcontractors, since most of the disputes about adherence to labor standards arise in connection with work done by different corporate entities—that is, subcontractors—for major firms in the United States. Illustrative of these firms are Nike, Levi Strauss, the GAP, Sears, JCPenney, and Wal-Mart.

Concern about labor problems that could be characterized as sweatshop conditions in industries such as clothing and footwear produced the Apparel Industry Partnership Agreement in the Clinton administration. The overriding objective is to produce a labeling system as the result of monitoring that could determine which countries abide by fair labor practices. The objective here is to create sufficient transparency and competition between firms, which are concerned about loss of business as the result of changes in consumer practices, so that working conditions could be improved worldwide.[161]

V. Conclusion

Whatever the validity of the argument about a "race to the bottom" within a country's own borders[162]—and it must be said that the fact that relatively successful Canadian labor law is provincial and not national creates a measure of skepticism about this—there is no general evidence that the same phenomenon exists internationally. To repeat, there is no evidence of a "race to the bottom" internationally in the labor arena. Indeed, the OECD evidence is that countries adopting the so-called core standards of the ILO have not been harmed, and they may well have benefited economically as their trade performance has been enhanced.

But there are substantial arguments for international regulation. The moral high ground for human rights properly includes labor rights. The idea associated with such human rights has moved beyond national borders. And the outlier countries coupled with China make it possible that the "race to the bottom" phenomenon could yet become a pressing one.

Yet the child labor issue demonstrates the care and selectivity that must be exercised in this area. The absence of cash payments—a matter that must be addressed through a substantial expansion of foreign assistance beyond present policies and proposals—seriously erodes advancement for the families the child labor policies are presumably designed to protect. International labor regulation can only move forward in tandem with major revisions and expansion of foreign assistance from the rich countries—particularly the United States.

The world has long recognized that labor rights are an important part of the idea of democracy accepted throughout the world. The United States must be an important part of the world and take responsibility for international regulation. Whatever the success of private initiatives, the argument for international regulation, initially at the regional trade level, is important. As noted, it must be undertaken with care and caution. It will not diminish as this century's globalization process moves forward. But the necessary confluence of labor and the financial assistance demonstrates how uneasy the case is for this admittedly vital objective.

Notes

I am most grateful to Brian Bercusson, Professor of Law at King's College, University of London, and Herman Phleger Visiting Professor of Law at Stanford Law School, for extensive comments on an earlier draft. Similarly, I express my appreciation to Professor Richard Steinberg of UCLA Law School who improved my understanding of World Trade Organization procedures through both discussion and a memorandum on this subject with which he provided me. Of course, I take full responsibility for any deficiencies or errors in this article. I also express my appreciation for valuable research assistance provided by Michael Dominic Meuti, Stanford Law School,

2003; Sarah Preston, Brown University, A.B., 1999; Nina-Louisa Arold, Stanford Law School, 2002.

This article is based upon the Wayne Morse Public Lecture provided by the author on Feb. 28, 2001, when serving as the Wayne Morse Chair of Law and Politics at the University of Oregon. It was reshaped and revised for the Lane Lecture presented at the University of Nebraska College of Law on Apr. 8, 2002. My ideas were sharpened by virtue of seminars that I presented on the themes articulated in this article to my colleagues at Stanford Law School in Jan. 2002 and at a seminar organized by Professor Gary Williams, Stanford Law School '76, at Loyola Law School in Los Angeles in Feb. 2002. This title is borrowed from *The Uneasy Case for Progressive Taxation*, by Walter J. Blum and Harry Kalven, Jr. (1953).

1. William Jefferson Clinton, "Remarks by the President to the International Labor Organization Conference," United Nations Building, Geneva, Switzerland (June 16, 1999) (transcript available at http://clinton2.nara.gov/WH/New/Europe-9906/html/Speeches/990616.html).

2. 15 U.S.C. § 17 (2000) (recognizing that "[t]he labor of a human being is not a commodity or article of commerce"). See Paul O'Higgins, "'Labour Is Not a Commodity'—An Irish Contribution to International Labour Law," *Industrial Law Journal* 26 (1997): 225, for a description of the Irish origin of and Australian contribution to the idea that labor is not a commodity. This article provides understanding about American Federation of Labor President Samuel Gompers's promotion of the idea both in 1914 at the time of the Clayton Antitrust Act and shortly thereafter at the Treaty of Versailles, discussed below.

3. Smoot-Hawley Tariff Act of 1930, ch. 497, Pub. L. No. 71–361, 46 Stat. 590 (codified as amended in scattered sections of 19 U.S.C.).

4. Reciprocal Trade Agreements Act of 1934, pt. III, Pub. L. No. 316, 48 Stat. 943 (current version at 19 U.S.C. §§ 1351–54 [2000]).

5. John O. McGinnis and Mark L. Movsesian, "The World Trade Constitution," *Harvard Law Review* 114 (2000): 511, 516; Douglas A. Irwin, *Free Trade under Fire* (Princeton, NJ: Princeton University Press, 2002).

6. Organisation for Economic Co-operation and Development, *Trade, Employment and Labour Standards: A Study of Core Workers' Rights and International Trade* (Paris, 1996), p. 124 [hereinafter OECD 1996].

7. McGinnis and Movsesian, "The World Trade Constitution," pp. 521–22.

8. See, e.g., *Allen Bradley Co. v. Local 3, IBEW*, 325 U.S. 797 (1945).

9. *Loewe v. Lawlor*, 208 U.S. 274 (1908); *Duplex Printing Press Co. v. Deering*, 254 U.S. 443 (1921); *Coronado Coal Company v. United Mine Workers*, 268 U.S. 295 (1925).

10. Interestingly, the free-trade camp has recently picked up on the use of morality rhetoric as well. See, e.g., Marc Lacey, "Bush Declares Freer Trade a Moral Is-

sue: Chides Critics," *New York Times*, May 8, 2001, p. A11. Yet this rhetoric lost its spring when the Bush administration fashioned a substantial steel industry tariff in early 2002. See David E. Sanger, "Bush Puts Tariffs of as Much as 30% on Steel Imports," *New York Times*, Mar. 6, 2002, p. B1; Richard W. Stevenson, "Steel Tariffs Weaken Bush's Global Hand," *New York Times*, Mar. 6, 2002, p. C1; "Playing Politics with Trade," *New York Times*, Mar. 5, 2002, p. A24; Greg Rushford, "Bush Steps into a Steel Trap," *Wall Street Journal*, Mar. 6, 2002, p. A16; Edward Alden, "Republicans Sacrifice Free Trade Rhetoric to Bat for US Workers," *Financial Times* (London), Mar. 7, 2002.

11. See, generally, Stanley L. Engerman, "The History and Political Economy of International Labor Standards" (paper presented at a seminar on international labor standards in Stockholm, Sweden, Aug. 23–24, 2001, organized by the Swedish Ministry for Foreign Affairs and the Expert Group on Development Issues).

12. *Adkins v. Children's Hospital*, 261 U.S. 525 (1923) (holding that a District of Columbia regulation setting minimum wages for female workers violated economic due process). See also *Adair v. United States*, 208 U.S. 161 (1908).

13. *Muller v. Oregon*, 208 U.S. 412 (1908) (upholding against a Fourteenth Amendment challenge against a statute setting a limitation on the number of hours women could work in a day).

14. See *ILO History*, available at http://www.ilo.org/public/english/about/history.htm (accessed Mar. 6, 2002). See, generally, Edward C. Lorenz, *Defining Global Justice: The History of the U.S. International Labor Standards Policy* (Notre Dame, IN: University of Notre Dame Press, 2001).

15. See *ILO History*.

16. William B. Gould IV, *Japan's Reshaping of American Labor Law* 30 (Cambridge, MA: MIT Press, 1984).

17. Convention 87 delineates guarantees of freedom of association including employees' right to establish and join organizations of their own choosing, to draft the constitutions and rules of such organizations, ILO gloss grafted on by virtue of the ILO Freedom of Association Committee relating to the right to strike, and to do all of this without prior authorization. See also OECD 1996, pp. 31–32.

18. By guaranteeing employees' right to engage in collective bargaining, Convention 98 gives teeth to Convention 87. See ibid., p. 32. Convention 98 guarantees the right to collective bargaining by requiring that workers be protected against anti-union discrimination and that the law provide "adequate protection against acts of interference between workers and employers organizations." Ibid.

19. ILO Constitution, available at http://www.ilo.org/public/english/about/iloconst.htm#pre.

20. Ibid.

21. OECD 1996, p. 11.

22. See 29 U.S.C. § 151 (2000). Interestingly, in enacting the NLRA, Congress announced that a primary purpose of this policy was to remove the downward pressure on wages that a failure to protect collective bargaining rights produces. Congress stated:

> The denial by some employers of the right of employees to organize and the refusal by some employers to accept the procedure of collective bargaining lead to strikes and other forms of industrial strife or unrest, which have the intent or the necessary effect of burdening or obstructing commerce by . . . causing diminution of employment and wages in such volume as substantially to impair or disrupt the market for goods flowing from or into the channels of commerce. Ibid.

Congress also noted: "The inequality of bargaining power between employees . . . and employers . . . tends to aggravate recurrent business depressions, by depressing wage rates and the purchasing power of wage earners . . . and by preventing the stabilization of competitive wage rates and working conditions within and between industries." Ibid.

23. See, e.g., Organisation for Economic Co-operation and Development, *International Trade and Core Labour Standards* 39 (2000) [hereinafter OECD 2000] (reviewing the "race to the bottom" literature), available at http://www.oecd.ord/ pdf/m00005000/M00005860.pdf.

24. See Joseph Kahn, "Losing Faith: Globalization Proves Disappointing," *New York Times*, Mar. 21, 2002, p. A6; "Globalisation—Is It at Risk?" *The Economist*, Feb. 2, 2002, p. 65; Tim Weiner, "More Entreaties in Monterrey for More Aid to the Poor," *New York Times*, Mar. 22, 2002, p. A10; Joseph Kahn and Tim Weiner, "World Leaders Rethinking Strategy on Aid to Poor," *New York Times*, Mar. 18, 2002, p. A3; Kofi A. Annan, "Trade and Aid in a Changed World," *New York Times*, Mar. 19, 2002, p. A27. And see also some of the pernicious consequences of free trade set forth in Marc Edelman, "Price of Free Trade: Famine," *Los Angeles Times*, Mar. 22, 2002; Louis Uchitelle, "Challenging the Dogmas of Free Trade," *New York Times*, Feb. 9, 2002, pp. A15, A17; Alice H. Amsden, "Why Are Globalizers So Provincial?" *New York Times*, Jan. 31, 2002, p. A25; Jeffrey E. Garten, "Free Trade Has to Be Managed," *New York Times*, July, 18, 2002, p. A23; Joseph Kahn, "Globalism Unites a Many-Striped Multitude of Foes," *New York Times*, Apr. 15, 2000, p. A5. Nonetheless, open trade policies, on balance, do seem to have better results than where they are absent. "Aid Effectiveness: Help in the Right Places," *The Economist*, Mar. 16, 2002, p. 73.

25. See Tim Weiner, "More Aid, More Need: Pledges Still Falling Short," *New York Times*, Mar. 24, 2002, p. 4; George Melloan, "In Monterrey, Getting Real about Foreign Aid," *Wall Street Journal*, Mar. 26, 2002, p. A23; "Forging the Monterrey

Consensus," *New York Times*, Mar. 24, 2002, p. 14; Chris Kraul and Edwin Chen, "U.S., Europe to Tout Pledges of Development Aid at Summit," *Los Angeles Times*, Mar. 21, 2002, p. A3; Elisabeth Bumiller, "Bush, in Monterrey, Speaks of Conditional Global Aid," *New York Times*, Mar. 23, 2002, p. A7. But see Thomas L. Friedman, "Better Late than . . . ," *New York Times*, Mar. 17, 2002, p. 15; Jorge Castañeda, "US Aid Pledge Puts a New Spin on Mexico Conference," *Financial Times* (London), Mar. 18, 2002, p. 14.

26. "Security over Succor," *National Journal* 32 (June 10, 2000): 1824.

27. Henri Migala, "Development's Role in Ensuring Global Security," *San Diego Business Journal*, Dec. 17, 2002, p. 39.

28. "Indicators," *The Economist*, Feb. 14, 1998, p. 104.

29. "Foreign Aid: Stingy Sam," *The Economist*, Mar. 25, 1989, p. 26.

30. Migala, "Development's Role in Ensuring Global Security," p. 39.

31. "The Social Summit: Worlds Apart," *The Economist*, Mar. 11, 1995, p. 42.

32. Henrik Bering, "Denmark, the Euro, and Fear of the Foreign," *Policy Review*, Dec. 1, 2000, p. 63.

33. "France's Changing View of the World," *The Economist*, Feb. 10, 1996, p. 47.

34. Ibid.

35. Unfortunately, the poorest developing nations receive surprisingly little of the foreign aid provided by industrialized countries. According to the UN Development Programme, ten nations that contain two-thirds of the world's poorest people receive only one-third of the world's foreign aid. "Foreign Aid, The Kindness of Strangers," *The Economist*, May 7, 1994, p. 19. The rest of the aid is directed toward countries that are, by comparison, rather wealthy. For example, between 1982 and 1991, Israel and Egypt received the lion's share of U.S. aid. During that period, Israel received $29.9 billion and Egypt received $23.2 billion from the United States. "Foreign Aid: Kind Words, Closed Wallet," *The Economist*, Mar. 27, 1993, p. 26. By way of comparison, Turkey ranked third on the U.S. list for that time period, receiving only $6.9 billion. Ibid. Since that time, the pattern has continued. Israel receives the most aid per capita, with about $400 of aid going to Israel for every citizen. "Indicators," *The Economist*, Feb. 14, 1998, p. 104.

36. John Cassidy, "Helping Hands: How Foreign Aid Could Benefit Everybody," *New Yorker*, Mar. 18, 2002, p. 64.

37. Alan Beattie and Carola Hoyos, "US Blocks Move for Big Rise in Aid to Poor Countries," *Financial Times* (London), Jan. 28, 2002, p. 5.

38. Cassidy, "Helping Hands," p. 66.

39. Ibid., p. 63.

40. "But opening up markets makes little difference if countries lack the capability to produce for them—if, for instance, they do not have the transport to bring

their goods to market. By the same token, the mantra that countries should turn to the private sector is misleading. Foreign investment is important, but it goes to relatively few countries and in relatively few sectors. Foreign direct investment misses out on rural roads, on health, and education—all important to developing countries.

"The Monterrey conference was long on rhetoric, but, especially because of Washington's refusal to make serious commitments either on aid or trade, it was short on action." Joseph Stiglitz, "Overseas Aid Is Money Well Spent," *Financial Times*, Apr. 15, 2002, p. 13.

41. Alan Beattie, "Raw Deal for Poor Nations Limits Backing for Free Trade," *Financial Times* (London), Apr. 12, 2002, p. 3.

42. Universal Declaration of Human Rights, G.A. Res. 217(A), U.N. GAOR, 3d Sess., pt. 1, at 71, U.N. Doc. A/810 (1948).

43. International Covenant on Civil and Political Rights, opened for signature Dec. 19, 1966, 999 U.N.T.S. 171, 6 I.L.M. 368 (entered into force Mar. 23, 1976, adopted by the United States, Sept. 8, 1992).

44. International Covenant on Economic, Social, and Cultural Rights, opened for signature Dec. 16, 1966, 993 U.N.T.S. 3, 6 I.L.M. 360 (entered into force Jan. 3, 1976).

45. See Robert J. Peterson, "Political Realism and the Judicial Imposition of International Secondary Sanctions: Possibilities from John Doe v. Unocal and the Alien Tort Claims Act," *University of Chicago Law School Roundtable* 5 (1998): 277, 291 (noting the Carter administration's "stated . . . concern over international human rights").

46. The European Court of Human Rights has jurisdiction over forty-three member-states both within and outside the European Union. The court, among its duties, resolves disputes involving the interpretation of and adherence to Article 11 of the Convention which protects the right to join unions. For a discussion of the comparable law in the European Union, see, generally, Brian Bercusson, *European Labour Law* (London and Charlottesville: Butterworths, 1996), pp. 58–63; P. L. Davies, "The Emergence of European Labour Law," in *Legal Intervention in Industrial Relations: Gains and Losses,* ed. William McCarthy, pp. 313, 318–42 (Cambridge, MA: Blackwell Publishers, 1992).

47. See, generally, James K. Galbraith, *Created Unequal: The Crisis in American Pay* (New York: Free Press, 1998); Derek Bok, *The Cost of Talent: How Executives and Professionals Are Paid and How It Affects America* (New York: Maxwell International, 1993). Increases in wealth inequality are further evidence of the increasing inequality in America. For instance, between 1983 and 1998, the bottom 40 percent of Americans' share of national wealth dropped from 0.9 percent to 0.2 percent. *Facts and*

Figures, available at http://www.inequality.org/factsfr.html (accessed Mar. 6, 2002) (citing Edward N. Wolff, "Recent Trends in Wealth Ownership, 1983–1998," Apr. 2000, Economics Working Paper Archive at Wustl(?) Macroeconomics Series, #0004047). During the same time period, the middle 20 percent of Americans' share dropped from 5.2 percent to 4.5 percent (ibid.). The extent of inequality growth is better illustrated by the following figure: between 1983 and 1998, the bottom 40 percent of Americans experienced a 76.3 percent decrease in household net worth, while the top 1 percent of Americans enjoyed a 42.2 percent gain (ibid.).

48. The weakness of our social safety net is evidenced by the fact that the United States has the highest percentage of children in poverty (20.5 percent) of any industrialized nation. See Sylvia Ann Hewlett and Cornel West, *The War against Parents: What We Can Do for America's Moms and Dads* (Boston: Houghton Mifflin, 1998), p. 47.

49. See Robin Toner and Robert Pear, "Bush's Plan on Welfare Law Increases Work Requirement," *New York Times,* Feb. 26, 2002, p. A23.

50. See, generally, Peter H. Lindert and Jeffrey G. Williamson, *Does Globalization Make the World More Unequal?* NBER Working Paper No. 8228 (Apr. 2001).

51. See, generally, John Cassidy, "Who Killed the Middle Class?" *New Yorker,* Oct. 16, 1995.

52. For a sample of the debate surrounding the decision to grant normal trade relations treatment to China, see "Providing for Further Consideration of H.R. 4444, Authorizing Extension of Nondiscriminatory Treatment (Normal Trade Relations Treatment) to People's Republic of China," 146 *Congressional Record H* 3652, 106th Cong., May 24, 2000; "Authorizing Extension of Nondiscriminatory Treatment (Normal Trade Relations Treatment) to People's Republic of China," 146 *Congressional Record H* 3662, 106th Cong. May 24, 2000.

53. A similar argument has led to national legislation on the doctrine of preemption in connection therewith in American labor law. See, generally, Archibald Cox, "Federalism in the Law of Labor Relations," *Harvard Law Review* 67 (1954): 1297.

> National labor legislation is also warranted in many instances by the need to prevent competition based upon differences in state law. . . . Today enterprises located in states where unionization is fought by the whole business community and where there are repressive laws against strikes and picketing frequently enjoy advantages which influence the location of new industries and even the migration of established concerns. Ibid.

See also William B. Gould IV, "The Garmon Case: Decline and Threshold of Litigating Elucidation," *University of Detroit Law Journal* 39 (1962): 539. The same doctrine affects state legislation in the international labor policy arena. See Crosby, *Sec-*

retary of Administration and Finance of Massachusetts v. National Foreign Trade Council 530 U.S. 363 (2000).

54. McGinnis and Movsesian, "The World Trade Constitution," p. 559.

55. Robert J. Flanagan, paper entitled "The Race to the Bottom?" presented at the International Labor Standards Conference, Stanford Law School, May 20, 2002.

56. Gary S. Fields, "The Role of Labor Standards in U.S. Trade Policies," in *Social Dimensions of U.S. Trade Policies*, ed. Alan V. Deardorff and Robert M. Stern (Ann Arbor: University of Michigan Press, 2000), pp. 178–79.

57. Daniel W. Drezner, "Bottom Feeders," *Foreign Policy*, Nov./Dec. 2000, p. 67.

58. Ibid. However, the shantytowns and worker dislocation in that country represent another more somber side of the Mexican picture. See, for instance, Tim Weiner, "Monterrey's Poor Sinking in Rising Economic Tide," *New York Times*, Mar. 21, 2002, A6; Joel Millman, "Mexican Border Workers Suffer as Plants Relocate South," *Wall Street Journal*, Mar. 26, 2002, p. A20.

59. OECD 2000, p. 14 (arguing that because core and noncore labor standards differ in the economic outcomes they produce, studies based on labor standards generally cannot be easily compared with studies based on core labor standards).

60. See, generally, Nancy H. Chau and Ravi Kanbur, "The Adoption of International Labor Standards Conventions: Who, When and Why?," presented at Brookings Trade Forum 2001, available at http://www.brook.edu/dybdocroot/es/events/tradeforum/200105/papers/04_chau_kanbur.pdf; Virginia A. Leary, "Workers' Rights and International Trade: The Social Clause (GATT, ILO, NAFTA, U.S. Laws)," in *Fair Trade and Harmonization Prerequisites for Free Trade?* ed. Jagdish Bhagwati and Robert E. Hudec (Cambridge, MA: MIT Press, 1996), p. 177; Jonas Malmberg and David Johnson, "Social Clauses and Other Means to Promote Fair Labour Standards in International Fora—A Survey," *Arbetslivsrapport* 25 (1998).

61. Ibid., 18, 20 (listing the fundamental principles and rights at work).

62. Ibid. (including eliminating child labor among the fundamental principles and rights at work). See also OECD 1996, p. 13. But, as we shall see, the child labor issue carries with it special problems that bump up against economic issues directly.

63. See OECD 2000, p. 17.

64. Ibid., p. 33. But see Jagdish Bhagwati, *Free Trade Today* (Princeton, NJ: Princeton University Press, 2002), p. 71, decrying the selective use of core standards so as to disadvantage developing countries.

65. See Novotel New York, 321 NLRB 624 (1996), which stresses the connection between labor rights and constitutional rights relating to freedom of expression protected by the First Amendment.

66. See *Declaration Concerning the Aims and Purposes of the International Labour Organization*, Art. III(e), available at http://www.ilo.org/public/english/about/

iloconst.htm#annex (accessed Mar. 6, 2002) (committing the ILO to "further world programmes which will achieve . . . the effective recognition of the right of collective bargaining, the cooperation of management and labour in the continuous improvement of productive efficiency, and the collaboration of workers and employers in the preparation and application of social and economic measures").

67. OECD 1996, p. 37.

68. But see ibid. (noting that in Kuwait, Malaysia, Singapore, Thailand, and Turkey, real wages have outpaced productivity gains).

69. Ibid., p. 41.

70. See ibid., p. 42 (citing U.S. International Trade Commission, "International Trade and the Role of Labor Standards," *International Economics Review* [1995]).

71. Ibid., p. 43.

72. Ibid., p. 45.

73. Ibid. Accord, Bhagwati, *Free Trade Today*, p. 87.

74. Ibid., p. 46 (arguing that "the enforcement of core standards is likely to strengthen the long-term economic performance of all countries").

75. Ibid., p. 49.

76. Ibid.

77. Ibid.

78. OECD 2000, p. 34.

79. Ibid.

80. See Erik Eckholm, "Workers' Rights Are Suffering in China as Manufacturing Goes Capitalist," *New York Times*, Aug. 22, 2001, p. A8 (chronicling the Chinese government's hostility to independent unions). See also Erik Eckholm, "A Mining Town's Sullen Peace Masks the Bitter Legacy of China's Labor Strategy," *New York Times*, Apr. 14, 2002, p. 6.

81. William B. Gould IV, "The World's Workers May Yet Unite," *Los Angeles Times*, Sept. 1, 1975. Compare William B. Gould IV, "Multinational Corporations and Multinational Unions: Myths, Reality and the Law," *International Lawyer* 10 (1976): 655; William B. Gould IV, "The Rights of Wage Earners: Of Human Rights and International Labor Standards," *Industrial Relations Law Journal* 3 (1979): 489.

82. Bhagwati, *Free Trade Today*, p. 68.

83. See, e.g., J. Bhagwati, *A View from Academia, in International Labor Standards and Global Integration: Proceedings of a Symposium*, ed. G. Schoepfle and K. Swinnerton (Washington, DC: U.S. Department of Labor, Bureau of International Labor Affairs, 1994).

84. Bhagwati, *Free Trade Today*, pp. 79–80.

85. Since 1997, the United States has lost 180,000 jobs in textiles. In 2002, 116 plants closed. "Free Trade Tangled up in Textiles," *The Economist*, Mar. 30, 2002, p. 25.

86. Adrian Wood, *North-South Trade, Employment, and Inequality: Changing Fortunes in a Skill-driven World* (Oxford: Clarendon Press, 1994; New York: Oxford University Press, 1994).

87. See note 10 for articles dealing with the increased tariffs in the steel industry.

88. See "High Price of Fast-track," *Financial Times* (London), Dec. 17, 2001, p. 14.

89. See *Sure-Tan, Inc. v. NLRB*, 467 U.S. 883 (1984).

90. *Hoffman Plastic Compounds, Inc. v. NLRB*, 535 U.S. 137 (Mar. 27, 2002). The Court's statement that it was attempting to enforce immigration law is undercut by virtue of the fact that immigration law is not being enforced in any event. See Louis Uchitelle, "I.N.S. Is Looking the Other Way as Illegal Immigrants Fill Jobs: Enforcement Changes in Face of Labor Shortage," *New York Times*, Mar. 9, 2000, pp. A1, A14. The position of the dissenters was first articulated by my NLRB in APRA Fuel Oil Buyers Group Inc., 320 NLRB 408 (1995), enforcement granted *NLRB v. APRA Fuel Oil Buyers' Group*, 134 F.3d 50 (1997). For some of the institutional and political limitations and pressures presented by this issue for the NLRB, see William B. Gould IV, *Labored Relations: Law, Politics, and the NLRB—A Memoir* (Cambridge, MA: MIT Press, 2000), pp. 182, 134.

91. "Ruling Makes Immigrant Abuse More Likely: Justices' 5–4 Decision Sets Back Efforts to Unionize Undocumented Workers," *San Jose Mercury News*, Mar. 29, 2002, p. 10B.

92. OECD 2000, pp. 22–23.

93. Ibid., p. 21 (noting that nations with federal forms of government, such as the United States and Switzerland, may be limited in their abilities to bind their states as a result of the decentralization of political authority). Although this "federalism prevents passage of fundamental standards" argument makes sense, comparing the performance of different federalist nations demonstrates that some other factors must be at work. Canada has ratified four of the ILO's seven fundamental conventions; Australia has ratified six; and Switzerland has ratified all seven. Ibid., p. 25. If it were the case that federalism were the determinant factor, then one would expect these nations' totals to be closer to the measly U.S. total of two.

94. I am indebted to Professor Brian Bercusson for making this point to me.

95. See 29 U.S.C. § 152(3) (2000) ("The term 'employee' . . . shall not include any individual employed as an agricultural laborer. . . ."). The Supreme Court has rejected the view that the statutory exclusion of agricultural workers represents an unconstitutional denial of the right to organize. *Babbitt v. United Farm Workers Nat'l Union*, 442 U.S. 289 (1979). For a contrasting view under Canadian law, see *Dunmore v. Ontario (Attorney General)* 2001 SCC 94, File No. 27216 (Dec. 20, 2001).

96. James A. Gross, "A Human Rights Perspective on United States Labor Rela-

tions Law: A Violation of the Right of Freedom of Association," *Employee Rights and Employment Policy Journal* 3 (1999): 65.

97. See Bob Davis, "Bradley to Propose Plan for Laid-Off Workers," *Wall Street Journal,* Feb. 23, 2000, pp. A2, A8; David Wessel, "Trade Balance: Tipping Scales to Help Workers," *Wall Street Journal,* Aug. 30, 2001, p. A1 (arguing in support of "wage insurance" to support employees who lose their jobs because of foreign trade).

98. "Free Trade Tangled up in Textiles," *The Economist*; Lael Brainard, "Textiles and Terrorism," *New York Times,* Dec. 27, 2001, p. A19. Compare the Swedish approach in Nicholas George, "Swedish Union Body Wants 'Buffer Fund,'" *Financial Times* (London), Mar. 3, 2002, p. 4.

99. McGinnis and Movsesian, "The World Trade Constitution," p. 525.

100. J. F. Hornbeck, "Trade Adjustment Assistance for Firms: Economic, Program, and Policy Issues," *CRS Report* RS20210, July 2, 2001; Ethan Kapstein, "Trade Liberalization and the Politics of Trade Adjustment Assistance," *International Labor Review* 137 (1998): 501.

101. "Tariffs on Steel: George Bush, Protectionist—The President's Decision to Place High Tariffs on Imports of Steel Is Disgraceful," *The Economist,* Mar. 9, 2002, p. 13.

102. See, e.g., Thomas Friedman, "Foreign Affairs: America's Labor Pains," *New York Times,* May 9, 2000, p. A25.

103. International Longshoremen's Ass'n, 323 NLRB 1029, 1034 (1997) (Chairman Gould, dissenting), on remand from International Longshoremen's Ass'n, AFL-CIO v. NLRB, 56 F.3d 205 (D.C. Cir. 1995), cert. denied 516 U.S. 1158 (1996).

104. *First National Maintenance Corp. v. NLRB,* 452 U.S. 666 (1981); Q-1 Motor Express, 323 NLRB 767, 769 (1997) (Chairman Gould, concurring).

105. *NLRB v. Transportation Management,* 462 U.S. 393 (1983).

106. *Aguayo v. Quadratech Corp.,* 129 F.Supp.2d 1273 (C.D. CA 2000).

107. *Labor Union of Pico Korea, Ltd. v. Pico Products, Inc.,* 968 F.2d 191 (2d Cir. 1992).

108. The Civil Rights Act of 1991 is different in explicitly establishing extraterritorial jurisdiction in connection with that statute. See William B. Gould IV, "The Supreme Court and Employment Discrimination Law in 1989: Judicial Retreat and Congressional Response," *Tulane Law Review* 64 (1990): 1485; William B. Gould IV, "The Law and Politics of Race: The Civil Rights Act of 1991," *Labor Law Journal* 44 (1993): 323. Congress there reversed *EEOC v. Arabian American Oil Co.,* 499 U.S. 244 (1991).

109. See note 103, above. Compare *MuCulloch v. Sociedad Nacional de Marineros de Honduras,* 372 U.S. 10 (1963); *Longshoremen ILA v. Allied International,* 456 U.S. 212

(1982); *Jacksonville Bulk Terminals, Inc. v. International Longshoremen's Association,* 457 U.S. 702 (1982).

110. Richard B. Freeman and James L. Medoff, *What Do Unions Do?* (New York: Basic Books, 1984).

111. The debate surrounding pay equity/comparable worth in the United States is evidence of the thorniness of this issue. See, e.g., *County of Washington v. Gunther,* 452 U.S. 161, 166 note 6 (1981); *AFSCME v. Washington,* 770 F.2d 1401 (9th Cir. 1985). Compare William B. Gould IV, "The Supreme Court's Labor and Employment Docket in the October 1980 Term: Justice Brennan's Term," *University of Colorado Law Review* 53, 1: 63–74. For a review of the U.S. experience with pay equity, see M. Neil Browne and Michael D. Meuti, "Individualism and the Market Determination of Women's Wages in the United States, Canada, and Hong Kong," *Los Angeles Internaional and Comparative Law Review* 21 (1999): 355, 365–72.

112. Thus I am skeptical about the Bhagwati argument that gender discrimination will not be fast-tracked as a core standard. Bhagwati, *Free Trade Today,* p. 71.

113. See, generally, James Gray Pope, "The Thirteenth Amendment versus the Commerce Clause: Labor and the Shaping of American Constitutional Law, 1921–1957," *Columbia Law Review* 102 (2002): 1; James Gray Pope, "Labor's Constitution of Freedom," *Yale Law Journal* 106 (1997): 941.

114. International Labour Organization, "The Elimination of All Forms of Forced or Compulsory Labour" 59 (2001), available at http://www.ilo.org/public/english/standards/decl/publ/reports/index.htm; Jonathan M. Cowen, "One Nation's Gulag Is Another Nation's Factory within a Fence: Prison Labor in the People's Republic of China and the United States of America," *UCLA Pacific Basin Law Journal* 12 (1993): 190, 201–3 (briefly reviewing the states' laws on contracting out prison labor). Cowen notes that in the nineteenth century and through 1929, the practice of states' permitting private enterprises to operate factories in their prisons was common. Ibid., p. 201. Since 1979, this practice has again come into fashion. Ibid., p. 202. See also OECD 1996, *Trade, Employment and Labour Standards,* p. 34.

115. See ibid., p. 32 (noting that the ILO's Convention 29 prohibits prison labor performed for private agents). Interestingly, to the extent that prison labor is performed "in the interest of the community when there is imminent necessity," it does not violate Convention 29.

116. Ibid., p. 28.

117. Kaushik Basu, "Compacts, Conventions, and Codes: Initiatives for Higher International Labor Standards," *Cornell International Law Journal,* 34 (2001): 487, 490–96; Drusilla K. Brown, "Labor Standards: Where Do They Belong on the International Trade Agenda?" Tufts University Economics Working Paper Series No. 2001–13, available at http://ase.tufts.edu/econ/papers/200113.pdf.

118. Convention 138, passed in 1973, requires each member nation to establish a minimum age for workers. That age should be at "a level consistent with the fullest physical and mental development of young persons," ILO Convention No. 138, Art. I, available at http://ilolex.ilo.ch:1567/cgi-lex/convade.pl?query=c138&query0=138, and no lower than fifteen, ibid. at Art. II § 3. The Convention further establishes that the minimum age in jobs "likely to jeopardise the health, safety or morals of young persons" should be eighteen. Ibid., Art. III § 1. These provisions notwithstanding, Convention No. 138 states that member nations may permit children between the ages of thirteen and fifteen to perform work that is "not likely to be harmful to their health or development" and "not such as to prejudice their attendance at school, their participation in vocational orientation or training programmes approved by the competent authority or their capacity to benefit from the instruction received." Ibid., Art. VII, § 1.

119. ILO Declaration on Fundamental Principles and Rights at Work, Art. 3(b) available at http://www.ilo.org/public/english/standards/decl/declaration/text/index. htm.

120. But see Elizabeth Olson, "I.L.O., Long in Eclipse, Regains Some Prominence," *New York Times*, Mar. 23, 2000, p. C4; "The Collapse in Seattle," *New York Times*, Dec. 6, 1999, p. A28.

121. Bhagwati, *Free Trade Today*, p. 79.

122. Ibid., p. 173.

123. The connection between effective child labor policies and cash assistance is clear from the ILO experience itself. See, for instance, Christian von Mitzlaff, "ILO Technical Paper 1: Monitoring and Verification Systems in Garment Factories and the Placement of Child Workers in Education Programmes," presented at ILO/Japan Asian Regional Meeting on Monitoring Child Labour at the Workplace, Dhaka, Bangladesh (Oct. 24–26, 2000) (available at http://www.ilo.org/public/english/ region/ asro/bangkok/paper/dhaka/tpaper1.pdf), where it is noted that the "provision of an instant income loss alternative is crucial for the ex-child worker to accept social assistance by the project." The same document points out that "lack of funds forced the project management to halt stipend payment twice. Part of the dropout is related to this interruption of payment." All too frequently the essential cash payments are minuscule or lacking. See Fred Hiatt, ". . . And the Children," *Washington Post*, Nov. 16, 1997, p. C07. See, generally, International Labour Office, International Programme on the Elimination of Child Labour, "IPEC Action against Child Labour 2000–2001: Progress and Future Priorities" (Jan. 2002), available at http://www. ilo.org/public/ english/standards/ipec/about/implementation/ipecreport.pdf; International Labour Office, "International Programme on the Elimination of Child Labour," *IPEC Highlights 2000* (Oct. 2000), available at http://www.ilo.org/public/ english/standards/

ipec/publ/imprep99/report2000/draft7.htm; International Labour Office, "International Programme on the Elimination of Child Labour," *ILO-IPEC Highlights of 1998* (Oct. 1998), available at http://www.ilo.org/public/english/standards/ipec/publ/policy/high-98/index.htm. The attendance of children in the schools apparently due to inadequate cash payments is set forth in "The Invisible Children," *New York Times*, Feb. 20, 2000, p. 1. See also Juan Forero, "In Ecuador's Banana Fields, Child Labor Is Key to Profits," *New York Times*, July 13, 2002, pp. A1, A6.

124. "Former NLRB Chairman Reflects on Freedom of Association as ILO Celebrates Major Milestones," *ILO Focus* 12 (1999) (interview with William B. Gould IV) available at http://us.ilo.org/news/focus/991/FOCUS-4.htm.

125. My assistant Sarah Preston points out to me that trade sanctions could operate unevenly and harm the interests of developing countries that do not have resources or economic power comparable to the industrialized world. Assuming *arguendo* the accuracy of this point, this strengthens support for other remedies such as fines that can transcend national boundaries.

126. Article XX(e) of GATT provides,

> Subject to the requirement that such measures are not applied in a manner which would constitute a means of arbitrary or unjustifiable discrimination between countries where the same conditions prevail, or a disguised restriction on international trade, *nothing in this* Agreement shall be construed to prevent the adoption or enforcement by any contracting party of measures:
>
> . . .
>
> (e) relating to products of prison labor.

General Agreements on Tariffs and Trade, opened for signature Oct. 30, 1947, 61 Stat. A3, 55 U.N.T.S. 1887, quoted in Patricia Stirling, "The Use of Trade Sanctions as an Enforcement Mechanism for Basic Human Rights: A Proposal for Addition to the World Trade Organization," *American University Journal of International Law and Policy* 11, 1 (1996): 36.

127. See Steven Greenhouse and Joseph Kahn, "U.S. Effort to Add Labor Standards to Agenda Fails," *New York Times*, Dec. 3, 1999, p. A1; Joseph Kahn and David E. Sanger, "Impasse on Trade Delivers Stinging Blow to Clinton," *New York Times*, Dec. 4, 1999, p. A1; Richard W. Stevenson, "Clinton Defends His Role at the Seattle Trade Talks," *New York Times*, Dec. 9, 1999, p. A12; David E. Sanger, "Clinton Criticizes World Trade Body in Stormy Seattle," *New York Times*, Dec. 2, 1999, pp. A1, A14; Guy De Jonquieres, "Clinton's Demands Threaten Turmoil at Seattle Talks: Call for Sanctions to Enforce Trade Links to Labour Standards," *Financial Times* (London), Dec. 2, 1999, p. 1.

128. See Louis Uchitelle, "Challenging the Dogmas of Free Trade," *New York Times*, Feb. 9, 2002, p. B7.

129. McGinnis and Movsesian "The World Trade Constitution," pp. 564–65 (footnotes omitted).

130. Nicholas D. Kristof and Sheryl Wu Dunn, "Two Cheers for Sweatshops," *New York Times Magazine,* Sept. 24, 2001, p. 70.

131. For discussion of a wide variety of instruments containing labor clauses, see Brian Bercusson, "Labour Regulation in a Transnational Economy," *Maastricht Journal of European and Comparative Law* 6: 244.

132. The mechanisms are described in more detail in M. J. Bolle, *NAFTA Labor Side Agreement: Lessons for the Worker Rights and Fast-Track Debate, CRS REPORT* 97–861 (Jan. 11, 2002).

133. See William B. Gould IV, *Agenda for Reform: The Future of Employment Relationships and the Law* (Cambridge, MA: MIT Press, 1993); Lance A. Compa, *Unfair Advantage: Workers' Freedom of Association in the United States under International Human Rights Standards* (New York: Human Rights Watch, 2000).

134. LCF, Inc. 322 NLRB 774 (1996), enforcement denied 129 3d.1276 (D.C. Cir. 1997).

135. National Administrative Office of Mexico for North American Agreement on Labor Cooperation, Report on Review of Public Submission 9501/NAO, Staff translation, Mexico, Fed. Dist. (May 31, 1995). Compare Sarah Lowe, "The First American Case under the North American Agreement for Labor Cooperation," *University of Miami Law Review* 51 (1997): 481.

136. Clyde Summers, "NAFTA's Labor Side Agreement and International Labor Standards," *Journal of Small and Emerging Business Law* 3 (1999): 173. See, generally, Henry H. Drummonds, "Transnational Small and Emerging Business in a World of Nikes and Microsofts," *Journal of Small and Emerging Business Law* 4 (2000): 249.

137. See Joe Klein, *The Natural: The Misunderstood Presidency of Bill Clinton* (New York: Doubleday, 2002), p. 10.

138. Thomas L. Friedman, "The New American Politics," *New York Times,* Nov. 13, 1997.

139. See Joseph Kahn, "Labor Praises New Trade Pact with Jordan," *New York Times,* Oct. 25, 2000, pp. C1, C12. For a discussion of this agreement during the Bush administration, see Marc Lacey, "Bush Seeking to Modify Pact on Trade with Jordan," *New York Times,* Apr. 11, 2001, p. A5; David Armstrong, "U.S., Jordan Expand Economic Ties," *San Francisco Chronicle,* Nov. 10, 2001, pp. B1, B2; Richard W. Stevenson, "Senate Approves Bill to Lift Barriers to Trade with Jordan," *New York Times,* Sept. 25, 2001, pp. C1, C6.

140. Lenore Sek, "Trade Promotion Authority (Fast-Track Authority for Trade Agreements): Background and Developments in the 107th Congress," CRS *Issue Brief* IB10084, Jan. 18, 2002, p. 6.

141. Ibid., p. 10.

142. The compromise to grant Mr. Bush so-called trade promotion authority won the support of the Senate Democratic leadership only after weeks of partisan haggling. It would triple the money spent on aid for displaced workers to $1.2 billion annually. The government would also begin paying 70 percent of the health insurance costs for people whose jobs disappear because of imports. Joseph Kahn, "Senate Approves Bill Giving Wider Trade Authority to Bush," *New York Times*, May 24, 2002, p. A19. See also Kathy Chen and Neil King, Jr., "Workers Gain in Trade Equation: Bush Gets Closer on 'Fast Track' Bill by Agreeing to More Aid," *Wall Street Journal*, May 13, 2002, p. A4; Richard W. Stevenson, "Partisan Fight on Job Losses Casts Shadow on Trade Bill," *New York Times*, May 1, 2002, p. A19; Neil King, Jr., "Senate May Tie Jobless Health Care to Trade Deal," *Wall Street Journal*, Apr. 24, 2002, pp. A2, A16.

143. Neil King, Jr., "Converting Democrats Is Key to Trade Bill: West Coast Representatives Are in Spotlight as Fast-Track Legislation Hangs in Balance," *Wall Street Journal*, June 19, 2002, p. A4; Shailagh Murray and Michael Phillips, "Fast-Track Bill Runs into Hurdle; Talks Are Delayed," *Wall Street Journal*, June 21, 2002, pp. A3, A5.

144. See, generally, "Promoting the Noble Cause of Commerce," *The Economist*, Aug. 3, 2002; Guy de Jonquieres and Edward Alden, "A Deal, at Last," *Financial Times*, Aug. 1, 2002, p. 14; David Firestone, "Senate Approves Bill to Give Bush Trade Authority," *New York Times*, Aug. 2, 2002, pp. A1, A8.

145. "Trade Act of 2002, Conference Report," *Congressional Record* 148, S7768-S7769 (2002).

146. Paul Blustein, "Trade Bill to Help Laid-Off Workers; Victims of Imports Win Added Benefits," *Washington Post*, Aug. 3, 2002, p. E1.

147. Arnold Zack has proposed a mediation unit in conjunction with the ILO that would promote compliance with international labor standards:

There seems to be little prospect of governments in developing countries enforcing their own national—workplace laws—if it means losing factories, employment and taxes, let alone conforming to the conventions of the ILO. And private monitoring is too often a public relations sham—with little incentive for companies to effectively police their own violations of basic workplace protections. The multinational corporations are increasingly sensitive, however, to the power the consumer market and other organizations may impose, and willing under pressure, for the short term at least, to provide the accommodation that will perpetuate sales to the protesting markets. That measure of persuasion more than enforcement may be effective. The institutionalization through the ILO of a mediating facility might be a way of bringing compliance when international political will is now lacking. The NGOs, the consumers, the unions and many responsible retailers are increasingly alert to the deprivations of workplace protections, and yet they are largely ineffective in enforcing employers to live up to their international workplace obligations. Arnold Zack, "How to Improve Labor Standards while Checking Corporate Flight," address at the National Policy Forum of the IRRA, Washington, D.C. (June 2001) (transcript on file with the author).

148. A confidentiality demarcation line between conciliation and adjudication was drawn by the NLRB during my chairmanship. The rule prohibits disclosure of discussions, representations, and positions taken in conciliation but requires disclosure in adjudication. See John T. Delaney and Lamont E. Stallworth, *An Evaluation of the NLRB's Settlement Judge Program* (2001) (unpublished, on file with the author).

149. See "Agreement Establishing the World Trade Organization, Annex 2, Understanding on Rules and Procedures Governing the Settlement of Disputes" (1994); "The Procedures for the Circulation and Derestriction of WTO Documents" (1994), WT/L/160/Rev. 1 (July 26, 1996). See Memorandum from Professor Richard Steinberg to the author (Mar. 21, 2002)(on file with the author).

150. Doha WTO Ministerial 2001: Ministerial Declaration, WT/MIN(01)/DEC/1 Paragraph 10 (Nov. 20, 2001).

151. Daniel T. Griswold, "Trade, Labor, and the Environment: How Blue and Green Sanctions Threaten Higher Standards," Cato Institute Trade Policy Analysis No. 15 (Aug. 2, 2001).

152. Joseph Kahn, "To Aid Trade Bill, Democrat Creates Plan for Rights Panel," *New York Times*, May 4, 2000, p. A8.

153. 19 U.S.C. § 2462 (2000).

154. See Sarah H. Cleveland, "Book Review: Global Labor Rights and the Alien Tort Claims Act," *Texas Law Review* 76 (1998): 1533, 1547–50.

155. 19 U.S.C. § 2702(c)(8) (2000) (requiring consideration of whether a country "has taken or is taking steps to afford to workers in that country [including any designated zone in that country] internationally recognized worker rights" in extending duty free status to twenty-seven Caribbean nations).

156. Helen Cooper, "Dropped Stitches: A Trade Deal Helps Cambodian Workers, But Payoff Is Withheld," *Wall Street Journal*, Feb. 28, 2000, pp. A1, A13.

157. Office of the United States Trade Representative, "U.S.-Cambodia Textile Agreement Links Increasing Trade with Improving Workers' Rights," Press Release, Jan. 7, 2002; "First Synthesis Report on the Working Conditions Situation in Cambodia's Garment Sector," Nov. 2001, available at http://www.ilo.org/public/english/dialogue/cambodia.htm; Frederik Balfour and Sheri Prasso, "Bumps in Road to Cambodian Labor Reform: A U.S. Trade Deal Becomes a Test Case in Global Standards," *Businessweek* (international edition), Sept. 11, 2000; John A. Hall, "Human

Rights and the Garment Industry in Contemporary Cambodia," *Stanford Journal of International Law* 36 (2000): 119.

158. Cleveland, "Book Review: Global Labor Rights and the Alien Tort Claims Act."

159. *Labor Union of Pico Korea, Ltd. v. Pico Products, Inc.*, 968 F.2d 191 (2d Cir. 1992); *International Labor Rights Education and Research Fund v. Bush*, 752 F. Supp. 495 (D.D.C. 1990), aff'd 954 F.2d 745 (D.C. Cir. 1992). But see for some measure of success the decision by the Texas Supreme Court in *Dow Chemical Co. v. Castro Alfaro*, 786 S.W. 2d 674 (Tex. 1990).

160. Organisation for Economic Co-operation and Development, *Corporate Codes of Conduct: An Inventory* (1999; OECD, Trade Committee Report, http://64.49.225.236/documents/04E95110_.doc); Organisation for Economic Co-operation and Development, *Codes of Conduct—An Expanded Review of Their Contents* (2000; Working Paper on International Investment Number 2001/6, Directorate for Financial, Fiscal and Enterprise Affairs [May 2001], http://www.oecd.org/pdf/m00015000/m00015433.pdf); Compare William H. Meyer and Boyka Stefanova, "Human Rights, the UN Global Compact, and Global Governance," *Cornell International Law Journal* 34 (2001): 501.

161. Archon Fung, Dara O'Rourke, and Charles Sabel, "Realizing Labor Standards: How Transparency, Competition, and Sanctions Could Improve Working Conditions Worldwide," *Boston Review*, Feb./Mar. 2001, available at http://bostonreview.mit.edu/BR26.1/fung.html.

162. Cox, "Federalism in the Law of Labor Relations."

Why International Labor Standards?

SARAH H. CLEVELAND

D o we need international labor standards? Traditionally, regulating the terms and conditions of work has fallen to the domestic policies of sovereign states. Nevertheless, the last century and particularly the past two decades have seen an explosion of activity seeking to regulate labor conditions at the transnational and international level. This activity has progressed on three fronts: through the definition of international labor standards, through widespread ratification of core international labor instruments, and through increasing resort to such standards in the activities of the United Nations, international financial institutions, regional and bilateral trade systems, unilateral foreign assistance and trade measures, transnational litigation, and voluntary corporate codes of conduct and social labeling efforts. These developments have been stimulated in large part by a rapidly globalizing economy. The General Agreement on Tariffs and Trade (GATT)/World Trade Organization (WTO) system has lowered tariff barriers and increased transnational flows of goods and capital. The Internet and the international telecommunications revolution have made far-flung corporate activities possible. Multinational corporations now transcend any particular state, and goods for Western consumption are produced around the globe. All of these developments have given states and consumers a greater interest in labor conditions outside their borders. International labor standards nevertheless have been criticized as, at best, unnecessary interference with domestic markets and global trade expansion and, at worst, disguised protectionist measures designed to impose Western values on developing states and to deprive them of their comparative advantage in low wages.

This chapter examines the case for international labor standards: why they are necessary; what standards are necessary, and what they contribute to trade, social and economic development, and the overall human rights movement. Part I examines the current status of international labor standards and their use in international, regional, national, and private regulatory systems. Part II examines the case for international labor standards from seven perspectives: (1) the role of labor rights as fundamental human rights; (2) the role of labor standards in preventing labor exploitation as an unfair trade practice; (3) the role of labor standards in promoting high-wage economic development strategies; (4) their role in preventing and in avoiding a global race to the bottom in labor conditions; (5) the increasing difficulty of controlling corporate and employment structures through domestic legislation; (6) the special problems of migrant workers, and (7) the functional need for standardization in the international economy. Part III considers the most controversial aspect of international labor standards: efforts at enforcement through trade/labor linkage. Part IV concludes by arguing that a certain group of labor standards—the International Labor Organization's (ILO's) core labor standards, plus subsistence wages, protection from ultrahazardous working conditions, and protection of migrant workers—are particularly important to securing fundamental protections for workers within the global economy.

I. The Current State of Play

The ILO

After decades of relative inaction and criticism as ineffective, the International Labor Organization has made significant progress in recent years, both in rallying global support for international labor standards and in promoting compliance.[1] The ILO has promulgated over 180 binding labor conventions, establishing standards in areas ranging from the rights of seamen to migrant worker health and safety. The ILO recently launched a highly successful effort to obtain universal commitment to four "core" labor standards: freedom of association and collective bargaining, nondiscrimination, the prohibition against forced labor, and the prohibition against child labor. These standards in turn are supported by eight core ILO conventions.[2] Since 1995 the number of countries that have ratified all the core ILO conventions has more than doubled.[3] Ratification progress has been especially notable in the area of child labor. As recently as 1998, only 51 states had ratified the ILO's Minimum Age Convention (No. 138).[4] Both that convention and the new Worst Forms of Child Labor Convention (No. 182) have now received at least 116 ratifications.[5] Moreover, the ILO's 1998 Declaration on Fundamental Principles and Rights at Work makes commitment to these labor standards obligatory as a political matter on all ILO members.[6] Although actual implementation lags significantly behind state ratifications, the ILO has become more aggressive in providing technical assistance to improve member state compliance with the core conventions, and in denouncing noncompliant members. The ILO has developed new initiatives for implementing labor standards, including establishing a Working Party on the Social Aspects of Globalization and a World Commission on the Social Dimension of Globalization, and adopting a follow-up program for implementing the Declaration. For the first time, the ILO has invoked Article 33 of its constitution to suspend Burma from participating in the ILO and receiving technical assistance, because of that country's pervasive forced labor practices.[7] As part of its more aggressive stance, the ILO has called upon its members to ensure that their actions did not perpetuate Burma's system of forced labor and to take additional actions to stop the use of forced labor in that state.[8] In the future, the ILO may authorize the imposition of economic sanctions under Article 33 as part of its enforcement efforts.[9]

Regional and Bilateral Labor Standards Oversight

In addition to the ILO's efforts at the international level, regional and bilateral mechanisms have been established for developing transnational labor standards and encouraging compliance. The European Union (EU) has taken the most advanced steps toward regional economic integration, and has established a regional legal framework for the definition and enforcement of labor standards, establishing communitywide standards in a range of worker rights areas. Through the European Works Council of 1994, the European Union required multinational enterprises (MNEs) operating in the European Union to establish worker councils to address questions such as working conditions.[10] The European Union also has negotiated industrywide codes of conduct in a range of industrial sectors.[11] The European Community (EC) has taken steps as well to promote labor rights compliance abroad.

The EC recently reached an agreement with the African, Caribbean, and Pacific (ACP) countries reaffirming the signatories' commitment to the core ILO conventions, and it has reached a similar agreement with South Africa.[12]

The North American Agreement on Labor Cooperation (NAALC),[13] the labor side agreement to the North American Free Trade Agreement (NAFTA), does not require labor standard harmonization. It does, however, obligate member states to enforce their own labor standards in eleven areas such as freedom of association, employment discrimination, minimum wages, and forced and child labor. Over twenty-five petitions have been filed under the NAALC alleging failure of the member states to enforce their domestic labor laws relating to freedom of association, sexual discrimination, minimum wages, and other rights.[14] Although the NAALC obligates member states to enforce only their own domestic labor laws, these laws include international labor standards that members have embraced by treaty. Several NAALC cases have alleged violations of a member state's international obligations.[15]

Nor are regional efforts limited to North and Central America and Europe. In 1998, members of the Common Market of the South (MERCOSUR) adopted a declaration on social and labor issues that commits member states to promote the ILO core labor standards, the rights of migrant workers, health and safety standards, and other workplace rights.[16] The fourteen-member South African Development Community (SADC) also is taking steps to formulate a Social Charter of Fundamental Rights, including observance of the ILO core labor rights.[17]

Certain commodity agreements have contained labor rights protections for a number of years.[18] More recently, labor rights provisions have appeared in bilateral trade agreements. Canada and Chile have reached an Agreement on Labor Cooperation with provisions similar to the NAALC.[19] The United States reached an understanding with China regarding the use of prison labor in 1992,[20] and it has entered bilateral agreements with Jordan and Cambodia that expressly require respect for labor rights.[21] The Trade Act of 2002, which granted the President trade promotion authority, directs the President to promote respect for worker rights in the negotiation of new trade agreements.[22]

International Financial Institutions

International labor standards also have begun to permeate international financial institutions. After years of resistance, the World Bank, the International Monetary Fund (IMF), the Inter-American Development Bank, the African Development Bank, and other international finance and development institutions have begun to consider the impact of their lending decisions on labor practices.[23] The World Bank also has directly targeted development assistance toward eliminating substandard labor practices such as child labor.[24]

Unilateral Measures

U.S. statutes promoting respect for human rights abroad include a number of laws that condition economic assistance, trade, and investment on worker rights compliance.[25] Section 307 of the U.S. Tariff Act of 1930 bars the importation of goods produced with convict, forced, or indentured labor, including "forced or indentured child labor,"[26] and has been applied to exclude the importation of certain Mexican and Chinese products.[27] A 1999 executive order bars agencies of the U.S. government from purchasing products made with forced or indentured child labor.[28] Assistance from the Overseas Private Investment Corporation (OPIC) is conditioned on compliance with international labor standards.[29] U.S. representatives to the Multilateral Investment Fund,[30] the IMF, and other international financial institutions are directed to use their "voice and vote" to encourage respect for internationally recognized worker rights.[31] In 2003, countries failing to meet minimum standards relating to slavery will be subject to suspended foreign assistance and U.S. opposition to international financial institution loans.[32]

The United States also conditions tariff benefits to developing countries on compliance with "internationally recognized worker rights" through the Generalized System of Preferences (GSP)[33] and a number of related programs.[34] Since 1984, forty-seven countries have been cited in petitions challenging their GSP status for worker rights violations.[35] GSP privileges have been withheld from at least thirteen countries, with others placed on continuing review status.[36]

Since 1994, the EU has had a similar system for promoting labor standards abroad through its GSP system.[37] The EU system ties additional tariff reductions beyond the GSP baseline to developing countries that can demonstrate that they effectively implement the core ILO conventions: Nos. 87 and 98 (freedom of association and collective bargaining), nos. 29 and 105 (forced labor), No. 111 (employment discrimination), and nos. 138 and 182 (child labor).[38] EU GSP benefits may be suspended for the use of slavery, forced labor, or the export of goods made with prison labor, and the EU has suspended tariff benefits to Burma in response to that state's forced labor practices.[39]

Litigation

Transnational litigation promoting compliance with international labor standards has increased significantly in the past few years, particularly in the United States.[40] Suits by foreign workers employed by U.S. companies abroad to enforce contract and tort rights have been brought in the United States for some time. Examples include a suit by Korean workers seeking to enforce their collective bargaining agreement against the U.S.-based parent corporation,[41] suits by Central American banana workers for pesticide exposure,[42] and suits by Mexican maquiladora workers for sexual harassment and wrongful death.[43] These more traditional suits have been supplemented in recent years by efforts to use the Alien Tort Claims Act[44] and other legal mechanisms to directly enforce international labor standards through the courts. Lawsuits have been filed challenging the Unocal Corporation's complicity in Burma's use of forced labor,[45] challenging sweatshop conditions in apparel manufacturing operations in Saipan,[46] seeking damages for abuse of union leaders in Guatemala[47] and Colombia,[48] and seeking compensation for the use of forced labor and slavery by Japan and Germany in World War II.[49] International labor standards also have been utilized in forced labor and servitude claims in the United States by housekeepers and other domestic workers as well as by garment and agricultural workers.[50]

Corporate Codes of Conduct and Social Labeling

International organizations, regional and national governments, nongovernmental organizations (NGOs), and private corporations all have been involved in drafting voluntary codes of conduct or guidelines on corporate behavior. The ILO Tripartite Declaration of Principles Concerning MNEs and Social Policy[51] and the Organisation for Economic Co-operation and Development (OECD) Guidelines for Multinational Enterprises[52] have been revised and strengthened. UN Secretary-General Kofi Annan recently instituted a Global Compact setting forth general guidelines for corporate responsibility in the labor rights area,[53] and the UN Sub-Commission on Promotion and Protection of Human Rights is drafting a declaration on Fundamental Human Rights Principles for Business Enterprises that includes labor rights.[54] The European Union has taken steps toward developing a model code of conduct,[55] and the European apparel and construction industries have adopted codes of conduct in cooperation with union representatives.[56] The UK-sponsored Ethical Trading Initiative has adopted a code through the participation of government, union, industry, and NGO representatives.[57] The Clinton Administration sponsored the development of the Fair Labor Association for the U.S. apparel industry, which developed a voluntary code of conduct through the collaboration of industry, labor, human rights, and government representatives.[58]

Private corporations, industry associations, and NGOs have developed voluntary codes of conduct addressing labor standards in global manufacturing operations. The U.S. Worker Rights Consortium, which monitors the compliance of its member companies, and the Social Accountability (SA-8000) effort are notable NGO-sponsored efforts. Private corporations have developed codes in response to NGO pressure exposing sweatshop conditions overseas, and to deflect efforts to tie labor standards to international trade rules in the WTO. Most U.S. Fortune 500 companies, including Nike, Levi-Strauss, the Gap, and Toys-R-Us, have adopted codes of conduct or internal guidelines addressing labor standards.[59] Over 60 percent of the top 500 companies in the United Kingdom have adopted similar codes, up from 18 percent a decade ago.[60] Social labeling efforts such as the "Rugmark" campaign to reduce child labor in the carpet industry and the International Fairtrade Labeling initiative, which encompasses labeling efforts for foodstuffs in seventeen countries, also have gained momentum in recent years.[61]

Linkages also are beginning to appear among the various forms of labor standards mechanisms discussed above. Corporate codes of conduct, for example, have been used in litigation to enforce labor standards, not as the direct basis for liability, but as evidence that the corporation purports to exercise control over the labor conditions of its subcontractors.[62] And The Netherlands recently has taken controversial steps to link government trade, export, and investment assistance to compliance with the OECD guidelines.[63]

In sum, international labor standards have become incorporated into a decentralized global network of international, regional, national, and private efforts to promote labor rights. This sheer level of activity alone suggests that international labor standards are serving an increasingly important function in the global economic system. Indeed, the *idea* of international labor standards, at least in core areas, is relatively uncontroversial. The fundamental ILO conventions have been ratified and are legally binding on the vast majority of nations, as noted above. As discussed in Part III, below, it is the international *enforcement* of labor standards, particularly through linkage to the international trading system, that has provoked the most strenuous opposition.

II. The Case for International Labor Standards

As the global activity surrounding labor rights suggests, international labor standards fill a number of important functions in the modern global community. This section considers seven reasons for the proliferation of international labor rights activity in recent years. Some labor standards are widely recognized as human rights. International standards help prevent states from suppressing labor rights as an unfair trade practice and encourage the pursuit of high-wage, high-productivity economic development strategies. They seek to prevent a race to the bottom in labor standards in the global economy. Their global reach helps overcome states' individual limitations in regulating increasingly flexible forms of employment and global corporate structures. They fill an important gap in the protections available to workers who migrate across borders in search of work. And finally they create a common language that facilitates consideration of labor rights in a range of contexts in the international economy. Each of these justifications and functions will be considered in turn.

1. Labor Rights as Human Rights

On the most basic level, the need for international labor standards is the same as the need for international human rights standards generally. The theory behind the international human rights movement (and correspondingly, the labor standards that constitute human rights) is that human beings are universally entitled to a certain minimum standard of treatment. Accordingly, many areas of human life that traditionally were viewed as falling within the domestic jurisdiction of sovereign states are now subject to international regulation, oversight, and scrutiny. These include the rights of women, children, persons in the criminal justice system, racial and religious minorities, and certain general labor rights. The modern idea of human rights, as set forth in the Universal Declaration of Human Rights, conceives of such rights as universal, equal and inalienable, deriving from the inherent dignity of human beings and necessary to the peace and security of nations.[64]

The human rights idea incorporates a number of basic labor rights. Indeed, the first international human rights movement—the effort to abolish slavery—was also a labor rights movement. The 1919 Treaty of Versailles called for domestic protection of freedom of association, reasonable wages, an eight-hour day, a forty-eight-hour work week, equal pay for men and women, equal rights for migrant workers, and the prohibition of child labor.[65] The Universal Declaration, which sets forth a "common standard of achievement for all peoples and all nations,"[66] includes in its protections a general prohibition against discrimination, the prohibition against slavery, the rights to freedom of association and to form and join trade unions, the right to work, to free choice of employment, to just and favorable conditions of work and protection against unemployment, equal pay for equal work, just and favorable remuneration sufficient to ensure an existence worthy of human dignity, leisure, a reasonable limit on working hours, paid vacation, and a standard of living adequate for the health and well-being of the individuals and their families. The International Covenant on Civil and Political Rights (ICCPR),[67] and the International Covenant on Economic, Social, and Cultural Rights (ICESCR)[68] were drafted to incorporate the rights in the Universal Declaration into binding treaty law. The ICCPR prohibits slavery, servitude, and forced labor, protects the right to freedom of association and to form and join trade unions, and prohibits discrimination. The ICESCR, in turn, prohibits gender discrimination, protects the rights to work and choice of employment, to just and favorable conditions of work (including fair wages sufficient to sustain a decent living), equal pay, safe and healthy working conditions, equal opportunities for promotion, rest, leisure, a reasonable limit on working hours, paid vacation, freedom of association, the right to join trade unions and to strike, the right to technical and vocational guidance and worker training, and the right to an adequate standard of living. The Convention on the Elimination of All Forms of Discrimination Against Women (CEDAW)[69] obligates states to abolish employment discrimination against women and to ensure safe and healthy working conditions and maternity leave with pay. The Convention on the Rights of the Child[70] obligates states to protect children from injury, abuse, or exploitation.

Given the widespread protection of certain fundamental labor rights in international human rights instruments, the ILO has identified its four "core" labor standards as fundamental human rights. The purpose of freedom of association, nondiscrimination, and the prohibitions on child labor is to protect the basic life and well-being of workers around the world. These core standards are incorporated in the major human rights treaties as well as in the eight widely ratified core ILO conventions.

2. Unfair Trade Practices

In addition to the values underlying the international human rights system, labor rights bring another card to the table. To the extent that they implicate competitiveness in international trade, substandard labor conditions can constitute an unfair trade practice.[71] The international prohibition against the use of prison, forced, and other coercive labor, for example, may be viewed from a human rights perspective as a fundamental protection of the right of the person not to be compelled to work under slavelike conditions. Coerced labor may also be viewed, from the perspective of international competitiveness, as a means of gaining an unfair advantage in the international trade arena.[72] International labor standards thus both protect the basic dignity of the human being in the workplace and prevent the exploitation of labor as a means of gaining a trade advantage.

3. High-Wage Development Strategy

Labor standards also are a means for compelling a high-wage rather than a low-wage economic development strategy. Left to its own devices, the market will always offer developing states the option of suppressing wages and other labor costs in order to gain a competitive advantage in the international economy. States thus can compete on the basis of low wages and poor working conditions to attract foreign capital. Lower wages resulting from countries' differing levels of development are, of course, an acceptable basis for competition. But wage competition also can encourage states to suppress wages and working conditions in order to compete in the global economy.[73] Such a strategy tends to attract investment in low-skill, highly mobile production methods by peripatetic industries that invest little in skills development within the country and move constantly in search of lower-wage production sites. By eliminating the option of suppressing labor costs as a basis for competition, international labor standards encourage states instead to seek higher-skill, more stable forms of investment. In other words, labor standards encourage states to compete through skills development and productivity, rather than through low wages.[74] Indeed, a substantial body of evidence suggests that adherence to the core labor standards (freedom of association/collective bargaining, nondiscrimination, and the prohibition of forced and child labor) may improve a nation's productivity.[75] This high-wage, high-skill development strategy in turn puts money into workers' pockets, strengthening the consumer economy and further stimulating the nation's economic development.

4. Globalization and the Race to the Bottom

The flip side of the high-wage development strategy is the concern that the absence of international labor standards creates downward pressure on global labor conditions. The preamble of the ILO Constitution provides that "the failure of any nation to adopt humane conditions of labour is an obstacle in the way of other nations which desire to improve the conditions of their own countries."[76] The premise of this statement is that differing levels of labor protection around the world, combined with capital mobility, will result in a race to the bottom, where capital naturally flows in a free market system to states with lower labor costs and cheaper labor protections.[77] Thus, countries—especially those whose comparative advantage lies in low labor costs—have an incentive to keep labor protections low in order to attract mobile capital. Developing states' desire to attract foreign investment through low labor costs combines with developed states' fear of capital flight to impose global downward pressure on national labor regulation. Even if market competition does not lead to suppression of labor protections, it may hold them static. Less developed countries may become unwilling to raise their level of labor protection for fear of discouraging foreign investment, while developed countries may oppose even modest legislative reform—such as increases in the minimum wage—for fear of losing capital to states with lower costs.

The extent to which the "race to the bottom" phenomenon plays out in reality is disputed.[78] Corporations take many considerations into account in making relocation decisions, including education and skill levels, labor market inflexibilities, political stability, bureaucratic structures, transportation and technological infrastructure, and other macroeconomic and cyclical factors.[79] To the extent that higher wages and labor standards reflect higher levels of productivity, as discussed above, the importance of labor cost differentials in attracting investment may be neutralized.[80] Moreover, the OECD's important 1996 study of the relationship between labor standards, trade, and economic development found that while a few countries may have deliberately denied core labor standards in an effort to improve trade performance or attract foreign investment, the economic benefits gained from such policies were likely to be short-lived,[81] and that "host countries may be able to enforce core labour standards without risking negative repercussions of [foreign direct investment] flows."[82] The OECD report concluded (after noting the difficulties involved in conducting empirical work on the issue) "that core labour standards do not play a significant role in shaping trade performance."[83] The OECD's 2000 follow-up report again found "no robust evidence that low-standard countries provide a haven for foreign firms," and export processing zones with poor working conditions were "unlikely to attract *sustained*, long-term investment."[84] Accordingly, countries aggressively pursuing a low wage/low labor standard development strategy are likely to receive only highly transient investment that utilizes unskilled labor and will move quickly to take advantage of cheaper opportunities elsewhere.[85]

The glaring exception to these conclusions is China, which has been the object of significant foreign investment and trade in recent years, despite its refusal to allow independent unions and other systematic violations of core labor rights. Although China is the only state that fails to respect the core labor rights and still receives significant flows of global capital,[86] it is a sufficiently giant exception to be of concern.

Pressure for a race to the bottom in labor rights has been exacerbated in recent years by the increasing mobility of international investment. Reduction in tariff levels under the GATT/WTO and the streamlining of international finance have made movement of corporate activities across national borders easier than ever before. Multinational corporations accordingly are more able to respond to developing countries' voracious need for trade and foreign capital. The rise of Export Processing Zones (EPZs), many of which are subject to reduced national labor regulation, is evidence of this impulse.[87] Some states, such as Bangladesh and Pakistan, exclude EPZs from national labor legislation altogether, while other states, such as Panama, have adopted weaker legislation for EPZs.[88] EPZs are often subject to reduced enforcement activity as well, since labor ministries may lack resources to monitor the zones effectively and view them as a low priority.[89]

International labor standards can counterbalance these pressures on domestic working conditions by removing certain intolerable labor conditions from the labor rights/production costs calculus. Universal standards create a floor below which states and managers cannot legitimately go to compete.

5. The Limits of National Regulation: Employment and Corporate Flexibility

International labor standards also have become necessary as globalization has undermined the ability of national law to effectively regulate the workplace. Flexible corporate structures, corporate mobility, and the increasing political and economic power of multinational corporations have combined with employment flexibility and new conceptions of the employment relationship to exacerbate the inherent limitations of states in maintaining and enforcing labor standards.

Corporate and financial mobility has led multinational corporations to adopt increasingly global corporate organizations, which may be headquartered in one state, have shareholders in others, and operate worldwide.[90] Accordingly, "[c]ompanies, industries, products, technologies and jobs no longer depend upon the strengths and weaknesses of any one nation's economy or economic base."[91] As corporate decision-making is decentralized and the lines between firms are blurred, transnational corporate activities are increasingly difficult to regulate.[92] States where corporations are headquartered are generally reluctant to regulate corporate activities abroad, due to political concerns about disadvantaging their own corporations in the international economy as well as traditional concepts of limited territorial jurisdiction.[93] Host states, in turn, may be reluctant to regulate out of a desire not to deter foreign investment.

Growing corporate wealth also undermines the willingness and ability of national governments to regulate. Many multinational corporations now have resources greater than the states in which they operate and thus can exert substantial political and economic pressure on the policies of host states. As noted above, the desire of developing countries to attract and retain foreign investment may compete with their interest in regulating fundamental worker rights protections. States may even cooperate with corporations in labor rights violations, as in Burma's use of forced labor to provide security and develop infrastructure for the Yadana natural gas pipeline.[94] In extreme cases, states may cede statelike control to corporations over large tracts of territory, as with the operations of Freeport McMoran in Irian Jaya, Indonesia; or Texaco in the Ecuadorian rain forest.[95] Complex corporate structures and the fiscal clout of large transnational corporations accordingly combine to place many corporate activities beyond the reach of the sovereign nation-state.[96]

Finally, changes in the employment relationship have challenged traditional domestic regulation. States historically have regulated the workplace through collective bargaining agreements, whereby workers and employers in a particular firm negotiate the terms of employment in a private contract, and through the common law and state legislation, which impose general obligations on employers and employees. These models, in turn, are based on certain traditional assumptions about the nature of employment that may no longer pertain. Collective bargaining models rely on strong unionization, and national labor laws traditionally assume the existence of relatively long-term employment with an individual firm in a traditional employer-employee relationship. But unionization is on the wane in many states, and "flexible," multitiered, and disparate employment relationships, which have long shielded agricultural and garment employers from liability for domestic labor law violations, are now proliferating through employment forms such as temporary and leased employees and so-called independent contractors. Thus, "janitors, truck drivers, taxi drivers, limousine drivers, parking lot workers, banquet waiters, carpet and cable television installers, building service workers, and security guards have been subjected to such practices designed to relieve the real employers of liability under labor-protective and employment tax laws."[97] Developments in computers, telecommunications, and information technology have facilitated both the creation of more flexible forms of employment and greater global corporate mobility.[98] Nor has this transformation been limited to low-skill employment sectors. In high-performance workplaces as well, skill distinctions between employees and management are blurring, and employment insecurity has invaded high tech and management levels.[99] Employment precariousness is also spurred by flexible just-in-time production methods, which rely on an increasingly flexible, multiskilled, and versatile work force to produce customized goods to meet rapidly changing consumer demands.[100] Thus, the increasingly diffuse nature of employment and labor relationships may evade the state's ability to apply traditional legal categories to the workplace.

Employment flexibility alone would not necessarily require an international solution. National governments could respond by revising labor laws within their own borders to address these developments. But together, corporate mobility and layering, MNE economic power, and employment flexibility may create an employer-employee relationship that eludes national regulation. As Manuel Castells has put it, "Who are the owners, who the producers, who the managers, and who the servants, becomes increasingly blurred in a production system of variable geometry, of teamwork, of networking, outsourcing, and subcontracting."[101] International labor standards that transcend national boundaries thus are an important response to the developments in transnational corporate and employment relationships. International standards are both uniform and universal, and cannot be evaded through corporate restructuring or relocation abroad.

6. The Special Case of Migrant Workers

The establishment of international standards may be particularly important for migrant workers, who are uniquely impervious to domestic protection. Migrant workers who travel to a foreign state in search of work are notoriously underprotected by the countries in which they labor—through both lack of legal rights and underenforcement. Migrant workers are a peculiarly vulnerable population, who are generally very poor, often illiterate, may not speak the language of the host country or understand its laws, and work in low-skill, unattractive sectors. They may have a tenuous immigration status and be subject to deportation if they complain. Perhaps most important, they lack any political or economic voice in the host country.

In the United States, for example, a number of factors conspire to undermine legal protections for migrant workers. First, migrant workers tend to be found in sectors with unusually low legal protection, such as agriculture and domestic housekeeping. Under U.S. law, agricultural workers are excluded from the rights to organize, bargain collectively, and strike,[102] and from overtime protections.[103] Federal law imposes a lower age requirement for child labor in agriculture,[104] and many agricultural workers are excluded from unemployment compensation.[105] Farmworkers are also excluded from workers' compensation laws in many states.[106] Agricultural workers employed by small farms are further exempt from minimum wage,[107] Title VII nondiscrimination,[108] and OSHA health and safety protections.[109] Finally, migrant agricultural workers who are employed under H–2A and H–2B visa programs are excluded from Social Security,[110] Title VII,[111] and the Migrant and Seasonal Agricultural Workers' Protection Act (AWPA)[112] (the primary federal statute protecting farmworkers), and are barred by their visas from changing employers. The situation is little better for domestic workers such as housekeepers, nannies, and cooks, who similarly are excluded from the rights to organize, bargain collectively, and strike, from overtime, and from OSHA regulations.[113]

Enforcement resources also tend to be underallocated in these sectors (or relatively nonexistent, in the case of domestic workers), because of the disparity in political power between U.S. citizen employers and their noncitizen employees.

Although it has been difficult to obtain international agreement on the rights of migrant workers because of the conflicting interests of sending and host states,[114] international standards are uniquely capable of protecting this group.

7. The Functional Value of Harmonization

Finally, like all systems of standardization, international labor standards play an important role in encouraging efficiency and creating a basis for effective dialogue among transnational actors. International standards create a common language and baseline of acceptable employment behavior against which the international, regional, national, and private oversight, enforcement and compliance efforts discussed in Part I can be measured.

Universally accepted standards create a uniform benchmark against which organizations such as the World Bank and the IMF can determine whether their investment projects are adversely affecting labor conditions or whether working conditions in a country (such as child labor) are at levels warranting investment and technical assistance. International standards also give these institutions a transparent common language through which they can communicate with the ILO and effectively draw upon the ILO's expertise and resources. International standards facilitate negotiations on labor standards in regional and bilateral agreements by providing all parties a common, consistent measure against which to compare their own compliance and that of others.

International labor standards also are essential to preventing unilateral oversight and enforcement mechanisms from undermining the international economic system. International standards help prevent unilateral trade and foreign assistance measures from being abused for protectionist purposes or undermining the legitimate comparative advantages of developing states. If tied to internationally recognized standards, for example, import prohibitions on goods produced with forced, prison, or exploitative child labor can properly serve their legitimate purposes. Conversely, in the absence of uniform, transparent international standards, unilateral enforcement may disintegrate into a tower of Babel, with every state determining for itself what will be the baseline of acceptable labor conditions for its global trading partners.[115]

The U.S. GSP worker rights provisions, for example, have been criticized as self-serving, unilateralist measures that are not tied to any international benchmark.[116] The GSP "internationally recognized worker rights" are not expressly tied to the ILO standards, and are both under- and overinclusive of the ILO core labor rights.[117] The United States recently has made some improvements in this area. The GSP statute, for example, incorporates the ILO definition of the worst forms of child labor,[118] and section 307 of the Tariff Act of 1930 mirrors the ILO definition of forced labor.[119] Such disharmony between national and international standards exposes a state's policies to criticism as self-serving, imperialist, and protectionist, and undermines that state's ability to encourage other states to comply with recognized international standards.[120] In short, international standards could play an important role in responding to critics of unilateralism and trade/labor linkage by helping to eliminate discriminatory or protective use of these enforcement mechanisms.

International standards also make possible the use of transnational public litigation to hold both domestic and foreign corporations accountable for labor rights violations. International standards establish a universal baseline for corporate behavior, providing a consistent measure for assessing transnational corporate activity. They overcome limits on the extraterritorial reach of domestic standards and allow norms articulated in one forum to be transferred and enforced in another.[121]

International standards may be especially important to legitimize corporate codes of conduct and other private mechanisms for regulating corporate behavior. At present, most codes of conduct adopted by private corporations are not expressly tied to the ILO core labor standards (IKEA's code is a rare exception).[122] And many codes, such as those of Levi-Strauss and Wal-Mart, do not protect freedom of association and collective bargaining.[123] Codes of conduct and social labeling schemes rely on the expression of consumer preferences through market choice. Codes and labels therefore can be effective only if they communicate information accurately and efficiently to consumers about labor conditions. Standardized, universally accepted definitions of appropriate working conditions are critical to this process.[124] International standards also are critical to effective monitoring of corporate compliance. Monitoring is the linchpin of the codes of conduct movement; it distinguishes mere corporate public relations campaigns from codes capable of improving working conditions. Yet, meaningful, independent monitoring cannot occur absent an objective measure for assessing corporate practices. If every company simply incorporates its own definition of appropriate working conditions into a code of conduct, the codes will be meaningless.

Finally, the proposed efforts to link international trade and labor rights cannot occur in the absence of international labor standards. If trade is to be conditioned on acceptable labor practices, there must be a defined, accepted basis for determining whether a state or its corporations are in compliance. International standards are necessary in order for international bodies such as the ILO and the WTO to evaluate the legitimacy of a labor rights norm and determine whether that norm has been violated.[125] With international standards as a point of reference, for example, the ILO could assist the WTO in determining whether a labor rights value should be recognized as a legitimate exception under GATT Article XX.[126] The ILO also could evaluate the relative importance and severity of the labor rights violation to assist the WTO in determining whether the violation rose to a level warranting application of sanctions.[127]

In sum, international standards play an important role in advancing the human rights system, in preventing the suppression of labor conditions as an unfair labor practice, in promoting high-wage forms of economic development and preventing a race to the bottom in labor standards, in counterbalancing the ability of flexible corporate and employment structures to elude national regulation, in protecting migrant farmworkers, and in facilitating the transnational regime of global labor rights enforcement. While there is no expectation that international standards will replace national instruments, they complement and supplement national activity in important ways.

III. Trade- Labor Linkage

As the previous discussion has demonstrated, international labor standards currently are being embraced and utilized by international organizations, regional entities, states, and private actors in a wide variety of contexts, and many current unilateral, bilateral, and regional enforcement mechanisms seek to promote labor rights through linkage with trade. Nevertheless, it is

the concept of trade/labor linkage, especially at the international level
through the WTO, that remains highly controversial.

Linkage between labor rights and trade for enforcement purposes has
been an issue on the agenda of the international labor rights movement since
its inception. An early British proposal suggested that the ILO conventions
should be enforceable through trade sanctions:

> one of the principal objectives of international labour Conventions is to elimi-
> nate unfair competition based on oppressive working conditions. . . . [T]he ap-
> propriate penalty should be that, when a majority of two thirds of the conference
> is convinced that the terms of the convention have been broken, the signatory
> states should place an embargo on goods produced in those conditions of unfair
> competition unless those conditions are remedied.[128]

During the original negotiations to establish the GATT and International
Trade Organization (ITO), which was to oversee implementation of the
GATT, the United States pressed for including broad international labor
standards as part of the agreement. Article VII of the ITO accordingly provided that

> The Members recognize that measures relating to employment must take fully
> into account the rights of workers under inter-governmental declarations, con-
> ventions, and agreements. They recognize that all countries have a common in-
> terest in the achievement and maintenance of labour standards related to pro-
> ductivity, and thus in the improvement of wages and working conditions as pro-
> ductivity may permit. The Members recognize that unfair labour conditions,
> particularly in production for export, create difficulties in international trade,
> and accordingly, each Member shall take whatever action may be appropriate
> and feasible to eliminate such conditions within its territory.[129]

Although signed by the United States, the ITO agreement was never ratified
by the Senate, and only the GATT came into existence. In 1953, the United
States again unsuccessfully sought to incorporate language similar to ITO
Article VII as an enforceable GATT obligation.[130]

While support for international labor standards has strengthened in the
past fifty years, the consensus for trade/labor linkage has eroded as developing states have joined the international GATT/WTO trade system and free
market economic policies have gained ascendance. Since the establishment
of the WTO in 1994, a number of Western states have urged the adoption of

a social clause or other mechanism for linking the WTO trade enforcement regime with compliance with core labor standards. This proposal was rejected at the 1996 Singapore Ministerial.[131] At the 1999 Seattle Ministerial, the Clinton Administration put forward a more modest proposal for the establishment of a working group to examine the possible relationship of core labor standards and free trade.[132] This proposal also was resoundingly rejected by the WTO membership.[133] The Doha Ministerial Conference in November 2001 reaffirmed the Singapore Ministerial Declaration and otherwise refused to address labor standards.[134]

Notably, the developing nation's stated objection to trade/labor rights linkage at Singapore was not to the idea of binding labor standards per se. Instead, the WTO membership pronounced that we "renew our commitment to the observance of internationally recognized core labour standards" and that "the WTO and the ILO Secretariats will continue their existing collaboration."[135] Their stated objection was simply to "the use of labour standards for protectionist purposes" and to undercut "the comparative advantage of . . . low-wage developing countries."[136]

This position can be interpreted in two ways. The United States accepted the Singapore Declaration with the understanding that the Declaration recognized the validity of international labor standards and only precluded trade/labor linkage when used for protectionist purposes or to undermine developing countries' comparative advantage.[137] Presumably this view is relatively noncontroversial, since Western states agree that developing countries are entitled to a comparative trade advantage in lower labor costs based on their relative stage of development. From this perspective, the Singapore Declaration advances the cause of trade/labor linkage by affirming the commitment of WTO members to respect the ILO core labor standards. Indeed, Robert Howse has suggested that the Singapore Declaration may constitute "soft law" supporting the imposition of trade sanctions for noncompliance with the core labor rights.[138]

A more cynical reading of the Declaration suggests a rejection of any trade/labor linkage as necessarily protectionist and offensive to comparative advantage. Indeed, many developing states, as well as academic opponents of trade/labor linkage such as Jagdish Bhagwati, contend that "the real aim of the rich countries' trade unions and governments is to deter competition" and that trade/labor linkage is merely "protectionism hiding behind a moral mask."[139] Bhagwati views the developed world's protection of agriculture and textiles and its obsession with child labor—a largely developing world phenomenon—rather than with more universal problems such as gender discrimination and freedom of association, as proof of underlying protectionist motives.[140]

At this point, the debate over trade/labor linkage has deteriorated into a standoff in which developing countries disingenuously deny the existence of any relationship between labor rights and trade, for fear that even discussing the issue will prove the camel's nose in the free trade tent. Western countries, on the other hand, equally disingenuously deny the protectionist potential of trade/labor linkage, while they themselves pursue protectionist policies.

Protectionist activity by the United States and other Western countries unquestionably has seriously impaired the credibility of efforts to build an international labor rights regime and promote global compliance. Measures such as the recent steel tariffs in the United States,[141] and agricultural and textile provisions, are easy targets for those who wish to view labor rights measures as inherently protectionist.[142] The desire to protect domestic jobs and working conditions in some of these provisions is overt.[143] The particular preference of the United States for the stick of economic sanctions, rather than the carrot of foreign assistance to address entrenched economic problems such as child labor,[144] also raises questions about the altruism of U.S. support for trade/labor linkage.

The assumption that trade/labor linkage inherently is protectionist or designed to undermine foreign states' comparative advantage, however, improperly conflates all labor standards with their realistic potential for abuse. Bhagwati is incorrect that Western states are solely concerned with primarily Third World problems such as child labor.[145] Child labor is the example most frequently raised by those who oppose trade/labor linkage, who contend that child labor is primarily an issue of poverty, which can be resolved only through positive incentives such as debt forgiveness and development assistance, rather than through trade sanctions. Child labor does raise broad developmental and cultural issues that other labor standards, such as the prohibition on forced labor, do not.[146] But it is in many ways a red herring for the trade/labor linkage debate. The vast majority of child labor in the world occurs in informal and nonexport sectors, and therefore would not be affected by enforcement efforts targeting labor abuses in production for international trade. Furthermore, advocates of trade/labor linkage do *not* contend that trade sanctions are a complete solution to the issue of child labor (or any other labor standards violations, for that matter). They recognize that negative sanctions must be augmented by substantial education and development programs. But in order to be most effective, carrots may need to be coupled with sticks against those in the export sector who employ children in the worst forms of child labor.

Nor are Western trade unions, at least, unconcerned about the substantial violations of international labor standards that occur at home.[147] Moreover, steel tariffs and agricultural subsidies *do not*, in fact, demonstrate that labor rights measures are necessarily protectionist. Measures such as the steel tariffs do not purport to promote labor rights abroad, and simply demonstrate what all presumably would acknowledge: that states do sometimes act to protect their own workers, industries, and markets. But the international trade system has mechanisms in place for scrutinizing trade behavior for protectionist measures, and labor rights measures should be equally subject to such scrutiny. In other words, not all labor rights trade measures linking trade and labor rights are protectionist. Most are genuinely motivated by concern for workers and working conditions abroad, and ordinary mechanisms for guarding against protectionist motives should be applied to them equally with other conditions on foreign trade.

The ideas of acceptable comparative advantage and universal labor standards coexist in some tension. The ILO's 1998 Declaration recognized this fact, stressing "that labour standards should not be used for protectionist purposes, and that . . . the comparative advantage of any country should in no way be called into question by this Declaration and its follow-up."[148] But the whole idea of international labor standards rests on the proposition that a baseline exists below which working conditions no longer constitute a valid trade advantage, but are unacceptable human exploitation. Slavery and exploitative child labor, in short, are not "advantages" to be respected by free trade. Nor were these standards adopted in order to raise the costs of production for developing states. Ultimately, the fundamental purpose of labor standards is to protect the life and health of working men and women around the world and to alleviate poverty. ILO conventions are not primarily aimed at raising labor costs or eliminating unfair trade practices.

The simple fact is that the core labor rights already are legally binding obligations on almost all WTO members through ILO conventions and fundamental human rights instruments, and political obligations under the 1998 ILO Declaration. The assertion of comparative advantage as an objection to conditioning trade privileges on these rights, therefore, appears to have much less to do with protecting legitimate trade advantages than with avoiding enforcement and compliance with international obligations that member states have already embraced.

Moreover, as Brian Bercusson has noted, the failure to reach agreement on global linkage between labor standards and trade in the WTO has been bypassed by widespread linkage of labor standards with trade in other areas. Labor rights and trade have become linked through a disparate range of subglobal mechanisms, including regional and bilateral trade agreements, industrywide commodity agreements, unilateral legislation, and public and private codes of conduct and labeling schemes, as noted above. Indeed, the OECD identified sixty-six incidents of trade/labor standards linkage between 1990 and 1996.[149] Perhaps ironically, the WTO's insistence that labor standards be relegated to the ILO has spurred new innovation and confidence within the ILO. All of this extra-WTO activity may ultimately render the WTO's recalcitrance on trade/labor linkage less significant.

IV. Which International Labor Standards?

Assuming that international labor standards have a role to play in the globalized economy, what core protections should they encompass? What standards are critical to creating a baseline of acceptable working conditions that should be respected in all countries?

The ILO resolved these questions by adopting the four core standards of freedom of association, nondiscrimination, and forced and child labor. These four standards have been embraced in a variety of other fora as well, including the 1995 World Summit for Social Development in Copenhagen[150] and the OECD.[151] Other commentators have urged that the list of core labor rights should include occupational health and safety,[152] limits on hours of work, rights to periods of rest, and protection against abusive treatment.[153] Lance Compa argues that a "core" or "expanded core" of labor protections should include "wages, benefits, health and safety protection, social insurance, and other working conditions below levels of dignity that workers' labor should yield them in a decent workplace with a fair distribution of wealth in the society."[154] As a pure policy matter, setting aside the political considerations involved in achieving international consensus around any particular cluster of fundamental labor standards, it would appear that core standards at a minimum should include the ILO core standards plus protection from ultrahazardous working conditions, subsistence wages, and protection for migrant workers.

One justification often offered for the ILO core labor standards is that they do not raise labor costs, and thus do not negatively impact a country's comparative advantage. In contrast to restrictions on working time and minimum wages, which may negatively affect trade performance,[155] the OECD notes, the prohibitions against forced and exploitative child labor and discrimination simply eliminate artificial distortions in the allocation of labor, and thus improve the efficiency of market outcomes and overall productivity.[156] These standards, so the argument goes, are either cost neutral, or may in fact improve efficiency and productivity, while other "non-core" standards, such as raising minimum wages, impose clear costs on firms.

The neutral economic impact argument, however, can be dangerous to labor standards. It is not obvious that the core labor standards are so readily distinguished from other labor rights. For one thing, prohibiting forced and exploitative child labor may also have the short- and medium-term effect of raising labor costs (since autonomous, voluntary adult workers must be employed, and compensated, instead). Although eliminating forced and child labor undoubtedly benefits a country's economic and social development over the long term,[157] studies also have shown that prison and child labor provide cost advantages to firms that use them.[158] Freedom of association may have an even greater impact on labor costs, though it may contribute toward long-term productivity increases as well. As the OECD has noted, freedom of association and collective bargaining can counterbalance the disparate power of employers, encourage workers to contribute to efficiency improvements in the firm, and generally improve productivity.[159] But presumably one purpose of allowing workers to organize collectively in their relations with management is to improve wages and working conditions, and thus to raise absolute labor costs (though productivity may increase as well). Lance Compa has noted that even enforcing the prohibition against discrimination in the workplace, which is generally viewed as having positive long-term benefits to an economy's overall productivity,[160] would impose substantial costs on individual companies.[161]

The critical question for identifying core labor standards, therefore, should not be whether the standard has a neutral impact on labor costs, but whether the standard is sufficiently fundamental to the life and well-being of employees to warrant status as a core labor standard. It is appropriate to ask whether any given standard will impact the comparative advantage of developing countries in low labor costs. But standards should be set at a level below which it is unacceptable for any country to claim a comparative advantage. As the OECD concluded, "[C]ore labour standards cannot be considered primarily as a means to improve market efficiency, as they are fundamental rights of workers."[162] Ultimately, it is the human rights justification that controls. Labor rights that constitute fundamental human rights should be included in any set of core international labor standards.

Appropriate international standards themselves may break into two subcategories. Some labor standards may be sufficiently fundamental that they must be honored, regardless of a country's level of economic development. Other standards may be tied to a country's level of development, but nevertheless constitute human rights violations or unfair trade practices if suppressed below a certain (flexible) level.

Three of the ILO's four core labor standards—freedom of association, nondiscrimination, and forced labor—appear to fall into the first category. These are fixed standards that are sufficiently fundamental to be universally obligatory, regardless of a country's level of development. Freedom of association, nondiscrimination, and the prohibition against forced labor are sufficiently central to worker autonomy and dignity to be core human rights norms. States and companies should not be able to derogate from these protections based on their level of economic development.

All three of these standards are widely recognized as fundamental human rights. The rights to freedom of association and to organize and bargain collectively are recognized in major human rights instruments,[163] as noted in Part I. In addition to being core political and civil rights, these associational process rights undergird the entire system of domestic and international labor protection. They are the mechanisms that give meaning and voice to the interests of workers, both in the political system and in labor/management relations, and they are critical to modifying the unequal bargaining power between workers and their employers. Associational rights may be particularly crucial in low-skill, high-unemployment economies, where most workers are fungible and have no individual leverage with their employers.

The prohibition against gender and racial discrimination in the workplace likewise is respected in widely ratified human rights instruments, including the ICCPR, ICESCR, CEDAW, and the Race Discrimination Convention.[164]

Both human rights and international trade instruments bar slavery and other forms of coerced labor. The prohibition against slavery is widely regarded as one of the most fundamental *jus cogens* principles of customary international law.[165] Servitude, forced and bonded labor, and other slavelike practices are prohibited by the UDHR and the ICCPR, as well as by specialized international treaties.[166] Moreover, coerced labor is widely recognized as an unfair trade practice. In fact, the prohibition of goods made with prison labor is the only human or labor rights protection expressly set forth in the GATT.[167]

In contrast to the three core rights discussed above, the prohibition against child labor is widely acknowledged to be a relative and somewhat flexible standard that is contingent on a country's level of development. While all countries are obligated immediately to eliminate the worst forms of child labor,[168] the ILO Minimum Age Convention expressly allows developing nations to use age fourteen as the minimum age for employment whereas for developed countries the minimum is fifteen.[169]

The prohibition against child labor finds less clear support in general human rights instruments than the other core ILO rights. In contrast to the ILO Minimum Age Convention, none of the major human rights instruments attempt to define an appropriate age for the employment of children. Nevertheless, a general prohibition against exploitative forms of child labor has broad-based international support. The Convention on the Rights of the

Child, which has been ratified by all UN member states except the United States and Somalia, prohibits exploitative child labor.[170] The international prohibition against servitude and forced and bonded labor applies to coercive forms of child labor. And both the ILO Minimum Age Convention and the Worst Forms of Child Labor Convention have been ratified by the majority of nations.[171]

Beyond the ILO fundamental labor standards, a number of other labor protections appear entitled to status as core labor rights, including rights to freedom from ultrahazardous working conditions, a right to subsistence wages, and protection for migrant workers. The rights to a subsistence wage and to a safe and healthy workplace were considered for inclusion as core rights in the 1998 ILO Declaration but were rejected at the insistence of employer groups.[172] Protections for migrant workers have never enjoyed a substantial international consensus. Putting these political considerations to one side, however, these rights are sufficiently critical to protecting a worker's basic existence, and share sufficient characteristics with the other core labor rights, to entitle them to core labor status.

Ultrahazardous Conditions and Subsistence Wages

Health and safety and wage levels both are contingent to a substantial degree on a country's level of development. But both also surely have a relative baseline below which it should be unacceptable for any country to fall. All workers should be entitled to protection from ultrahazardous working conditions, where human life itself is at risk.[173] Likewise, it should be both a human rights violation and an unfair trade practice for goods to be produced for wages that are insufficient to feed and sustain an individual and his or her family. I should note that I am *not* advocating a universal minimum wage, at a fixed rate that would apply to all countries. Low wages remain one of the most sacred comparative advantages of developing countries. Unquestionably, any internationally embraced wage standard would have to accommodate different costs of living and stages of development among states.

Outside the ILO, a substantial international consensus supports the view that provision of subsistence wages and protection from ultrahazardous working conditions should constitute core labor standards. Occupational health and safety in general are recognized as human rights by numerous international instruments, including the UDHR, the ICESCR, CEDAW, and the Convention on the Rights of the Child.[174] The right to fair remuneration and a decent standard of living likewise is recognized by the Universal Declaration and the ICESCR.[175] Of the eleven labor rights areas encompassed by the NAALC, minimum wages and protection of occupational health and safety are considered among the most important, and are among the three labor rights that are potentially subject to sanctions (the third area being child labor). The ILO, OECD, and UN model codes for corporate responsibility recognize obligations in both areas.[176] The MERCOSUR countries also have committed to protect healthy and safe working conditions (though not minimum wages).[177] And fully three-fourths of private corporate codes of conduct include protection for health and safety.[178]

In short, it should be possible to agree on the *principle* that workers should be entitled to protection against life-threatening workplaces and below-subsistence wages. The difficulty with both standards, therefore, is definitional. How should one define ultrahazardous working conditions or subsistence wages? The ILO's Convention Concerning Occupational Safety and Health and the Working Environment (No. 155), and Minimum Wage Fixing Convention (No. 131) are generally worded and have not been widely ratified.[179] The ILO's recent Worst Forms of Child Labor Convention could provide a model for thinking about the worst workplaces, the worst health and safety threats, and how to counter them.

Much work has been done on the international level to devise minimum wage standards that would accommodate the definitional concerns by tying the right to a fair wage to a country's relative level of development and cost of living. In addition to the ILO's Minimum Wage Fixing Convention,[180] the European Social Charter Committee of Experts defined a "decent standard of living" for the EU as 68 percent of a nation's average wage, and has formally found European nations in noncompliance.[181] Stephen Herzenberg has proposed a formulaic minimum wage, under which workers would be paid a minimum percentage of the value added in manufacture (such as 40 percent), and the local minimum wage would be set at half that amount.[182]

Labor Rights NGOs also have worked on trying to define "living wages," and their results, while perhaps more comprehensive and ambitious than a standard for subsistence wages, are illustrative of some of the considerations involved. The Worker Rights Consortium's Model Code of Conduct would require manufacturers of collegiate apparel and their subsidiaries to pay "dignified living wages" that meet the basic needs of workers. The WRC defines a living wage as providing

> for the basic needs (housing, energy, nutrition, clothing, health care, education, potable water, childcare, transportation, and savings) of an average family unit of employees in the garment manufacturing employment sector of the country divided by the average number of adult wage earners in the family unit of employees in the garment manufacturing employment sector of the country.[183]

The Living Wage Working Summit's Draft Formula for Calculating Living Wages requires considering average family size, the average number of adult wage earners per family, and the local costs of basic needs (nutrition, clothing, health care, education, potable water, childcare, and transportation).[184] What constitutes a subsistence wage would also depend upon the hours of work allowable in a week—another internationally controversial issue.

Wage proposals remain a flashpoint for international disagreement over labor standards, in part because of the definitional difficulties noted above, and in part because of developing countries' insistence that any matter relating to wages treads improperly upon their low-wage comparative advantage. The definitional problem is real, and it invites further study. But it is simply disingenuous for countries to dismiss the payment even of subsistence wages as protectionist or infringing on their legitimate low-wage competitive advantages.

Migrant Workers

Finally, protection for migrant workers should be included among the core labor rights, because of the peculiar vulnerability of these workers. ILO and UN Conventions,[185] the European Union,[186] the MERCOSUR Socio-Labor Declaration of 1998,[187] and the NAALC[188] all recognize the need for a range of international protections for migrant workers. These include, in particular, a right to treatment equal to that afforded domestic nationals.[189] The international system, however, has been neglectful of migrant workers, in large part because of the standing disagreement between migrant-sending and migrant-receiving countries. Protection of migrant workers is not included among the ILO's core conventions, and the principal ILO conventions relating to migrant workers have been ratified by no more than forty-five countries.[190]

International law nevertheless accords migrant workers greater protection than U.S. national law in some respects. Migrant workers are entitled to rights to freedom of association under the core ILO conventions. International rules regarding forced and bonded labor and servitude offer workers greater protection than U.S. domestic laws regulating peonage.[191] The NAALC obligates NAFTA member states to provide migrant workers "to the maximum extent possible . . . with the same legal protection as the party's nationals in respect of working conditions."[192] The Inter-American Court of Human Rights also is currently considering the extent of employment protections enjoyed by migrant workers in the Americas under international law.[193]

Western migrant-receiving states seek to encourage developing countries to embrace international labor standards regarding primarily developing world problems such as child and forced labor, but are themselves reluctant to embrace an international standard that would grant migrants from those same developing countries national treatment. A workable compromise to this stalemate might be a quid pro quo—Western states would agree to international protections for migrants, and developing states in turn would accept meaningful enforcement of the other core labor standards.

Conclusion

This chapter has argued that international labor standards are now operative through a disparate range of mechanisms at the international, regional, bilateral, national, and private levels, that they fill important and legitimate functions in protecting the fundamental rights of workers in the global economy, and that a comprehensive set of worker protections should include the ILO core standards as well as protection for subsistence wages, fundamental health and safety, and the rights of migrant workers. International labor standards, however, are not a complete solution to labor conditions around the globe. Standards alone are incapable of accomplishing the most difficult work in labor rights enhancement—that of eliminating substandard practices. To the extent that lack of enforcement, rather than lack of adequate domestic legal protections, is the cause of poor working conditions, labor standards have little to contribute. States may lack resources to promote positive solutions, such as development and education strategies to help poor economies escape the cycle of child labor. Lack of either the political will or adequate resources for enforcement cannot be remedied by international standards alone. Nevertheless, international standards have become an important complement to domestic standards and provide the basic sinews that can make the international labor rights regime effective.

Notes

I am grateful to Lance Compa and Ray Marshall for assistance relating to this project, to Brian Bercusson, Jean-Claud Javillier, and Richard Steinberg for their comments at the Stanford International Labor Standards Conference, and for the thoughts of many other attendees. This project also benefited from the research assistance of Mike Tyler and the skilled library support of Jonathan Pratter.

1. See discussion in Virginia Leary, "Form Follows Function—Or Does It?" in this volume.

2. Convention Concerning Freedom of Association and Protection of the Right to Organize (No. 87), July 9, 1948, 68 U.N.T.S. 16 (entered into force July 4, 1950) (142 ratifications); Convention Concerning the Application of the Principles of the Right to Organise and to Bargain Collectively (No. 98), July 1, 1949, 96 U.N.T.S. 257 (entered into force July 18, 1951) (152 ratifications); Convention Concerning the Abolition of Forced Labour (No. 105), June 25, 1957, 320 U.N.T.S. 291 (entered into force Jan. 17, 1959) (159 ratifications); Convention Concerning Forced or Compulsory Labour (No. 29), June 28, 1930, 39 U.N.T.S. 55 (entered into force Jan. 5, 1932) (161 ratifications); Convention Concerning Discrimination in Respect of Employment and Occupation (No. 111), June 25, 1958, 362 U.N.T.S. 31 (entered into force June 15, 1960) (159 ratifications); Convention Concerning Equal Remuneration for Men and Women Workers for Work of Equal Value (No. 100), June 29, 1951, 165 U.N.T.S. 303 (entered into force May 23, 1953) (161 ratifications); Convention Concerning the Prohibition and Immediate Action for the Elimination of the Worst Forms of Child Labour (No. 182), June 17, 1999, 38 I.L.M. 1207 (entered into force Nov. 19, 2000) (132 ratifications); Convention Concerning Minimum Age for Admission to Employment (No. 138), June 26, 1973, 1015 U.N.T.S. 297 (entered into force July 19, 1976) (124 ratifications). Conventions and ratification information available from the ILO website, http://www.ilo.org/public/english/standards/norm/whatare/fundam/index.htm (accessed May 22, 2003).

3. Organisation for Economic Co-operation and Development, *International Trade and Core Labour Standards* (2000), p. 9 [hereinafter OECD 2000].

4. See Sarah H. Cleveland, "Global Labor Rights and the Alien Tort Claims Act," *Texas Law Review* 76 (1998): pp. 1533, 1540 (noting the relative lack of ratification support for the child labor convention at that time).

5. See note 2 above.

6. See ILO Declaration on Fundamental Principles and Rights at Work, 86th Sess. (June 1998), ¶2 (declaring that "all Members, even if they have not ratified the Conventions in question, have an obligation arising from the very fact of membership in the Organization to respect, to promote and to realize, in good faith and in accordance with the Constitution, the principles concerning the fundamental rights which are the subject of those Conventions"), available at http://www.ilo.org/public/english/standards/decl/declaration/text/index.htm (accessed Jan. 20, 2002).

7. ILO Resolution on the Widespread Use of Forced Labour in Myanmar, 87th Sess. (June 1999), available at http://www.ilo.org/public/english/standards/relm/ilc/ilc87/com-myan.htm (accessed Feb. 19, 2002).

8. In Nov. 2000, the ILO Governing Body reaffirmed its 1999 resolution and called upon ILO members to ensure that their relations with the Burmese government "do not perpetuate or extend the system of forced or compulsory labour in that country." Press release: "International Labour Organization, ILO Governing Body Opens the Way for Unprecedented Action against Forced Labour in Myanmar" (Nov. 17, 2000), available at http://www.ilo.org/public/english/bureau/inf/pr/2000/44.htm (accessed Feb. 18, 2002).

9. Francis Maupain, "The Settlement of Disputes within the International Labour Office," *Journal of International Economic Law* 2, 273 (1999): 281–85 (discussing possibility for economic sanctions under ILO procedures).

10. Council Directive 94/45/EC-1 of Sept. 22, 1994, on the establishment of a European Works Council or a procedure in community-scale undertakings and community-scale group undertakings for the purposes of informing and consulting employees.

11. OECD 2000, p. 74.

12. OECD 2000, p. 67.

13. North American Agreement on Labor Cooperation Between the Government of the United States of America, the Government of Canada and the Government of the United Mexican States, Sept. 13, 1993, 32 I.L.M. 1499 (entered into force Jan. 1, 1994), available at http://www.naalc.org/english/infocentre/NAALC.htm (accessed May 22, 2003).

14. See discussion in Lance Compa, "NAFTA's Labor Side Agreement and International Labor Solidarity," *Antipode*, 2001, p. 541; Clyde Summers, "NAFTA's Labor

Side Agreement and International Labor Standards," *Journal of Small and Emerging Business Law* 3 (1999): 173.

15. Compliance with international standards under the NAALC has been raised, inter alia, in the maquiladora sex discrimination complaint, which charged Mexico with failing to enforce its international obligations prohibiting pregnancy discrimination. See Submission Concerning Pregnancy-Based Sex Discrimination in Mexico's Maquiladora Sector to the United States National Administrative Office, Submission No. 9701 (May 15, 1997), available at http://www.dol.gov/ILAB/media/ reports/nao/submissions/Sub9701.htm (accessed Jan. 5, 2003). See also U.S. NAO Public Submission No. 940003, In re: Sony Corporation d/b/a/ Magneticos de Mexico (alleging violations of ILO Conventions 87 and 98 relating to freedom of association in a Mexican Sony plant), available at http://www.dol.gov/ILAB/media/reports/nao/submissions/Sub940003.htm (accessed Jan. 5, 2003).

16. Declaración Socio-Laboral del Mercosur (Dec. 10, 1998), available at http://www.mercosur-comisec.gub.uy/DOCUMENT/DECLARAC/ResDecSLaboral.htm (accessed July 1, 2002).

17. OECD 2000, p. 62.

18. The 1987 agreement on sugar, art. 28; the 1981 agreement on tin, art. 45; the 1986 agreement on cocoa, art. 64; and the 1987 agreement on rubber, art. 53, all include provisions for fair labor standards. Guy Claire, "Labour Standards and International Trade," in *International Labour Standards and Economic Interdependence,* ed. Werner Sengenberger and Duncan Campbell, pp. 287, 305 (Geneva: International Institute for Labour Studies, 1994). For a discussion of the efficacy of labor standards in commodity agreements, see Ulrich Kullmann, "'Fair Labour Standards' in International Commodity Agreements," *Journal of World Trade Law* 14 (1981): 527; Philip Alston, "Commodity Agreements—As Though People Don't Matter," *Journal of World Trade Law* 15 (1981): 455 (replying to Kullmann).

19. OECD 2000, p. 62.

20. China–United States Memorandum of Understanding on Prohibiting Import and Export Trade in Prison Labor Products, 31 I.L.M. 1071 (1992). The Memorandum of Understanding was supplemented in 1995 by a Statement of Cooperation between the United States and China that allowed U.S. embassy officials to visit prisons suspected of producing goods for export. OECD 2000, p. 68.

21. Agreement Relating to Trade in Cotton, Wool, Man-made Fiber, Non-Cotton Vegetable Fiber and Silk Blend Textiles and Textile Products between the Government of the United States of America and the Royal Government of Cambodia, 1999, ¶ 10, available at http://web.ita.doc.gov/Otexa (accessed Jan. 15, 2002); U.S.-Jordan Free Trade Agreement, Art. 5, available at http://192.239.92.165/regions/eu-med/middleeast/US-JordanFTA.shtml (accessed Oct. 14, 2002).

22. E.g., Trade Act of 2002, 19 U.S.C. §3802(b)(11)(C). Although the act directs the President to promote the "core labor standards of the ILO," 19 U.S.C. §3802(a)(6), like the GSP, it defines these rights differently from the ILO core rights, notably by including rights to minimum wages, hours of work, and occupational safety and health, and by failing to include a prohibition on discrimination in employment. 19 U.S.C. §3813(6).

23. E.g., World Bank Group, *Core Labour Standards and the World Bank* (July 2000).

24. Peter Fallon and Zafiris Tzannatos, *Child Labor, Issues and Directions for the World Bank* (Washington, D.C.: World Bank, 1998).

25. For a compilation of U.S. laws conditioned on international human rights or labor rights compliance, see Sarah H. Cleveland, "Norm Internalization and US Economic Sanctions," *Yale Journal of International Law* 26, 1 (2001): 92–102.

26. 9 U.S.C. §1307 (1994), as amended by Trade and Development Act of 2000, Pub. L. No. 106–200, §411, 114 Stat. 251 (2000).

27. 19 C.F.R. §12.42(h) (2001); 58 Fed. Reg. 32,746 (1993). A petition was filed on May 30, 2002, by the International Labor Rights Fund (ILRF), requesting that the Customs Service bar importation of cocoa from the Ivory Coast that was produced with child labor. "World Briefing," *New York Times*, May 31, 2002, p. A13. The petition is available on the ILRF website, http://laborrights.org (accessed May 21, 2003).

28. Exec. Order No. 13,126; 64 Fed. Reg. 32,383 (1999). (The order does not apply to products from countries that are parties to NAFTA or the WTO Agreement on Government Procurement.)

29. Overseas Private Investment Corp., 22 U.S.C. §§2191(a)(1) (2000).

30. Multilateral Investment Fund, 22 USC §290k-3(1) (2000) (instructing the U.S. Director to oppose investment support in countries barred from GSP treatment for failing to afford internationally recognized worker rights).

31. International Financial Institutions Act of 1977, 22 U.S.C. §262p-4p(a)(1) (2000).

32. See Todd S. Purdum, "Several U.S. Allies Criticized in Powell Report on Slave Trading," *New York Times*, June 6, 2002, p. A13.

33. 19 U.S.C. §2462(c)(7) (2002). The GSP statute defines "internationally recognized worker rights" as including: freedom of association and the right to organize and bargain collectively, the prohibition on forced or compulsory labor; "a minimum age for the employment of children, and a prohibition on the worst forms of child labor," and "acceptable conditions of work with respect to minimum wages, hours of work, and occupational safety and health." 19 U.S.C. §2467(4) (2002).

34. Similar tariff regimes include the Caribbean Basin Economic Recovery Act, 19 USC §2702(c)(8) (2002), as amended 19 USC §2703(b)(5)(B)(iii) and (iv) (2000)

(conditioning benefits on compliance with the GSP worker rights and elimination of the worst forms of child labor); the Andean Trade Preference Act (ATPA), 19 USC §§3202(c)(7), (d)(8) (2002) (applies the GSP labor rights provisions to Bolivia, Colombia, Ecuador, and Peru); and the Trade and Development Act of 2000, Pub L No. 106–200, §104(a)(1)(F), 114 Stat 251 (2000) (conditioning tariff preferences for Sub-Saharan Africa on compliance with internationally recognized human and worker rights).

35. OECD 2000, p. 67.

36. Romania (removed 1987, restored 1994); Nicaragua (removed 1987); Paraguay (suspended 1987, restored 1991); Chile (suspended 1987, restored 1991); Burma (suspended 1989); the Central African Republic (suspended 1989, restored 1991); Liberia (suspended 1990); Yugoslavia (suspended 1991); Sudan (suspended 1991); Syria (suspended 1992); Mauritania (suspended 1993); the Maldives (suspended 1995); Pakistan (partially suspended 1996). Pre-1993 sanctions remain in effect against North Korea for labor rights violations. In 1993, the United States also placed El Salvador, Guatemala, Indonesia, Thailand, Malawi, and Oman on "six-month continuing review status" to determine whether the countries made "substantial concrete progress" toward addressing worker rights. The Guatemalan review terminated in 1997, and the Thailand review terminated in 2000. In 2000, the U.S. Trade Representative recommended suspension of Belarus for labor rights violations.

37. Labor rights were first linked to the European GSP in 1994, Council Regulation No. 03281/94, OJ L 348, were reaffirmed in 1998, Council Regulation (EC) No. 2820/98 (Dec. 21, 1998), OJ L 357 of Dec. 1998, pp. 1–112, and were amended in 2001, Council Regulation 2501 of Dec. 10, 2001, 2001 O.J. (L346). General information on the European GSP can be found at http://europa.eu.int/comm/trade/miti/devel/gspguide.htm (accessed Jan. 8, 2003). For further discussion see OECD 2000, at 69; Diego Nogueras and Luis Martinez, "Human Rights Conditionality in the External Trade of the European Union: Legal and Legitimacy Problems," *Columbia Journal of European Law* 7 (2001): 307.

38. Council Regulation 2501/2001, see note 37 above.

39. Council Regulation (EC) No. 552/97 of Mar. 24, 1997 temporarily withdrawing access to generalized tariff preferences from the Union of Myanmar, OJ L 085 of Mar. 27, 1997, p. 8. See also *Human Rights Watch, World Report 1998, Burma,* (1997), pp. 161–62, available at http://www.hrw.org/worldreport/Table.htm (accessed Feb. 1, 2002).

40. Harold H. Koh, "Transnational Public Law Litigation," *Yale Law Journal* 100 (1991): 2347–49. For further discussion of many of the cases noted herein, see Lance Compa, "Pursuing International Labour Rights in U.S. Courts," *Industrial Relations* 57 (2002): 49, 55–57 (forthcoming).

41. *Labor Union of Pico Korea, Ltd. v. Pico Products, Inc.*, 968 F.2d 191 (2d Cir. 1992).

42. E.g., *Dow Chemical Co. v. Castro Alfaro*, 786 S.W.2d 674 (Tex. 1990) (rejecting defendants' forum non conveniens objection to suit). See discussion in Cleveland, "Book Review: Global Labor Rights and the Alien Tort Claims Act," p. 1555.

43. Compa, "Pursuing International Labour Rights in U.S. Courts," pp. 57–58.

44. 28 U.S.C. §1350 (2001) (establishing a cause of action and federal jurisdiction over "any civil action by an alien for a tort only, committed in violation of the law of nations or a treaty of the United States").

45. *Doe I v. Unocal Corp.*, _ F.3d _, 2002 WL 31063976 (9th Cir. 2002), vacated and rehearing en banc granted 2003 WL 359787 31063976 (9th Cir. 2002); *Doe v. Unocal Corp.* No. BC 237 980 (Ca. Super. Ct., June 10, 2002) (slip op.) (denying Unocal's motion for summary judgment on vicarious liability issues).

46. *Does I v. The Gap, Inc.*, No. CV-01-0031, 2002 WL 1000073 (D. N. Mar. I, May 10, 2002) (granting class certification).

47. *Villeda Aldana v. Fresh Del Monte Produce*, No. 01-3399-CIV (S.D. Fla. Filed Aug. 30, 2001). See discussion in Terry Collingsworth, "The Key Human Rights Challenge: Developing Enforcement Mechanisms," *Harvard Human Rights Journal* 15 (2002): 183, 193–95.

48. *Sinaltrainal v. Coca-Cola*, No. 01–03208-CIV (S.D. Fla. Filed July 21, 2001). See discussion in Collingsworth, "The Key Human Rights Challenge: Developing Enforcement Mechanisms," pp. 191–93.

49. *Iwanowa v. Ford Motor Company*, 67 F. Supp.2d 424 (D.N.J. 1999) (dismissing suit seeking damages under ATCA from German corporation for use of forced labor during World War II); In re World War II Era Japanese Forced Labor Litigation, 114 F. Supp.2d 939 (N.D. Cal. 2000) (dismissing claims as barred by treaty of peace with Japan); see also Stuart M. Kreindler, "Comment—History's Accounting: Liability Issues Surrounding German Companies for the Use of Slave Labor by Their Corporate Forefathers," *Dickinson Journal of International Law* 18 (2000): 343; Elisabeth Rosenthal, "Wartime Slaves Use U.S. Law to Sue Japanese," *New York Times*, Oct. 2, 2000, p. A1.

50. See, e.g., *Richards v. Runcie*, C.A. No. H-01-1072 (S.D. TX, complaint filed Apr. 2, 2001) (suit by Jamaican domestic worker held without pay for thirteen years alleging violation of international forced labor standards); *Manliguez v. Joseph*, No. 01 Civ. 7574 (E.D.N.Y. filed Nov. 13, 2001) (suit by Filipino domestic worker); *Hikabanze v. Shamapande*, No. 00 Civ. 9712 (S.D.N.Y., filed Dec. 22, 2000) (suit by Zambian domestic worker); *Okezie v. Udogwu*, No. 99 Civ. 3345 (S.D.N.Y., filed May 7, 1999) (suit by Nigerian domestic worker). For further discussion of recent suits to enforce international labor standards on behalf of workers in the United States, see

Michael J. Wishnie, "Immigrant Workers and the Domestic Enforcement of International Labor Rights," *University of Pennsylvania Journal of Labor and Employment Law* 4 (2002): 529, 533, and note 15, 540–43 (discussing cases); compare Cleveland, "Book Review: Global Labor Rights and the Alien Tort Claims Act," p. 1568, note 170 (discussing U.S. involuntary servitude cases).

51. ILO Tripartite Declaration of Principles concerning Multinational Enterprises (MNE's) and Social Policy, available at http://www.ilo.org/public/english/employment/multi/index.htm (accessed Oct. 27, 2002).

52. OECD, Guidelines for Multinational Enterprises, 2000, Part IV, available at http://www.oecd.org/daf/investment/guidelines/. The OECD Guidelines were completely revised in 1999 and 2001 to require member states, inter alia, to establish national contact points on implementation of the Guidelines and to submit annual reports on compliance.

53. The Global Compact Nine Principles, Principles 1–6, available at http://www.unglobalcompact.org/Portal/ (accessed Jan. 11, 2003).

54. See discussion in Virginia Leary, "Form Follows Function—Or Does It?" in this volume.

55. EU European Criteria for European Companies operating in developing countries/LDCs: Towards a European Code of Conduct. European Parliament Resolution, A4–0508/98 of Jan. 15, 1999, available at http://www3.europarl.eu.int/ (accessed Feb. 20, 2003).

56. OECD 2000, p. 74.

57. Ibid.

58. Fair Labor Association of the Apparel Industry Partnership, available at http://www.lchr.org/aipfull.htm (accessed Jan. 12, 2003). See also Michael Posner and Justine Nolan, "Can Codes of Conduct Play a Role in Promoting Workers' Rights?" in this volume.

59. OECD 2000, p. 73.

60. Ibid. For further discussion of private codes of conduct, see Robert Liubicic, "Corporate Codes of Conduct and Product Labeling Schemes: The Limits and Possibilities of Promoting International Labor Rights through Private Initiatives," *Journal of Law and Policy in International Business* 30 (1998): 111; R. Blainpain, ed., *Multinational Enterprises and the Social Challenges of the XXIst Century: The ILO Declaration on Fundamental Principles at Work, Public and Private Corporate Codes of Conduct* (London: Kluwer, 2000). For an overview of historical codes of conduct, see Christopher McCrudden, "Human Rights Codes for Transnational Corporations: What Can the Sullivan and MacBride Principles Tell Us?" *Oxford Journal of Legal Studies* 19 (1999): 167.

61. OECD 2000, pp. 75–78.

62. See *Does I v. The Gap*, note 46 above. Complaint ¶ 88 ("[Defendant] Retailers claim to have in place Codes of Conduct in which they take responsibility for over-seeing the conduct of the Contractor Defendants through monitoring programs these codes describe").

63. See discussion in Virginia Leary, "Form Follows Function—Or Does It?" in this volume.

64. The Preamble to the Universal Declaration of Human Rights provides as follows:

Whereas recognition of the inherent dignity and of the equal and inalienable rights of all members of the human family is the foundation of freedom, justice and peace in the world, . . .

Whereas the peoples of the United Nations have in the Charter reaffirmed their faith in fundamental human rights, in the dignity and worth of the human person and in the equal rights of men and women, and have determined to pro-mote social progress and better standards of life in larger freedom.

Universal Declaration of Human Rights (UDHR), preamble, G.A. Res. 217A (III), U.N. GAOR, 3d Sess., Supp. No. 16, U.N. Doc A/810 at 71 (1948).

65. Treaty of Versailles, Part XIII, 225 Consol. T.S. 288, 2 Bevans 43.

66. UDHR, preamble.

67. International Covenant on Civil and Political Rights, Dec. 16, 1966, 999 U.N.T.S. 171 (entered into force Mar. 23, 1976).

68. International Covenant on Economic, Social, and Cultural Rights, Dec. 16, 1966, 993 U.N.T.S. 3 (entered into force Jan. 3, 1976).

69. Convention on the Elimination of All Forms of Discrimination against Women, Dec. 18, 1979, 1249 U.N.T.S. 13 (entered into force Sept. 3, 1981).

70. Convention on the Rights of the Child, Nov. 20, 1989, 1577 U.N.T.S. 3 (entered into force Sept. 2, 1990).

71. Section 301 of the Trade Act of 1974, for example, defines unreasonable trade practices warranting the imposition of trade sanctions as including a persistent pat-tern of conduct that denies internationally recognized worker rights. 19 U.S.C. §2411(d)(3)(B)(IV)(iii) (2000).

72. It is unclear, for example, whether the prohibition on the importation of goods made with coerced, forced, or prison labor in §307 of the Tariff Act of 1930, see note 27 above, was motivated by concern over human rights conditions, unfair trade practices, or both. See Christopher S. Armstrong, "American Import Controls and Morality in International Trade: An Analysis of Section 307 of the Tariff Act of 1930," *NYU Journal of International Law and Policy* 8 (1975): 19. The exception for the prod-ucts of prison labor under GATT article XX(e) reflects a similar ambiguity. Ibid., pp. 25–26 (discussing GATT negotiating history).

73. See Organisation for Economic Co-Operation and Development, *Trade, Employment, and Labour Standards: A Study of Core Workers' Rights and International Trade* 123 (Paris, 1996) [hereinafter OECD 1996] (finding that "some governments in non-OECD countries have restricted labour rights (especially in EPZs) in the belief that doing so would help attract inward FDI both from OECD and non-OECD investors").

74. See, e.g., Ray Marshall, "The Importance of International Labour Standards in a More Competitive Global Economy," in *International Labour Standards and Economic Interdependence*, ed. Sengenberger and Campbell, pp. 65, 69 ("In forcing companies to compete by increasing efficiency rather than by reducing labour standards, ... [labour standards] shifted resources to more efficient uses and allowed countries to protect and develop human resources"); M. Piore, "International Labor Standards and Business Strategies," in *International Labor Standards and Global Integration: Proceedings of a Symposium*, ed. G. Schoepfle and K. Swinnerton, p. 21 (Washington, D.C.: U.S. Dept. of Labor, 1994), p. 23 (concluding that early labor standards foreclosed "sweating" strategies and thus operated to promote economic development and industrialization); Richard B. Freeman, "International Labor Standards and World Trade: Friends or Foes?" in *The World Trading System: Challenges Ahead*, ed. Jeffrey J. Schott (Washington, D.C.: Institute for International Economics, 1997), p. 87. See also OECD 1996, p. 113 ("higher standards may very well work as an incentive to raise productivity through investment in both human and physical capital, thus contributing in the longer run to greater cost competitiveness of companies").

75. OECD 2000, pp. 32–33.

76. ILO Constitution, preamble, 15 U.N.T.S. 35, 49 Stat. 2713.

77. Capital does not invariably flow to countries with the *cheapest* labor costs. As Liz Claiborne's General Manager in China has noted, Liz Claiborne operates in China, rather than in lower wage Asian countries such as Cambodia, because skill levels are higher in China. Comment of Diane E. Long, General Manager, Liz Claiborne International, Inc., at Stanford International Labor Standards Conference, May 20, 2002. Nevertheless, it is fair to assume that Liz Claiborne produces in China rather than in the United States or Europe because of China's significantly lower labor costs.

78. See Robert J. Flanagan, "Labor Standards and International Competitive Advantage," in this volume (finding that ratification of ILO standards does not impact economic competitiveness); but see John P. Martin, "Comments on the Paper by Robert J. Flanagan, 'Labor Standards and International Competitive Advantage'" (on file with the author) (challenging methodology); and Steve Beckman, "Comments on 'Labor Standards and International Competitive Advantage'" (on file with the author). For a discussion of the empirical evidence regarding the relationship

between labor standards, trade, and investment, see OECD 1996, pp. 77–148; OECD 2000, pp. 39–42 (reviewing recent empirical literature regarding a race to the bottom with respect to the core labor standards and finding the results "inconclusive").

79. See United Nations Conference on Trade and Development, *World Investment Report 1994: Transnational Corporations, Employment and the Workplace* (New York: United Nations, 1994), p. xxvii (observing that "transnational corporations do not often close down, on account of low labor cost considerations *alone*") (emphasis added).

80. Bob Hepple, "A Race to the Top? International Investment Guidelines and Corporate Codes of Conduct," *Comparative Labor Law and Policy Journal* 20 (1999): 347, 348 ("Enterprises are not likely to relocate to another state with lower nominal labor costs if these costs simply reflect lower productivity of workers in that state"). See also Stephen S. Golub, *Labor Costs and International Trade* (Washington, D.C.: AEI Press, 1999), p. 48 ("Differences in wages largely reflect differences in labor productivity and are not a form of unfair competition").

81. OECD 1996, p. 105.

82. Ibid., p. 124.

83. See ibid., p. 105; see also ibid., p. 123 (finding that "core labour standards are not primary factors in the majority of investment decisions in OECD companies").

84. OECD 2000, p. 34; ibid., p. 36 (noting that "Smart" EPZs in Singapore and Malaysia are focusing on human resource development to constantly upgrade labor productivity and encourage stable, long-term investment).

85. Ibid., p. 36.

86. Ibid., p. 34.

87. As of 2000, 850 EPZs were operating outside of China, employing twenty-seven million people, while China had several hundred additional EPZs in operation. Ibid., p. 13.

88. Ibid., p. 36 (discussing ILO studies of export processing zones).

89. Ibid.

90. See discussion in Steven R. Ratner, "Corporations and Human Rights: A Theory of Legal Responsibility," *Yale Law Journal* 111 (2001): 443, 462.

91. Edward E. Potter, "International Labour Standards, the Global Economy and Trade," in *International Labour Standards and Economic Interdependence*, pp. 357, 359.

92. Susan Strange, *The Retreat of the State: The Diffusion of Power in the World Economy* (New York: Cambridge University Press, 1996), pp. 49–50.

93. Not all countries are so hesitant in all contexts. The U.S. Foreign Corrupt Practices Act, for example, regulates the extraterritorial activities of U.S. corporations. Foreign Corrupt Practices Act of 1977, Pub. L. No. 95–213, 91 Stat. 1494 (codified as amended in scattered sections of 15 U.S.C.).

94. See *Does I v. Unocal Corp.*, note 45 above.

95. See discussion in Ratner, *Corporations and Human Rights*, note 90 above, p. 462 and note 58.

96. H. W. Arthurs, "Labour Law without the State?" *University of Toronto Law Journal* 46 (1996): 1, 44–45.

97. Bruce Goldstein et al., "Enforcing Fair Labor Standards in the Modern American Sweatshop: Rediscovering the Statutory Definition of Employment," *UCLA Law Review* 46 (1999): 983, 988. See, generally, Ozay Mehmet, Errol Mendes, and Robert Sinding, *Towards a Fair Global Labour Market: Avoiding a New Slave Trade* (London: Routledge, 1999), pp. 40–69 (discussing the impact of international trade on the precariousness of employment).

98. See, e.g., Louis Uchitelle, "Answering 800 Calls Offers Extra Income but No Security," *New York Times*, Mar. 27, 2002, p. A1 (noting the proliferation of call centers, which employ mainly women, and "can be relocated easily to lower-wage cities, or even overseas. All it takes is to ship the computers and communications gear somewhere else").

99. Potter, "International Labour Standards, the Global Economy and Trade," pp. 357, 359.

100. Patrick Macklem, "Labour Law Beyond Borders," *Journal of International Economic Law* 5 (2002): 605, 606 .

101. Manuel Castells, "The Information Age: The Rise of the Network Society" (1996), p. 475, quoted in Macklem, "Labour Law Beyond Borders," pp. 610–12.

102. A few states, however, provide these protections under state law. See, e.g., Maine's Agricultural Employees Labor Relations Act (MAELRA), Me. Rev. Stat. Ann. tit. 26 §1321–34 (West Supp. 1998) (protecting, inter alia, the right to organize and bargain collectively, but not to strike, for agricultural workers excluded from the National Labor Relations Act); California's Agricultural Labor Relations Act (CALRA), West's Ann. Cal. Lab or Code §§1140–66, §1154(d)(1)-(4) (West 2003) (protecting the right to organize and bargain collectively, including a limited right to strike).

103. Commission for Labor Cooperation, "Legal Background Paper, Protection of Migrant Agricultural Workers in Canada, Mexico and the United States" (2000), p. 63, available at http://www.naalc.org/english/pdf/migrant_worker.pdf (accessed Jan. 13, 2003).

104. Ibid., p. 63 (the Fair Labor Standards Act [FLSA] allows children as young as ten to work in agriculture under certain conditions).

105. Ibid., p. 66.

106. Twelve states exclude agricultural workers from workers' compensation laws; five states provide for elective coverage, and a number of other state laws ex-

empt agricultural workers in certain circumstances, such as those who work part-time or on small farms. Ibid., p. 65.

107. Ibid., p. 63 (FLSA does not apply to employers who use fewer than five hundred worker days of agricultural labor per year).

108. Ibid., p. 62 (Title VII applies only to employers with fifteen or more employees).

109. Ibid., p. 64.

110. Ibid., p. 67.

111. Ibid., p. 62.

112. Ibid., p. 68.

113. Human Rights Watch, "Hidden in the Home: Abuse of Domestic Workers with Special Visas in the United States," (June 2001), p. 3, available at http://www.hrw.org/reports/2001/usadom/ (accessed Jan. 13, 2003).

114. Three major ILO conventions specifically protect the rights of migrant workers, all of which have very low ratification levels. Convention Concerning the Safety and Health in Agriculture (No. 184), adopted June 21, 2001, not yet entered into force (2 ratifications); Convention Concerning Migrations in Abusive Conditions and the Promotion of Equality of Opportunity and Treatment of Migrant Workers (No. 143), adopted June 24, 1975 (entered into force Dec. 9, 1978) (18 ratifications); Convention Concerning Migration for Employment (No. 97) (Revised 1949), adopted July 1, 1949, entered into force Jan. 22, 1952 (42 ratifications). ILO conventions and ratification information are available at http://ilolex.ilo.ch:1567/english/convdisp2.htm (accessed Jan. 13, 2003). The UN Convention on the Protection of the Rights of All Migrant Workers (1990), available at http://untreaty.un.org/English/millennium/law/index.html (accessed Jan. 13, 2003), is not yet in force.

115. Sarah H. Cleveland, "Human Rights Sanctions and International Trade: A Theory of Compatibility," *Journal of Economic Law* 5 (2002): 133, 188–89 (arguing that linking trade and international human rights standards can improve the effectiveness of both regimes and protect them from corrosive unilateral action).

116. Philip Alston, "Labor Rights Provisions in U.S. Trade Law, 'Aggressive Unilateralism'?" in *Human Rights, Labor Rights, and International Trade,* ed. Lance Compa and Stephen Diamond (Philadelphia: University of Pennsylvania Press, 1996), pp. 71–95.

117. "[I]nternationally recognized worker rights" in the U.S. GSP system include minimum wages, hours of work, and health and safety, which are not among the ILO's core labor rights, and fail to include the prohibition against nondiscrimination, which is a core labor right. See note 33 above. This deficiency is replicated in the President's new trade promotion authority. See note 22 above.

118. 19 U.S.C. §2467(6) (2002).

119. 19 U.S.C. §1307 (1994) (as amended) (defining forced labor as "all work or service which is extracted from any person under the menace of any penalty for its nonperformance and for which the worker does not offer himself voluntarily").

120. See Cleveland, "Norm Internalization and US Economic Sanctions," p. 85 ("reliable interpretation and application of international norms by transnational actors is critical to encouraging nations to recognize, internalize, and obey international law").

121. See Harold H. Koh, "Transnational Public Law Litigation," *Yale Law Journal* 100 (1991): 2347, 2347–49 (describing the process of norm transfer and enforcement through litigation).

122. Agreement between IKEA and the International Federation of Building and Wood Workers, reprinted in *Multinational Enterprises and the Social Challenges of the XXIst Century*, ed. Blainpain, pp. 359–60.

123. Liubicic, "Corporate Codes of Conduct and Product Labeling Schemes," pp. 128–29. An ILO survey of 215 private codes of conduct found that "relatively few codes addressed freedom of association and collective bargaining." "Overview of Global Developments and Office Activities concerning Codes of Conduct, Social Labeling and Other Private Sector Initiatives Addressing Labor Issues," Working Party on the Social Dimensions of the Liberalization of International Trade, GB.273/WP/SDL/1(Rev.1), 273rd Sess., ILO Governing Body, Geneva (Nov. 1998), Para. 48, available at http://www.ilo.org/public/english/standards/relm/gb/docs/gb273/ (accessed May 21, 2003).

124. Liubicic, "Corporate Codes of Conduct and Product Labeling Schemes," pp. 131–34. See also Philip Alston and James Heenan, "The Role of International Labor Standards within the Trade Debate: The Need to Return to Fundamentals," in *Human Rights and Non-State Actors*, ed. P. Alston (Oxford: Oxford University Press, 2004) (forthcoming) (arguing that lack of a unified approach to codes of conduct will erode the universality of standards and allow the most powerful actors to determine the extent to which worker rights will be protected).

125. For further discussion, see Cleveland, *Human Rights Sanctions and International Trade*, p. 187.

126. Ibid.

127. Ibid.

128. Claire, *Labour Standards and International Trade,* p. 287 (the proposal was withdrawn, presumably due to fear that it would undermine states' willingness to adopt ILO conventions).

129. Havana Charter for an International Trade Organization, pt. II, art. VII, opened for signature Mar. 24, 1948, UN Doc. E/Conf.2/78 (1948).

130. Elissa Alben, "GATT and the Fair Wage: A Historical Perspective on the La-bor-Trade Link," *Columbia Law Review* 101 (2001): 1410, 1432–40.

131. WTO Singapore Ministerial Declaration, ¶ 4. For an overview of historical efforts to incorporate labor standards into the GATT system, see Elissa Alben, "GATT and the Fair Wage," pp. 1410 et seq.; Clyde Summers, "The Battle in Seattle: Free Trade, Labor Rights, and Societal Values," *University of Pennsylvania Journal of International Economic Law* 22 (2001): 61, 62–63; Christopher McCrudden and Ann Davies, "A Perspective on Trade and Labor Rights," *Journal of International Economic Law* 3 (2000): 43, 44–48.

132. "WTO's Forward Work Programme: Proposed Establishment of a Working Group on Trade and Labor: Communication for the United States," WTO Doc. WT/GC/W/382 (Nov. 1, 1999) (urging the establishment of a Working Group on Trade and Labour). The European Union has taken the position that the WTO should "encourage positive incentives to promote observance of core labour rights," but "opposes any sanctions-based approaches" and urges that "the comparative advantage of . . . low-wage developing countries must in no way be put into question." "Core Labour Rights: EU Negotiating Position," in *House of Lords, Select Committee on the European Union, The World Trade Organisation: The EU Mandate after Seattle* (Session 1999–2000, 10th Report, HL Paper 76-I).

133. See, e.g., Joint Communiqué: The Thirteenth ASEAN Labour Ministers Meeting, Yangon, Myanmar (May 14–15, 1999), available at http://www.aseansec.org/ (accessed Jan. 15, 2002). See also Steven Greenhouse and Joseph Kahn, "U.S. Effort to Add Labor Standards to Agenda Fails," *New York Times*, Dec. 3, 1999, pp. A1, A12 (noting that opposition to the proposal was solidified by Clinton's suggestion that the WTO should at some point use sanctions to enforce core labor rights).

134. According to the ILO, at the Doha Ministerial, Cuba, Egypt, India, Malaysia, Pakistan, and Zimbabwe, among others, expressed firm opposition to trade/labor linkage, while Namibia, the United Arab Emirates, and others simply stressed that the ILO was the competent body to address labor standards. Germany and Guatemala expressed their opposition to labor/trade linkage for protectionist purposes, while South Africa, Venezuela, and New Zealand all supported some form of recognition in the WTO of the relationship between trade and social or labor issues. ILO, "The ILO and Globalization: Fourth Ministerial Conference of the World Trade Organization," para. 12, available at http://www.ilo.org/public/english/bureau/exrel/ global/wto-doha.htm (accessed May 21, 2003).

135. WTO Singapore Ministerial Declaration, ¶ 4.

136. Ibid.

137. Trebilock and Howse, for example, have described the Singapore Declara-

tion as follows: "The use of labour standards for 'protectionist purposes' is rejected, which implies some openness to trade measures that are demonstrated to have non-protectionist purposes, i.e., not aimed at neutralizing the comparative advantage of developing countries, but rather at insuring compliance with core standards." Michael Trebilock and Robert Howse, *The Regulation of International Trade* (London: Routledge, 2nd ed. 1999), p. 457. I owe special thanks to Richard Steinberg for bringing this point to my attention.

138. Robert Howse, "The World Trade Organization and the Protection of Workers' Rights," *Journal of Small and Emerging Business Law* 3 (1999): 131, 169.

139. Jagdish Bhagwati, *Free Trade Today* (Princeton and Oxford: Princeton University Press, 2002), pp. 70–71.

140. Ibid., pp. 71–72.

141. "Dangerous Activities—Trade Disputes—Trade Disputes between Europe and America," *The Economist*, May 11, 2002, Special Report (2), p. 63 (discussing the President's imposition of up to 30 percent tariffs on foreign steel as "America's most protectionist single action for two decades").

142. The recent legislative battle over the House bill granting President George W. Bush trade promotion authority, for example, resulted in protectionist provisions for citrus and specialty agriculture, as well as a retreat from past trade-promotion commitments to Africa and the Caribbean. Speech of Representative Sander M. Levin delivered at Stanford Law School, May 19, 2002 (on file with author), p 4.

143. Barriers to imports of Vietnamese catfish, for example, were erected, among other things, to protect U.S. catfish producers from foreign competitors with "cheap labor and loose environmental standards." See ibid., p. 8.

144. See William B. Gould IV, "Labor Law for a Global Economy: The Uneasy Case for International Labor Standards," *Nebraska Law Review* 80 (2001): 715, 720–23 (discussing low levels of Western, and particularly U.S., foreign assistance).

145. Indeed, child labor has only recently been added to a number of unilateral U.S. provisions, such as §307 of the 1930 Tariff Act. See note 27 above. Both the European and U.S. GSP systems address a number of other core labor standards, including freedom of association and forced labor. See notes 33, 38, 39 above and accompanying text.

146. Drusilla Brown has done excellent work examining the causes of child labor and the impact of recent policy initiatives. See Drusilla K. Brown, "Child Labor in Latin America: Policy and Evidence," Working Paper No. 2001–10, Discussion Paper Series, Department of Economics, Tufts University, available at http://ase.tufts.edu/econ/papers/20010.pdf (accessed Feb. 19, 2003); Drusilla K. Brown, Alan V. Deardorff, and Robert M. Stern, "Child Labor: Theory, Evidence and Policy" (Research Seminar in International Economics, School of Public Policy, University of Michi-

gan), No. 2001–11, Discussion Paper Series, Department of Economics, Tufts University, available at http://ase.tufts.edu/econ/papers/ (accessed July 7, 2002).

147. See, generally, Human Rights Watch, *Unfair Advantage: Worker's Freedom of Association in the United States under International Human Rights Standards* (Human Rights Watch, Aug. 2000), available at http://www.org/reports/2000/uslabor (accessed Feb. 19, 2003).

148. ILO Declaration on Fundamental Principles and Rights at Work, note 6 above, ¶5.

149. Comments of Brian Bercusson at Stanford International Labor Standards Conference, May 2002.

150. "Report of the World Summit for Social Development, Copenhagen," Mar. 6–12, 1995, U.N. Doc. A/Conf.166/9 (1996), p. 12, Commitment 3(i) (listing freedom of association, forced and child labor, and nondiscrimination), available at http://www.un.org/esa/socdev/wssd/documents/ (accessed May 22, 2003)

151. The OECD has recognized freedom of association, forced labor, *exploitative* child labor, and nondiscrimination as core worker rights. OECD 1996, p. 26.

152. Gary Fields, *Trade and Labour Standards: A Review of the Issues* (OECD 1994), p. 11.

153. Summers, "The Battle in Seattle," p. 68. Summers also includes occupational health and safety as a potential core right.

154. Lance Compa, "Promise and Peril: Core Labor Rights in Global Trade and Investment," paper for the North American Conference, International Industrial Relations Association, Toronto, Canada (June 2002), p. 6 (on file with the author).

155. OECD 2000, p. 33.

156. OECD 1996, pp. 79–80.

157. The use of child labor is crippling to a country's long-term economic development. Child labor prevents human resource improvement and ensures that successive generations will remain unskilled and uneducated. OECD 2002, p. 32.

158. Gordon Lafer, "Captive Labor: America's Prisoners as Corporate Workforce," *American Prospect* (Sept.–Oct. 1999): 66 (discussing prison labor); Dani Rodrik, *Has Globalization Gone Too Far?* (Washington, D.C.: Institute for International Economics, 1997), pp. 45–46 (concluding, after controlling for productivity levels, that the use of child labor results in lower labor costs).

159. OECD 1996, pp. 80–82.

160. Studies demonstrate that rather than increasing a country's low-wage advantage, workplace discrimination is "costly and inefficient," obstructing both economic efficiency and social development. OECD 2000, p. 42, citing K. Maskus, "Should Core Labor Standards Be Imposed Through International Trade Policy?," World Bank Policy Research Working Paper No. 1817 (Aug. 1997).

161. *Compa*, "Promise or Peril," p. 8.

162. Ibid., p. 12.

163. See, e.g., UDHR, arts. 20, 23(4); ICCPR, art. 22; ICESCR, art. 8.

164. UDHR, art. 23(2) (right to equal pay); ICCPR, art. 26 (gender and race discrimination); ICESCR, art. 7(a)(1) (equal pay); CEDAW, art. 11 (gender discrimination); International Convention on the Elimination of All Forms of Racial Discrimination, art. 5(e)(i), 7 Mar. 1966, 660 U.N.T.S. 195 (entered into force Jan. 4, 1969); International Convention on the Suppression and Punishment of the Crime of Apartheid, Nov. 30, 1973, 1015 U.N.T.S. 243, 246 (entered into force July 18, 1976), available at http://www/unhchr.chhtml/menu3/b/11.htm (accessed May 22, 2003).

165. Cleveland, "Book Review: Global Labor Rights and the Alien Tort Claims Act," p. 1571 ("The prohibitions of forced labor and slave-like practices are now widely recognized in conjunction with slavery as customary international norms").

166. UDHR, art. 4; ICCPR, art. 8; Supplementary Convention on the Abolition of Slavery, the Slave Trade, and Institutions and Practices Similar to Slavery, Sept. 7, 1956, 266 U.N.T.S. 3; Convention to Suppress the Slave Trade and Slavery, Sept. 25, 1926, 46 Stat. 2183, 2191, 60 U.N.T.S. 253, 263.

167. General Agreements on Tariffs and Trade, opened for signature Oct. 30, 1947, 61 Stat A3, TIAS No. 1700, 55 U.N.T.S. 187, art. XX(e) (creating an exception to GATT trade liberalization requirements for measures relating to the products of prison labor). Technically the GATT 1947 never came into force but was incorporated via Article 1(a) of the General Agreement on Tariffs and Trade 1994 as part of the Uruguay Round negotiations that established the WTO. For further discussion of the GATT prison labor clause, see Cleveland, *Human Rights Sanctions and International Trade*, pp. 161–62; Francesco Francioni, "Environment, Human Rights and the Limits of Free Trade," in *Environment, Human Rights and International Trade*, ed. Francioni (Oxford: Hart Publishing, 2001), vol. 1, pp. 17–20; Federico Lenzerini, "International Trade and Child Labour Standards," in *Environment, Human Rights and the Limits of Free Trade*, ed. Francioni, pp. 287–312; Steve Charnovitz, "The Moral Exception in Trade Policy," *Virginia Journal of International Law* 38 (1998): 689, 740–42; Robert Howse, "The World Trade Organization and the Protection of Workers' Rights," p. 142.

168. ILO Convention No. 182, see note 2 above.

169. ILO Convention No. 138, note 2 above, art. 2(4). The Convention further allows any country "whose economy and administrative facilities are insufficiently developed" to initially limit the scope of its application of the Convention. Ibid., art. 5.

170. Convention on the Rights of the Child, see note 70 above, art. 19 (obligating states to protect children from all forms of physical or mental violence, injury or

abuse, neglect or negligent treatment, maltreatment or exploitation, including sexual abuse).

171. See discussion at notes 4 and 5 and accompanying text above.

172. Comments of Virginia Leary, Stanford International Labor Standards Conference (May 2002).

173. See Compa, "Promise and Peril," p. 8 (arguing that "[w]orking conditions free of grave risk of injury or illness" should be included among the core labor rights).

174. UDHR, art. 23(1) (just and favorable conditions of work); ICESCR, art. 7(b) (safe and healthy working conditions); CEDAW, art. 11(f) (health and safety in working conditions, including reproductive health); Convention on the Rights of the Child, art. 19 (freedom from all forms of injury or abuse).

175. UDHR art. 23(3) (just and favorable remuneration), art. 25 (right to a standard of living adequate for health and well-being of self and family, including food, clothing, housing, medical care, security for unemployment, old age, illness, and disability), ICESCR, art. 7(a)(ii) (a decent living for worker and family), art. 11 (adequate standard of living); art. 11(2) (fundamental right to be free from hunger).

176. ILO Tripartite Declaration of Principles concerning Multinational Enterprises and Social Policy, note 51 above; OECD, Guidelines for Multinational Enterprises, 2000, note 52 above; The Global Compact Nine Principles, note 53 above.

177. See Declaración Socio-Laboral del Mercosur, note 16 above, arts. 17 and 18.

178. See "Overview of Global Developments," note 123 above, ¶3.

179. Convention concerning Occupational Safety and Health and the Working Environment (No. 155), June 22, 1981 (entered into force Aug. 11, 1983) (40 ratifications); Minimum Wage Fixing Convention (No. 131), June 22, 1970 (entered into force Apr. 29, 1972 (45 ratifications). Convention text and ratification information is available at http://www.ilo.org/ilolex/english/convdisp1.htm (accessed May 22, 2003).

180. Article 3 of Convention No. 131 provides that a minimum wage should be based on "the needs of workers and their families, taking into account the general level of wages in the country, the cost of living, social security benefits, and the relative living standards of other social groups," as well as "economic factors, including the requirements of economic development, levels of productivity and the desirability of attaining and maintaining a high level of employment." Ibid.

181. Lamy Betten, *International Labour Law: Selected Issues* (Boston: Kluwer, 1993), pp. 213–14.

182. Stephen Herzenberg, "In from the Margins: Morality, Economics, and International Labor Rights," in *Human Rights, Labor Rights, and International Trade*, ed. Compa and Diamond, p. 109. The U.S. Department of Labor also has done work in this area. See U.S. Dept. of Labor: Bureau of International Labor Affairs, "Wages,

Benefits, Poverty Line and Meeting Workers' Needs in the Apparel and Footwear Industries of Selected Countries," (Feb. 2000), p. 7, available at http://www.dol.gov/ilab/media/reports/oiea/wagestudy/main.htm (accessed Feb. 21, 2003).

183. Worker Rights Consortium (WRC), Model Code of Conduct, ¶ IIC(1), available at http://www.workerrights.org/coc.asp (accessed Feb. 21, 2003).

184. Sweatshop Watch, "A Working Living Wage Methodology," available at http://www.sweatshopwatch.org/wages/formula.html (accessed Jan. 12, 2003).

185. See note 114 above.

186. The European Court of Justice has upheld a national treatment standard for migrant workers within the EU. In several cases, the ECJ has held that companies from low-wage member states (such as Portugal) operating in high wage states (such as France), are obligated to adhere to both national labor laws and applicable national collective bargaining agreements. See *Rush Portuguesa Lda v. Office National d'Immigration* (C-113/89), [1990] E.C.R. I-1417; *Finalarte Sociedade de Construção Civil Lda. v. Urlaubs- und Lohnausgleichskasse der Bauwirtschaft* (C-49/98) (Oct. 25, 2001), Official Journal, C3, Jan. 5, 2002, p. 1. I am grateful to Brian Bercusson for bringing these cases to my attention

187. Note 16 above, art 4.

188. Note 13 above.

189. Ibid., annex I, art. 11.

190. See note 114 above.

191. Article 8 of the International Covenant on Civil and Political Rights, and the ILO Forced Labor Conventions, for example, define forced labor as "all work or service which is extracted from any person under the menace of any penalty and for which the said person has not offered himself voluntarily." Compare *United States v. Kozminski*, 487 U.S. 931, 952 (1988) (limiting involuntary servitude to threat of legal or physical coercion).

192. See note 189 above.

193. See Request for Advisory Opinion OC-18, submitted to the Inter-American Court of Human Rights by the State of the United States of Mexico (May 10, 2002) (on file with the author).

"Form Follows Function": Formulations of International Labor Standards— Treaties, Codes, Soft Law, Trade Agreements

VIRGINIA A. LEARY

I. Introduction: What Form Should International Labor Standards Take?

Since 1919, legally binding labor conventions adopted by the International Labor Organization (ILO) have been the main form of instrument used to promote labor standards; 184 ILO conventions (and a greater number of recommendations) comprise the International Labor Code. In 1998, however, the International Labor Conference adopted, and gave particular emphasis to, a different form of instrument: a *Declaration on Fundamental Principles and Rights at Work* that is neither a treaty nor a recommendation. The Declaration enunciated for the first time within the ILO the concept of "core labor standards"—freedom of association and elimination of discrimination in employment, elimination of forced labor, and elimination of child labor—as obligations of membership in the organization, whether or not member states have ratified the relevant ILO conventions. Since the United States has ratified only two of the ILO conventions on these subjects (Convention No. 182 on the Elimination of Worst Forms of Child Labor and No. 105 on Forced Labor), the Declaration is of particular interest to the United States.

The adoption of the ILO Declaration is highlighted here as a focus for the subject of this paper: what form should international labor standards take? Why has the ILO adopted the concept of "core labor standards" and expressed the adoption in the form of a declaration? Does it evidence a trend away from legally binding conventions as the main form for labor standards? Trade unions and human rights organizations are focusing on other forms of instruments for promoting labor standards: links with trade and investment agreements and "soft law" nonbinding codes and declarations. Efforts to incorporate labor rights into the WTO system have not been successful; in the international climate of globalization, privatization, and trade liberalization, labor rights are viewed as protectionist measures that interfere with economic development. Developing countries are the strongest opponents of linking workers' rights with trade. Nevertheless, efforts continue to link workers' rights to trade agreements. Multinational enterprises are currently adopting private codes on social rights, following criticism of their activities.

The architectural maxim "form follows function" focuses our attention, however, away from *form* and toward the purpose or *function* of labor standards. Unfortunately, the use of this maxim, when applied in the "real world" of social policy, runs up against the realities of politics and national and personal interests; nevertheless, the maxim assists us in judging the efficacy of conventions, codes, and soft law, not on their form but on whether they contribute to the purpose of labor standards; the forms themselves may not be the crucial issue; particular forms may be more or less useful depending on the context.

A major portion of this paper focuses on the renewed relevance of the ILO and its efforts to promote labor standards through new initiatives and new forms; developments at the ILO are illustrative of the *problematique* of current labor standard setting and enforcement. The push to incorporate workers' rights in trade and investment agreements (WTO-GATT and NAFTA) and to promote working conditions through the adoption of declarations and codes, private as well as public, is also discussed in the paper. The actions of the trade union movement, human rights organizations, and other civil society organizations are referred to throughout the paper.

II. Function in Search of Form

A. The ILO and Labor Standards: New Initiatives

1. The United States and the ILO. Any discussion of international labor standards must focus primarily on the International Labor Organization, but this focus seems misplaced to many in the United States, where the ILO has never been well known, even among labor law scholars, and has been considered ineffective. The lack of attention to the ILO by the U.S. government and by Americans most concerned with working conditions has become a self-fulfilling prophecy. Inattention to an international organization by such a major power as the United States can only contribute to its lack of effectiveness. The United States has ratified only fourteen ILO conventions, and not the most fundamental conventions on freedom of association and collective bargaining. Most Western European countries have ratified between forty and seventy conventions.

There are many reasons why the U.S. government—as well the U.S. public—has focused so little attention on the ILO. Only a few will be cited here. The ILO emphasis, from its beginning in 1919, on adoption of international standards in the *form* of legally binding conventions, with a view to their incorporation in national legislation, seemed inappropriate in the U.S. context at the time, even to the labor leader Samuel Gompers, who was active in the establishment of the ILO. The approach of U.S. labor to workers' rights at the time favored collective agreements as the means of promoting such rights, with as little involvement of government as possible. The United States failed to ratify the Versailles Treaty, of which the ILO Constitution was a part, and there was no strongly active U.S. lobby urging the United States to join the ILO in the early years of its founding.

The United States became a member of the ILO only in 1934 as a result of Roosevelt's New Deal emphasis on social policy and the strong support of Frances Perkins, Secretary of Labor. In post–World War II years, U.S. interest in the ILO centered on Cold War issues. George Meany regarded the ILO as an organization with strong communist influence; his opposition led to U.S. withdrawal from the organization in 1977. Following his death in 1980 and the alleged improvement of ILO activities, the United States rejoined. Subsequent U.S. support focused on ILO criticism of the labor policies of Soviet bloc countries. With the end of the Cold War, that U.S. incentive to support the ILO faded.

Failure of the United States to ratify a larger number of ILO conventions has been attributed to the problem of federal/state relations, but the issue of ratification is less a constitutional problem than a political problem. Factors contributing to U.S. lack of support include, inter alia, the lack of interest in and knowledge of international organizations in the United States. Unilateralism is a deeply ingrained U.S. approach to international issues and organizations.

The U.S. lack of interest in the ILO is short-sighted. The ILO, like all organizations (and national governments!), has limitations and defects—some of them inherent in the present state of the development of the international community, and some peculiar to the ILO. But it remains the only international forum where the improvement of working conditions is a central focus.

In 2000, Human Rights Watch published an extensive report by Lance Compa entitled *Unfair Advantage: Workers' Freedom of Association in the United States under International Human Rights' Standards.* This excellent report cites numerous examples of violation of international labor standards by the United States, mentioning one example, the exclusion of agricultural workers from protection of the right to organize, as an instance of a clash with ILO norms. It quotes from a report to the ILO in 1999 in which the United States acknowledged for the first time that "there are aspects of this [U.S. labor law] system that fail to fully protect the rights to organize and bargain collectively of all employees in all circumstances. . . . [T]he United States is concerned about these limitations and acknowledges that to ensure respect, promotion and realization of the right to organize and bargain collectively, it is important to reexamine any system of labor laws from time to time to assure that the system continues to protect these fundamental rights."[1]

The Human Rights Watch Report points out that what is most needed

> is a new spirit of commitment by the labor law community and the government to give effect to both international human rights norms and the still-vital affirmation in the United States' own basic labor law for full freedom of association for workers. . . . One way to begin fostering such a change of spirit is for the United States to ratify ILO Conventions 87 and 98 [on Freedom of Association and Collective Bargaining]. This would send a strong signal to workers, employers, labor law authorities, and to the international community that the United States is serious about holding itself to international and human rights standards as it presses for the inclusion of such standards in new global and regional trade arrangements." (Pp. 17–18)

2. ILO Standard Setting: Form and Function of Labor Standards. In his classic 1961 treatise on The Law of Treaties, Lord McNair referred to treaties as the "only and sadly overworked instrument with which international society is equipped for the purpose of carrying out its multifarious transactions"—and this remains true to an extent today. ILO conventions and human rights treaties differ from many other treaties since their aim is to change the internal policies of states, but they continue to be the main form of instruments used for labor standards and human rights obligations. ILO conventions and human rights treaties are "law-making" rather than contractual and are intended for national application, rather than application in interstate relations; reciprocity cannot be relied on for their implementation. Implementation is promoted primarily through international supervision.

The most obvious value of a treaty or convention is that, once ratified, it creates a binding legal obligation and often becomes part of national law; the most obvious limitation of international labor conventions and human rights treaties is the lack of ratifications. A number of ILO conventions have not been widely ratified. This limitation of treaties has resulted in recourse to other forms, such as nonbinding declarations and codes, which may or may not be effective in improving labor standards depending on a number of factors referred to later in the paper.

From the beginning days of the ILO, it was recognized that the treaty *form* did not precisely fit the purpose or *function* of promoting labor rights. Hence, ILO conventions have characteristics that differentiate them from other conventions, leading some early commentators to consider them as international legislation or draft national laws. Unlike other conventions, nongovernmental organizations (workers' and employers' organizations) participate in their drafting, and conventions are adopted not by conferences of states but by the International Labor Conference, which includes worker and employer representatives. In addition to a requirement to submit the conventions for ratification, member states are required to submit labor conventions to the competent bodies in the member states for the enactment of legislation or other appropriate action. Conventions can come into force with as few as two ratifications; since they are not contractual treaties, there is no essential reason why they should not come into force on the basis of one ratification. The majority of ILO conventions are short in form and restricted to the formulation of a few broad obligations. When more precise and technical details are appropriate, they are generally elaborated in a recommendation and not a convention. A number of "flexibility devices" have been included in conventions to take into account differing levels of economic and social development. These aspects of ILO conventions, considered innovative in the early days of the ILO, are rarely remarked on today, with the exception of the participation of nongovernmental organizations. Yet, they exemplify the effort of the ILO from the beginning to adapt form to the function of the promotion of labor standards.

The variety in the content of ILO conventions is significant in the context of the issue raised in this paper concerning the *form* that labor standards should take. The treaty form appears to be remarkably adaptable, as exemplified, for example, in the recent use of very generally worded framework conventions for environmental obligations. The reluctance of the United States to ratify a greater number of ILO conventions may be due less to the content of the conventions than to an unwillingness to submit to international supervision.

The ILO Constitution lays down the basic rules concerning the adoption of conventions, and their adoption and supervision have been main functions of the ILO. Technical assistance and research are also major ILO activities, and, in the view of some observers, recent actions at the ILO downplay the centrality of the adoption and supervision of standards.

The ILO Constitution and subsequent developments have, however, created obligations concerning certain standards irrespective of the ratification of the relevant conventions. Thus, member states are required to report at regular intervals on the state of their law and practice in regard to matters dealt with in a convention (Article 19 of the Constitution). The Governing Body Committee on Freedom of Association considers freedom of association within member states whether or not the states have ratified freedom of association conventions. The United States, like other countries, has been criticized by the Committee for certain aspects of its law, particularly the "Mackay doctrine" permitting permanent replacement of workers during a strike, which was found by the Committee to be contrary to freedom of association.

3. *New ILO Initiatives.* While largely unremarked in the United States, the ILO has undertaken a number of new initiatives in recent years to reenforce its promotion of workers' rights in the contemporary international climate:

1. the establishment of a Working Party on Social Aspects of Globalization,
2. the adoption of the Declaration on Fundamental Principles and Rights at Work, and
3. the establishment of a World Commission on the Social Dimension of Globalization.

It has also attempted in recent years to collaborate with the WTO, the World Bank, and other development banks and organizations to promote a coherent approach to the protection of workers' rights. These efforts have often been rebuffed but currently seem to be leading to better relations. Some of the new ILO initiatives appear to be a response to the difficulty of achieving collaboration with these organizations in the promotion of labor rights. The repeated emphasis that it is the province of the ILO and not other organizations to promote labor standards has blocked efforts by the ILO to foster a coherent approach to labor standards in collaboration with other organizations—an approach that is obviously needed.

The refusal, by member states of the WTO at the Ministerial Conferences in Singapore, and more recently in Doha, to consider international labor standards in relation to the liberalization of trade, has led to the renewed relevance of the ILO. At the first WTO Ministerial Conference in Singapore an invitation to Michel Hansenne, then the ILO Director General, to address the ministers was withdrawn because of objections from developing countries. The ILO has received invitations to attend WTO Ministerial Conferences since Singapore, including the recent conference in Doha, but has not had any role other than attendance. The concluding statements at both Ministerial Conferences stressed that the WTO was not the correct body to deal with labor issues; such issues are the province of the ILO. Improved relations—at least courtesy relations—with the WTO may be heralded by the visit and address of Mike Moore, Director-General of the WTO, at the March 2002 meeting of the ILO Governing Body. Relations with the World Bank and other development banks also appear to be entering a new, more collaborative phase—for example, with ILO collaboration with the World Bank's Poverty Reduction Strategy.

Space does not permit extended discussion of all of the new ILO initiatives, but special mention should be made of the Declaration of Fundamental Principles and Rights at Work adopted by the International Labor Conference in 1998. As previously mentioned, the Declaration represents a departure from the traditional method of elaborating standards in ILO legally binding conventions. It is not in the form of a legally binding convention, and it is somewhat difficult to grasp its precise legal significance. The Declaration states that

> all Members, even if they have not ratified the Conventions in question, have an *obligation* arising from the very fact of membership in the Organization, to respect, promote and to realize, in good faith and in accordance with the Constitution, the principles concerning the fundamental rights which are the subject of those Conventions, namely (a) freedom of association and the effective recognition of the right to collective bargaining; (b) the elimination of all forms of forced or compulsory labour; (c) the effective abolition of child labour; and (d) the elimination of discrimination in respect of employment and occupation. (emphasis mine)

The adoption of the Declaration has been attributed to several causes: (1) the consensus following WTO meetings that the ILO was the body to set and supervise labor standards, (2) the influence of the World Summit on Social Development in Copenhagen in 1995, which concluded that all states should apply four basic principles of workers' rights (those later included in the Declaration), and (3) the search for ways to strengthen the ILO supervisory system to reach countries that have not ratified all the basic ILO labor standards.[2]

More significant perhaps than the Declaration's uncertain legal status is the emphasis given to it as a solemn commitment by the ILO and the follow-up procedure to the Declaration. The follow-up procedure provides for reports on the implementation of the core labor standards by ILO members who have not ratified the relevant conventions. An annual ILO report is then issued based on the reports of the governments. In 2001, the report on forced labor was published, based on government reports; it is interesting reading and an excellent summary of the law and practice of forced labor internationally.[3] Reports were received as well from countries that had abstained in voting for the Declaration, including China, which reported on its system of rehabilitation through labor. The Report referred to comments of the International Confederation of Free Trade Unions that the practice was a form of forced labor, and to criticisms of the practice by the United Nations Working Group on Arbitrary Detention.

In March 2002, Juan Somavia, Director-General of the ILO, announced the setting up of a World Commission on the Social Dimension of Globalization, to be led by two heads of state, Finnish President Tarja Halonen and President Benjamin Mkapa of Tanzania. It represents another ILO initiative to promote workers' rights in addition to the traditional approach of the adoption of standards. An unsuccessful effort was apparently made by Somavia to have such a commission set up through the United Nations with representation from other UN organizations. Members of the Commission, who serve in their personal capacity, include former Italian Premier Giuliano Amato; Joseph Stiglitz, winner of the 2001 Nobel Prize for Economics; Ann McLaughlinn Korologos, Vice Chairman of the Rand Corporation; John Sweeney, President of the AFL-CIO; and a number of other distinguished persons from a wide geographic group of states. Members will serve in their personal capacity.

While examining broader issues of globalization and social policy, the Commission will also focus on the impact of globalization on employment and decent work. A press release announcing the establishment of the Commission mentioned that it would also examine the perceptions of workers, enterprises, investors, and consumers, as well as different expressions of civil society and public opinion from all parts of the world. Thus, the Commission will reach out to broader categories than the traditional labor, employer, and government constituencies of the ILO. It is expected to issue a report in 2003.

4. A Limitation of the ILO Approach to Current World Working Conditions. The new initiatives of the ILO may be welcomed as partial responses to some of the limitations and inadequacies of the traditional ILO approach to the setting and implementation of labor standards. The full participation of nongovernmental entities—employers' and workers' organizations—in all ILO activities has traditionally been hailed as an important and useful exception to the usual limitation to participation only by states in such organizations. And, in many ways, it is an important exception to international organization activities. Ironically, however, the participation of these organizations in the activities of the ILO has also resulted in much less interest in and following of ILO activities by the currently most dynamic social movements, such as human rights and consumer organizations. It appears to observers that labor unions have felt that they sufficiently represented such civil society organizations and were not welcoming of their contribution to ILO activities. Given the current relative weakness of labor organizations in both the developing and developed world, their failure to enlist the active support of the human rights movement, for example, to support their efforts at the ILO, appears self-defeating.

It is not contended here that such organizations should be given the same full participation as employers' and workers' organizations at the ILO, but there are a number of means by which they could be encouraged to follow ILO activities and to make contributions to debates. States sometimes appear to be more amenable than labor and employer organizations to a limited participation of nongovernmental organizations in international organizations' activities. States are already accustomed to the contributions of nongovernmental organizations in many UN activities, particularly in human rights fora. Although such organizations are not full members of the United Nations they have been able through the limited participation accorded them to make substantial contributions. The membership of the new World Commission, including labor and employer representatives but not limited to them, is a welcome development. The human rights constituency, however, does not yet seem to have found a means for more active participation at the ILO.

The need for more input from civil society beyond the traditional ILO constituencies' is important in view of current issues relating to work. The ILO began at a time when the main economic actors were states and worker and employers' organizations; the situation in the world today is not the same—other actors and constituencies, such as environmental movements and human rights organizations, are also concerned with economic and work issues. The latter, for example, are more interested in improving the labor conditions of unorganized workers in the developed and developing world and the problems of women workers and migrant laborers than workers and employer organizations whose primary interest is organized labor.[4] Concern with child labor originated in large part from civil society groups that, in turn, influenced national governments. The excellent ILO Program on the Elimination of Child Labor (IPEC) was an initiative of Germany and has been made functional by the contributions of a number of countries. Labor unions and employer organizations had not demonstrated significant concern with child labor protection prior to the development of IPEC.

B. Linking Workers' Rights with Trade: An Issue That Won't Go Away—WTO, NAFTA

International labor standards were first conceived in the context of economic competitiveness. In the nineteenth century, European social reformers realized that there was little chance of a country shortening working hours or cutting down on child labor if such measures diminished its economic competitiveness. They urged all European countries to agree to the same social policies, specifically on working hours and child labor, so that none would have a comparative advantage in international trade; thus the idea of labor standards agreed to at the international level was born—leading eventually to the establishment of the ILO in 1919 and its emphasis on the adoption of international labor conventions. Later in the history of the ILO, the competition argument for labor standards was downplayed; labor standards were urged for their own sake or as human rights values.

Plus ça change, plus c'est la même chose. The problem of competitiveness and labor standards continues today, but on a worldwide scale: how can labor standards be improved in a world of fierce economic competition? Americans (both the U.S. government and American NGOs) are among the strongest proponents of the linking of labor standards to trade, but it is difficult for developing, and some developed, countries to believe that protectionism is not behind the policy of promoting labor rights, especially in view, inter alia, of the recent U.S. resort to protection against steel imports. American human rights organizations and even labor unions, genuinely pursuing improved international labor standards, are tarred with the same brush and viewed with suspicion. The unwillingness of many developed countries to adopt policies favoring import access for the products of developing countries is a further reminder that protectionism is alive and well and invocation of labor standards may serve as a pretext.

1. *The WTO and International Labor Standards.* This widespread suspicion of the agenda behind the advocacy of international labor standards, particularly by the United States, has effectively blocked consideration of labor standards at the WTO—and will likely continue to block any such consideration in the immediate future. As remarked earlier, ILO representatives have attended WTO Ministerial Conferences but have had no active partici-

pation at the WTO. The final Declaration at the Singapore Ministerial meeting stated, "We renew our commitment to the observance of internationally recognized core labour standards. The International Labour Organisation (ILO) is the competent body to set and deal with these standards, and we affirm our support for its work in promoting them. . . . We reject the use of labour standards for protectionist purposes, and agree that the comparative advantage of countries, particularly low-wage developing countries, must in no way be put into question."

A document prepared by the ILO secretariat reported on the discussion concerning the linking of labor standards to trade at the November 2001 Doha Ministerial Conference,

> Some 30 speakers made direct reference to the question of trade and labour standards. Many of these stated their firm opposition to linking trade negotiations to core labour standards. These included Cuba, Egypt, India, Malaysia, Pakistan, and Zimbabwe, while others, including the United Arab Emirates and Namibia, reiterated that the ILO was the competent body to set and deal with labour issues. South Africa stressed the need for a dialogue on social and labour standards and the world trade system, while Venezuela stressed the need for the WTO to include the social development dimension properly in the area of trade, and New Zealand wanted labour standards to be better integrated with trade agreements. Finally, some countries expressed their opposition to protectionist measures in this context (including Germany and Guatemala).[5]

The only reference to labor standards in the Declaration of the Doha Conference was succinct. It reads:

> We reaffirm our declaration made at the Singapore Ministerial Conference regarding internationally recognized core labour standards. We take note of work under way in the International Labour Organization (ILO) on the social dimension of globalization.

While the inclusion of a so-called social clause directly linking trade liberalization to WTO agreements is thus categorically rejected, labor issues have nevertheless been entering tangentially into the work of the WTO. In 2000, a panel of the WTO decided in the *Asbestos Case* between Canada and the European Communities (representing France) that France was entitled to prohibit the import of a certain type of asbestos from Canada on grounds of risk to health, under the provisions of Article XX(b) of the GATT, which permits exceptions to GATT rules in certain circumstances. In the absence of justification under Article XX, the panel concluded that France's barring of the asbestos would not have been acceptable under GATT rules.[6] The Appellate Body in April 2001 approved the finding of the panel but with different reasoning.[7] While the result has been welcomed by environmental and other groups, the panel's reasoning, in particular, was strongly criticized by some of these groups for reasons also not relevant here.

Although the *Asbestos Case* centered on health risk under Article XX, it also concerned labor issues, since the health risk associated with asbestos primarily affects workers; it is workers in the building trades who most frequently suffer serious health problems from exposure to asbestos. The EC attached two amicus curiae briefs to its submission, including one from the AFL-CIO. The panel report referred to ILO Convention No. 162 relating to the harmful effects of asbestos on workers and the need for replacement of its use wherever possible with alternative technologies. The panel, however, refused to permit a number of nongovernmental organizations to file amicus briefs, including Greenpeace International, World Wide Fund for Nature International, Ban Asbestos Network, the International Ban Asbestos Secretariat, the Foundation for International Environmental Law and Development, and the Center for International Environmental Law.

The Appellate Body subsequently published orderly procedures for amicus briefs in the *Asbestos Case* appeal: however, none of the some thirteen briefs filed by NGOs at that stage were accepted. The Appellate Body publication, indicating a theoretical openness to NGO amicus briefs, was severely criticized by member states at the WTO General Council meeting.[8]

Issues concerning the labeling of goods are increasingly raised at the WTO, particularly in the Committee on Trade and Environment where eco-labeling has been the subject of discussion. Labeling issues have also been discussed in the Committee on Technical Barriers to Trade. While discussions about eco-labeling are ongoing, the suggestion that labels relating to the labor conditions under which goods are produced might be acceptable under WTO rules has been summarily rejected.

In 2001 the Belgian government notified the WTO Committee on Technical Barriers to Trade that it had drafted a law that would create a label for goods and services produced in a socially responsible fashion that met criteria and standards recognized by the ILO. The draft law was intended to be voluntary, would not include sanctions, and would affect only Belgian goods and services. The Belgian government, through the EU, requested reactions from other WTO delegations. The reactions from ASEAN governments were particularly negative, but also those from Egypt, Brazil, and India. The Malaysian delegate said that the label was not a trade-related issue and that it would restrict trade, even if it were voluntary. It was a matter for the ILO and not the WTO.[9] The law has since been adopted by Belgium.

Despite the above developments, the issue of labor standards will continue to be raised at the WTO in various contexts, possibly in the context of investment issues newly being considered at the WTO. Pressure from consumer organizations, trade unions, and human rights activists will continue to focus on the WTO, believing that the reciprocity dispute settlement procedures at the WTO are more effective than efforts of other international organizations, including the ILO. In the meantime, however, the rejection of consideration of labor standards at the WTO has given new impetus to the work of the ILO.[10]

2. *North American Free Trade Agreement (NAFTA).* Other contributions to this volume discuss issues relating to trade and labor in Mexico, and I will therefore be brief on the subject of NAFTA, focusing on the inclusion of labor standards at the inception in the North American Agreement on Labor Cooperation (NAALC) appended to NAFTA.

Pressure primarily from American labor unions led to the adoption of NAALC and its attachment to NAFTA. The increasing tendency of American companies to move to the border regions of Mexico where parts imported from the United States could be assembled with low-wage Mexican employees and exported to the United States was already well underway in 1992 when the United States, Canada, and Mexico negotiated NAFTA. Proponents of the NAALC feared that more American jobs would be moving to Mexico, concluding that the Labor Agreement was necessary to assist workers in all three NAFTA countries.

An ironic aspect of the adoption of NAALC to improve labor rights was the observation that Mexico has ratified far more ILO labor conventions than the United States. Enforcement of its laws, however, has been uneven, and Mexico has frequently been criticized by the ILO for its failure to uphold labor standards. In 2001 the Report of the ILO Committee of Experts on the Application of Conventions and Recommendations made Observations (considered important criticisms) of Mexico concerning five conventions, including comments on the application of Convention No. 87 on freedom of association, stating that it had made similar observations over many years. It also made "direct requests" (less serious or less frequently reiterated comments) on five conventions. The deficiencies of the implementation of ILO standards by the United States have been referred to above.

The primary objective of the NAALC is the improvement in each party's territory of working conditions and the compliance with the enforcement of its *own* labor law. The emphasis is thus not on the application and enforcement of *internationally recognized labor standards* but on the application of each country's own labor laws. The phrase "internationally recognized labor standards" is nowhere found in the Agreement. The most important internationally recognized labor standards, freedom of association and collective bargaining, are referred to not as obligations of the parties but as "guiding principles that the Parties are committed to promote, subject to each Party's domestic law, but [that] do not establish common minimum standards for their domestic law. They indicate broad areas of concern where the Parties have developed, each in its own way, laws, regulations, procedures and practices that protect the rights and interests of their respective workforces" (Annex I of NAALC).[11]

A Conference Workshop, organized by the Cornell University School of Industrial and Labor Relations in 2000, reviewed the experiences under the NAALC, concluding that

> Results . . . have been mixed. Labor rights advocates have filed nine NAALC cases involving violations of workers' rights in Mexico, . . . five cases on violations in the United States and two cases on Canada. The procedures under the NAALC provide a good forum for public exposure of violations and the failure of labor law authorities to effectively enforce a country's laws, but they do not provide effective remedies. Remedial action is left to domestic authorities, which often fail to act.[12]

Efforts are ongoing to create a Free Trade Area of the Americas (FTAA) with the aim of arriving at an agreement no later than January 2005. The inclusion of a reference to labor standards is one of the many issues being raised in the negotiations.

C. Standards for Nonstate Actors: MNEs

1. *Non–Legally Binding Standards; International Organization: The ILO Tripartite Declaration on Multinational Enterprises and Social Policy.* The focus in international law on state action alone fails to address the influence of the activities of nonstate actors, such as multinational enterprises (MNEs), on labor and other social issues. This focus only on state activity by traditional international law has led to the increased adoption of voluntary non–legally binding guidelines and codes aimed at influencing corporate activities. An early effort by the United Nations to adopt a voluntary code on policies of transnational enterprises was aborted in the 1960s. Since that time, two nonbinding instruments have been adopted by international organizations setting standards for multinationals: the ILO has adopted a Tripartite Declaration and the OECD has adopted Guidelines. *The ILO Tripartite Declaration on Principles concerning Multinational Enterprises and Social Policy*, adopted in 1977, relates specifically to labor issues; the OECD Guidelines cover more general issues of social policy, as well as issues relating to investment.

The ILO Tripartite Declaration was adopted, not by the Annual ILO Conference composed of all ILO member states, but by the ILO Governing Body with a limited membership of governments and workers' and employers' organizations. Its adoption by the Governing Body and not the annual conference gives it a lesser standing than ILO conventions.

The ILO Declaration on Principles concerning Multinational Enterprises and Social Policy is "commended to the governments, the employers' and workers' organizations of home and host countries and to the multinational enterprises themselves." Its principles are intended "to guide" the governments, employers, and workers' organizations and multinational enterprises in adopting social policies. Paragraph 7 states that the principles are recommended for observation on a "voluntary basis." Use of the terms "encourage," "commended," and "recommended" in the Declaration emphasize its voluntary and nonbinding character. The norms contained in the Declaration concern employment, equality of opportunity, industrial relations, and collective bargaining.

The adoption of the Declaration as a voluntary nonbinding instrument was essentially due to political obstacles. The regulation of multinational enterprises remains today a controversial subject on which it is difficult to obtain agreement. Legal difficulties also created obstacles to adoption as a binding agreement: the definition of "multinational enterprise" was deliberately left vague, and attempting to affect the policies of nonstate entities, not subjects of international law, was also perceived as an obstacle.

The Declaration creates a procedure that requires governments to reply at regular intervals on its implementation, and also requests replies from workers' and employers' organizations. It provides for a system of interpretation of the provisions that has been rarely used. It also provides for the publication of a summary of the replies by the ILO. In March 2001, the ILO published the "Seventh Survey on the Effect Given to the Tripartite Declaration" based on replies from governments and employers' and workers' organizations to an ILO questionnaire.

The Report consists of two lengthy volumes and provides extensive detail on the activities of multinational enterprises in the countries from which replies were received. It deserves a detailed outside evaluation, but its length and the abundance of extensive footnotes referring to specific government reports militate against its use. The conclusions and recommendations of the Working Group of the Governing Body charged with recommending future work to the Governing Body on the basis of the secretariat Report are not analytical and are mostly routine recommendations for slight improvements in the organization of future surveys.

Nevertheless, even a cursory examination of the nonfriendly Report reveals frequent references to actions of multinational enterprises that are inimical to good labor and social policies. Many of the replies received, particularly from workers' organizations, apparently referred by name to particular enterprises; however, the names of specific multinationals are omitted in the ILO Report and replaced by the notation "(name given)" when a reply referred to a multinational by name. It is not clear why the ILO, a public international organization, feels called upon to omit part of the replies provided by its constituents, making it less useful to private efforts to focus attention on the activities of particular multinationals. Workers' organizations with access to the original replies could presumably provide such information. A positive step in enhancing the utility of the Declaration would be more complete reporting of the replies, including the names of multinational enterprises referred to, accompanied by an opportunity for named multinationals to reply, if desired. In the absence of the inclusion of the names of specific multinationals, the ILO might consider making the original complete reports available to the general public.

No independent extensive examination of the influence and effectiveness of the Tripartite Declaration appears to have been made. In 1994, the Chairman of the Workers' Group of the Governing Body observed,

> [T]he workers' group values the Tripartite Declaration of Principles on Multinational Enterprises and Social Policy as an important statement of good practice. However, there is no evidence that the Declaration has had substantial effect in influencing the behaviour of multinational enterprises. The procedural and other obstacles that have rendered very difficult the operation of the mechanism for interpretation of the Declaration have added to reservations concerning its credibility as a tool available to trade unionists in their dealings with multinationals.[13]

The timidity of the ILO twenty-two years ago when the Declaration was adopted was perhaps understandable, but it is less so today when the subject of labor rights and multinational enterprises is so clearly on the international agenda. At a minimum, the ILO might reconsider the manner in which the Report is written to make it more readable, more understandable, and more focused on issues. Since the Report is essentially a product of a Working Group of the Governing Body, the possibilities for improvement may be limited.

There is an indication that the ILO is interested in giving a larger profile to the Declaration. Until it does so, by bringing it to the attention of civil society, its effectiveness will probably remain limited.

The OECD Guidelines for Multinational Enterprises. The Organisation for Economic Co-operation and Development (OECD), headquartered in Paris, with thirty-three member states, has been referred to as a "rich man's club." As a follow-up to the Marshall plan, it originally consisted of the United States, Canada, and Western European nations. Today, the thirty-three member states are more diverse but consist primarily of major industrial powers; it now includes, inter alia, Turkey, Japan, and South Korea. Most multinational enterprises have their headquarters in member states of the OECD.

In 1976 the OECD Council of Ministers adopted the Declaration on International Investment and Multinational Enterprises. The overriding purpose of the Declaration was the promotion of international investment, but it also contained a section setting forth voluntary rules of conduct for MNEs, on the premise that the guidelines were necessary to "prevent misunderstanding and build an atmosphere of confidence and predictability between business, labour and governments."[14]

The Guidelines had some influence on conflicts over labor rights in Europe in the early days of their adoption, but eventually they began to be less important. They were amended several times and more completely revised in 2000. The revised Guidelines state that they are "recommendations jointly addressed by governments to multinational enterprises. They provide principles of good practice consistent with applicable laws. Observance of the *Guidelines* is voluntary and not legally enforceable."

Section IV of the Guidelines states that "enterprises should, within the framework of applicable law, regulations and prevailing labour relations and employment practices, respect freedom of association, contribute to the abolition of child labour, the elimination of all forms of forced labor, and not discriminate against employees on grounds of race, colour, sex, religion, political opinion, national extraction or social origin." The influence of the concept of "core labor standards" contained in the ILO Declaration on Fundamental Principles and Rights at Work is evident. The Preface refers to the development of an international legal and policy framework in which business should be conducted and mentions, specifically, the Universal Declaration of Human Rights, the ILO Declaration on Fundamental Principles, the Rio Declaration on the Environment, and the Copenhagen Declaration for Social Development.

In addition to the reference to the core labor standards, Section IV also states that enterprises should provide information to employee representatives as needed for meaningful negotiations, observe standards of employment and industrial relations not less favorable than those observed by comparable employers in the host country, and take adequate steps to ensure occupational health and safety in their operations. (Note: The failure to include occupational and safety standards in the ILO enumeration of core labor standards in the 1998 Declaration on Fundamental Principles and Rights at Work has been criticized by commentators.)

The Guidelines also state that reasonable notice should be given to employee representatives in case of closure of an entity involving collective dismissals and that enterprises should not threaten to transfer the whole or part of an operating unit from the country concerned nor transfer employees in order to influence negotiations unfairly. Paragraph II,2 is an innovation in the 2000 text. It states that enterprises should "[r]espect the human rights of their employees, as well as encourage the respect of human rights by business partners and in the societies in which they operate."

The Guidelines were originally adopted during the period when American multinationals were being criticized, inter alia, for their political role in Chile. "By setting out the rights and obligations of states and corporations, the architects of the code and its signatories hoped to create a stable and predictable framework. Firms would not abuse citizens or the environment in these countries, and governments would not try to control these firms," according to Susan Ariel Aaronson and James Reeves in *The European Response to Public Demands for Corporate Responsibility*.[15] The role of the Guidelines is intended to provide a political clarification process and not a legally enforceable means of contributing to the resolution of problems.

The Guidelines were revised in 2000 in an exceptionally open process. The advisory bodies to the OECD (the Business and Industry Advisory Council [BIAC] and the Trade Union Advisory Council [TUAC]) participated, as well as a Dutch nongovernmental organization charged with coordinating comments from civil society organizations. Comments on the draft Guidelines were received from a number of environmental and other groups, including Amnesty International.

The Guidelines require member states to develop a national contact point to publicize and implement the Guidelines and to resolve disputes over corporate behavior. Member states are to issue annual reports on their activities related to the Guidelines. It has been pointed out that

> The Guidelines' language is unclear on implementation. Some policymakers and observers disagree as to who can bring complaints about violations of the Guidelines; whether firms are responsible for the actions of their contractors and subcontractors. This last issue is extremely important because many companies have thousands of subcontractors. The Guidelines urge firms to be responsible for their contractors, but do not delineate how companies can be held responsible. Thus, the Guidelines leave much to the discretion of governments and multinational enterprises.[16]

The Guidelines are not well known in the United States, and the U.S. government has been little concerned with their implementation, in contrast to the attention paid to them in some Western European countries. A representative of the U.S. Council for International Business in a recent interview expressed the opinion that the Guidelines could be easily abused, and "business groups around the world are also worried about their ability to police their subcontracters."[17] Business groups emphasize that the Guidelines are voluntary.

The first Annual Report on the Guidelines was released in June 2001 and revealed that knowledge of the Guidelines and their implementation was mixed in OECD countries. Belgium, The Netherlands, and France were cited for their positive response to the Guidelines. Aaronson and Reeves have reported that the French, Swedish, and Belgian governments have cases under review at the national contact point. The Dutch Parliament in December 2000 requested the government to link the Guidelines to government subsidies for trade and investment and export credits. The linking of the Guidelines with the granting of government subsidies or guarantees in The Netherlands led to objections from the BIAC of the OECD, complaining that this action rendered the Guidelines obligatory.

Aaronson and Reeves have explained the lack of attention paid to the Guidelines in the United States as compared with the attention in European countries by referring to the different approaches to corporate social responsibility, to the differing "business culture." They argue that European businesses, such as Volkswagen and Nokia, have decided that corporate social responsibility makes good business. They also point out that European firms are more comfortable working with governments to improve social conditions and more comfortable in a regulated environment.[18]

Draft Declaration of UN Human Rights Sub-Commission. The UN Sub-Commission on Promotion and Protection of Human Rights, a subsidiary body of the Commission on Human Rights, has drafted a declaration on Fundamental Human Rights Principles for Business Enterprises that includes provisions on workers' rights. When officially adopted by the Sub-Commission, the Principles will be submitted to the governments making up the Human Rights Commission for endorsement. The Draft Principles state that although "governments have the primary responsibility to promote and protect human rights, transnational corporations and other business enterprises, as organs of society, are also responsible for promoting and securing . . . human rights."[19]

2. *Private Business Codes.* Enormous efforts are being undertaken by critics of multinational enterprises to encourage the adoption of codes by businesses pledging to promote good environmental, social, and labor policies. More attention has been given to the promotion of such codes in the United States than to the above described efforts of international bodies and organizations. These drafting efforts have been supplemented by the establishment of the Fair Labor Association and the Worker Rights Consortium in the United States to combat violations of workers' rights. Codes are useful in focusing attention on the issue of labor rights and documenting abuses, particularly, but not exclusively, in the U.S. context, where intergovernmental initiatives are not well known.

Another contribution to this volume focuses on these efforts, and provides a more comprehensive analysis of the codes. In the context of this presentation on the *form* that international labor standards should take, I refer here to criticisms concerning the efficacy of promoting labor standards through such private codes, which generally contain only passing reference to internationally adopted labor standards. Professor Philip Alston and James Heenan of the European University Institute, Florence, Italy, have compared these private initiatives with intergovernmental approaches and found them wanting:

> We. . . consider three ways in which these developments undermine the traditional conception of international labor standards. The first is the loss of a unified approach to the breadth and depth of labor standards as a variety of new actors attempt to establish labor standards regime. The resulting incoherence not only erodes the erstwhile universality of standards, but also allows the extent of the protection of workers rights in particular instances to be set according to the interests of the most powerful actors. . . .
>
> For the most part . . . they provide no substitute for the mobilizing power of internationally accepted rights, with their connotations of legitimacy, determinacy and solidarity. They generally discount the role of national governments and the responsibilities of other governments working through the international community and instead rely upon individual initiatives by key actors. . . .
>
> In particular, the consumer movement as it has manifested itself in a small range of cases working in or from the US is seen as the key to the future. . . . It is

touching to have such faith in consumers but it seems more likely that they will prove to be as fickle in their ability to maintain boycotts and selectivity as they are in their purchasing preferences.[20]

An ILO study of 215 available private codes of conduct found that a large number of private initiative codes were selective in the choice of labor issues referred to in the codes:

> The labour issues included in codes of conduct often, but not necessarily, appeared to reflect the nature of publicized labour problems in the various industry and service sectors. [Certain codes] tended to concentrate on child and forced labour. [T]hree-fourths of codes reviewed mentioned health and safety. . . . [T]wo-thirds . . . addressed the issue of employment discrimination. In contrast, relatively few codes addressed freedom of association and collective bargaining.[21]

Freedom of association is the most fundamental and important international labor standard; the failure to refer to it in the majority of private codes is thus a serious failing. The form here does not fulfill function.

Nicholas Howen, international human rights lawyer and former head of Amnesty International's legal office, while recognizing that voluntary codes have been a creative and essential step and that they will make any binding regulation more likely to succeed, believes that the time has come to "move beyond voluntarism" and "to draw together the strands of core human rights standards and voluntary accepted codes into a new and binding international regime."[22]

The "move beyond voluntarism" has also been echoed in an innovative and widely commented on publication by the International Council for Human Rights Policy. The 2002 publication entitled *Beyond Voluntarism: Human Rights and the Developing International Legal Obligations of Companies*, concluded:

> The debate on business and human rights has given too little attention to the role of law, and international human rights law in particular. Governments and companies have shown a distinct preference for voluntary approaches and self-regulation. However, it is increasingly clear that voluntary codes and non-official means of monitoring compliance should be complemented by legal rules and legal accountability. Voluntary approaches will remain ineffective and contested. In a world where business is increasingly global, only international law can provide this framework.[23]

Conclusion: Form and Function

How effective are the various forms of instruments purporting to strengthen international labor standards? Is it *form* that is primarily important? The conclusion of this paper is that form may indeed play a role, but that primary importance should be given to how well the *function* of protecting international labor standards is accomplished, whatever the form employed.

U.S. commentators frequently refer to the perceived ineffectiveness of the International Labor Organization and its efforts to promote international labor standards through conventions. It is evident that the ILO has not been as effective in influencing improvement of labor standards in the United States as it has been elsewhere. This may be due in part to the ILO, but the primary responsibility for failure to refer to international labor standards in the development of labor law in the United States is due to the U.S. government and the U.S. public and not to the effectiveness or lack of effectiveness of the ILO. There are numerous examples of the effectiveness of the ILO in other areas of the world.

Nevertheless, there are a number of aspects of the ILO that do not contribute to its effectiveness. The lack of participation by elements of civil society other than workers' and employers' organizations has been referred to previously. The dynamism of the human rights movement has not been felt at the ILO.[24] Labor organizations have thus not been assisted in improving the efficacy of the standards work at the ILO. Employers' organizations have often regarded their role at the ILO as one of "damage control," and the result has sometimes been a paralyzing stand-off between the labor organizations and the employers' group. Without changing the structure of the ILO, it seems that more could be done to enhance the contribution of human rights and other similar nongovernmental organizations to the work of the ILO.

Unlike the WTO, the ILO international labor standards system may not rely on reciprocity as an enforcement means for its conventions. To that extent, the ILO may be perceived as "ineffective"; it necessarily depends on member states to take seriously its International Labor Code. Its current efforts to emphasize "core labor standards," to collaborate with other international organizations in bringing more coherence to the protection of international labor standards, and to develop new initiatives such as the World

Commission on Globalization and Social Policy and the use of new instruments such as the Declaration on Fundamental Principals and Rights at Work are steps in the right direction.

The OECD Guidelines appear to be one of the most promising intergovernmental approaches to business social policy to date, despite their formulation in a non–legally binding instrument. They are linked to an important international organization whose members include nearly all major developed states and linked to investment issues. They were adopted through a process that relied on comments from civil society actors as well as governments, and they provide for a follow-up. But, most important, as explained above, they have been taken seriously by a number of the governments of member states in Europe. The involvement of civil society groups in their elaboration has attracted attention to the Guidelines. Their adoption was influenced by the ILO approach to core labor standards, and specific references are made in the Guidelines to ILO standards. Their effectiveness is primarily linked to the seriousness with which member states have taken the Guidelines, such as linking them to the grant of government subsidies.

It is the environment in which the Guidelines were adopted and the reaction of the governments to whom they are addressed that renders them effective. The *form* as a nonbinding guideline becomes less important than the *function* they fulfill.

Form and function are both important in the development of international labor standards, but the *function* and not the *form* remains primary.

Notes

Note: H. H. Richardson, an American architect of the last century, coined the maxim "Form Follows Function" to express his basic artistic philosophy. I have found it a particularly apt phrase for focusing on the issue of the form that international labor standards should take.

1. U.S. Report for the period ending Dec. 31, 1997, under Article 19 of the ILO Constitution on the position of national law and practice in regard to matters dealt with in Conventions 87 and 98.

2. "A Rights-Based Approach to Development, The ILO Experience, Stockholm," Oct. 18, 2000, unpublished memo in possession of author.

3. "Stopping Forced Labour," Global Report under the Follow-up to the ILO Declaration on Fundamental Principles and Rights at Work, ILO, 2001.

4. See Virginia A. Leary, "Human Rights at the ILO: Reflections on Making the

ILO More 'User-Friendly,'" in *The Modern World of Human Rights, Essays in Honor of Thomas Buergenthal*, ed. Antônio A. Cançado Trindade (San José, Costa Rica: Inter-American Institute of Human Rights, 1996), pp. 375–86.

5. ILO, GB.283-2002-02-0213-1-EN.

6. The Panel Report, WT/DS135/R is long and complex and involves a number of related issues that are not relevant here.

7. WT/DS135/AB/R, adopted Apr. 5, 2001. For a comprehensive treatment of the Appellate Body decision, see Gabrielle Marceau, "L'affaire 'CE—*Amiante*' et la nouvelle jurisprudence de l'Organe d'appel de l'OMC concernant les risques à la santé," *Annuaire canadien de droit international 2000*, 213–34.

8. See http://www.ciel.org/asbestospr.html.

9. See Carlos Lopez-Hurtado, "Labelling and WTO Law," study to be published in 2003 by the project on "Social Aspects of Trade Liberalization," Program for the Study of International Organization(s), Graduate Institute of International Studies, Geneva.

10. For an interesting but somewhat dated focus on the United States and WTO, see Brewster Grace, "In Focus WTO & Labor Standards," *Foreign Policy in Focus* 5 (Apr. 2000): 115.

11. Virginia A. Leary, "Workers' Rights and International Trade: The Social Clause (GATT, ILO, NAFTA, U.S. Laws)," in *Fair Trade and Harmonization*, ed. Jagdish Bhagwati and Robert E. Hudec, vol. 2 (Cambridge: MIT Press, 1996), pp. 177–230.

12. "Workers in the Global Economy," Project Papers and Workshop Reports, Cornell University School of Industrial and Labor Relations, Jan. 2001, p. 128.

13. Submission by William Brett, Chairman of the Workers' Group of the ILO Governing Body, to the Director-General, 1994, International Labour Conference.

14. See James Salzman, "Labor Rights, Globalization and Institutions: The Role and Influence of the Organisation for Economic Co-operation and Development," prepared for the Project on Social Aspects of Trade Liberalization, Program for the Study of International Organization(s), Graduate Institute of International Studies, Geneva, 2000.

15. Susan Aaronson and James Reeves, *The European Response to Public Demands for Corporate Responsibility* (National Policy Association, U.S.A., Feb. 5, 2002). The following section of this paper is primarily taken from the Aaronson and Reeves study.

16. Ibid., p. 12.

17. Interview of Aaronson and Reeves with the representative, ibid., pp. 14–15.

18. For an evaluation by a nongovernmental organization of the Guidelines, see Duncan McLaren, head of Policy and Research at Friends of the Earth, "Revised

OECD Guidelines—New Dawn or Old Wine?" *Human Rights and Business Matters* (autumn 2000/winter 2001): 3.

19. Draft for discussion, Draft Fundamental Human Rights Principles for Business Enterprises, Addendum 1, UN Doc. E/CN.4/Sub.2/2002/X/Add.l, E/CN.4/Sub.2/2002/WG.2/WP.1/ Add.1.

20. Philip Alston and James Heenan, "The Role of International Labor Standards within the Trade Debate: The Need to Return to Fundamentals," prepared for publication in 2004 by the Project on Social Aspects of Trade Liberalization, Program for the Study of International Organizations, Graduate Institute of International Studies, Geneva, Director, Virginia A. Leary; presented at the World Trade Forum 2001, World Trade Institute, Berne, Switzerland, Aug. 2001.

21. "Overview of Global Developments and Office Activities Concerning Codes of Conduct, Social Labelling and Other Private Sector Initiatives Addressing Labour Issues," Working Party on the Social Dimensions of the Liberalization of International Trade, GB.273/WP/SDL/l(Rev. l), 273rd Session, ILO Governing Body, Geneva. Nov. 1998.

22. Interview, "Human Rights and Business Matters," Amnesty International (UK) Business Group Newsletter, No. 5, 2001, p. 3.

23. *Beyond Voluntarism, Human Rights and the Developing International Legal Obligations of Companies*, ed. David Petrasek, International Council for Human Rights Policy, Versoix, Switzerland, Feb. 2002, p. 159.

24. See Leary, "Human Rights at the ILO."

Can Codes of Conduct Play a Role in Promoting Workers' Rights?

MICHAEL POSNER

JUSTINE NOLAN

In today's global economy, new mechanisms for protecting workers' rights and enforcing international labor standards are urgently needed. Multinational companies in pursuit of cheap labor—especially in labor-intensive, low-wage industries such as apparel and toys—now rely on complicated global webs of contractors and suppliers for their manufacturing. Violations of internationally recognized labor rights are common throughout this global assembly line, where no effective national or international framework for addressing these issues exists.

National governments have the primary responsibility for protecting human rights and ensuring that companies operating from or in their jurisdiction do not breach those standards. However, countries where human rights protections are most needed are often those least able to enforce them. In some countries, like Haiti or Cambodia, while laws may be on the books, governments devote few resources to enforcement. In other countries, like China or Vietnam, laws severely restrict freedom of association and preclude independent unions from operating. As a result, conditions in factories in much of the world are virtually unregulated, and violations of basic rights are endemic.

The growing chorus around the world about the downside of globalization is, in significant part, a reaction to what people in many parts of the world see as the unfair and unregulated conduct of multinational companies. The WTO has become a symbol of the problem, but it is not the place to start in the short term if one is building a practical model of accountability to protect workers. Although the International Labor Organization has developed a number of international conventions on labor rights issues, most of these assume action by national governments to regulate the practices of local employers. They have been less effective in situations where a government is unable or unwilling to sanction powerful commercial enterprises, which operate in other countries and jurisdictions.

So the question is: what can be done—and where is the leverage to create greater accountability? The void in enforcement of labor standards has brought codes of conduct to the fore as an additional way of trying to ensure accountability for workers' rights in the global economy. This article examines the role of voluntary codes of conduct and certification procedures in applying human rights norms to corporations (focusing primarily here on labor rights issues); then it discusses the characteristics that are important from the perspectives of procedure and monitoring; and finally it considers whether there is any potential interplay between private procedures and international, regional, and governmental procedures.

Role of Voluntary Codes of Conduct and Certification Procedures

Corporate codes of conduct and their certification procedures have been referred to as the "third way" to promote international labor rights, after government regulation and trade union organizing and collective bargaining.[1] Promoting global accountability for labor rights in today's borderless world means pursuing a multitude of methods that involve an array of nontraditional actors, and codes of conduct present a necessary additional model for promoting corporate accountability.

Codes of conduct assume many forms and roles. One function is in setting a standard to which companies publicly commit. Although codes are not generally legally enforceable, they are backed by the reputation of the company that adopts them, supported by the ever-present threat of media exposure. As such, codes can be useful advocacy tools for monitoring and assessing corporate performance, educating workers, mobilizing consumers and investors, and as a catalyst for debate about the need for stronger government and intergovernmental enforcement of labor rights.

These considerations are particularly strong for companies that rely heavily on the value of their brand to sell their product. Many of these companies have become, in essence, marketing and distribution companies that directly produce very little of what is sold under their brand name.[2] Protecting their brand name is critical to them, and as consumers in the United States and elsewhere become better informed about these issues, this creates possibilities to hold these companies accountable for activities throughout their entire supply chain. In the last five to ten years, aggressive campaigns in the United States by labor groups, nongovernmental organization (NGOs), and student activists have created an environment where companies, particularly brand-focused companies, have felt compelled to take responsibility for the labor practices of their principal contractors and suppliers. As a result, in some cases "voluntary" codes of conduct are not wholly discretionary, since they are sanctioned in varying measures by media, consumer, and investor pressure.[3]

Diversity of Codes

The proliferation of codes of conduct in the last decade has meant that hundreds of companies have now publicly committed to upholding basic labor standards.[4] These codes address issues such as child and forced labor, the right to organize, workplace health and safety conditions, wage and overtime issues, discrimination and harassment, and other persistent problems. But codes of conduct cannot provide meaningful improvements of working conditions unless they are effectively implemented and enforced. How to ensure that this happens systematically is one of the key challenges.

Part of that challenge is bound up in the fact that codes of conduct vary from company to company and among industries. While many codes are strong on more universally recognized labor rights, such as the prohibition of forced labor and child labor, and freedom from harassment and discrimination, the greatest differences are in standards on freedom of association and wages. Different standards on freedom of association are in part due to companies' practical concerns for their ability to ensure compliance when producing in countries such as China or Vietnam, where the rights of freedom of association and collective bargaining are severely restricted. Similarly, there is little consensus and a lot of debate about how to determine a standard floor for wages, particularly in countries where national minimum wages are at or below subsistence levels. In such cases, many companies prefer to adopt codes that simply require compliance with national laws and argue that applying human rights norms are not their business.[5] One challenge for activists, workers, and industry is to develop an environment where code standards ratchet upward rather than accepting the standards of the lowest common denominator.

Examples of codes and their certification procedures fall into several categories of varying effectiveness.[6] Codes are most effective when developed with wide support from industry, unions, and NGOs. The first category encompasses codes that are developed by companies for their individual use. These may be developed for a variety of reasons—activist pressure, brand preservation, and/or recognition of their responsibility to respect basic human rights. Such codes vary widely in the commitments they offer to protect human rights and the language they use.[7] Some will require compliance with the code from the company's subcontractors and suppliers, and others will remain quiet on this crucial issue.[8] Such company-specific codes have come under fire for both the lack of consultation in the development of standards with stakeholders external to the company and questions raised about the credibility of their internal code-monitoring systems, because of lack of transparency and independence.

In the wake of this failing, various industry or trade associations grouped together to develop common standards and reporting mechanisms. Examples of this second category include the 1996 framework agreement of the International Federation of Football Associations (FIFA) to prevent the use of child labor in the production of soccer balls,[9] and the more recent Worldwide Responsible Apparel Production (WRAP)[10] initiative to monitor working conditions in apparel members' factories. Again these closed-door initiatives have given rise to complaints about a lack of transparency and independence in reporting mechanisms and raise questions about the credibility of such standards when they are dictated solely at the discretion of industry.

The development of a third category involving multistakeholder codes and external monitoring initiatives now lies at the heart of the corporate accountability movement and will be the true test of the effectiveness of codes and monitoring. These multistakeholder code and certification initiatives involve an external party, such as an NGO, working in tandem with industry to develop standards and reporting mechanisms to monitor corporate compliance. The advantage of these efforts is the move to standardize and develop consensus among a variety of stakeholders—albeit on a limited basis initially—regarding the basic principles for ensuring greater respect of human rights in the workplace. Some of the better-known initiatives in the apparel industry include the Fair Labor Association (FLA),[11] Social Accountability International (SAI),[12] the Workers Rights Consortium (WRC),[13] and the Ethical Trading Initiative (ETI).[14]

The fourth category involves codes developed by international institutions with direct or indirect government involvement. Examples include the Organisation for Economic Co-operation and Development (OECD) Guidelines on Multinational Enterprises,[15] and the more recent efforts by the United Nations to promote its Global Compact.[16] Such codes are generally fairly broadly expressed and have limited reporting and transparency mechanisms.

Characteristics of Effective Monitoring

While codes can set valuable standards, they are meaningless if they are not implemented. Credible procedures for their monitoring and verification are crucial. Yet there is no one way to do this, and there are differing opinions on how it should be achieved. Private monitoring efforts (as opposed to government labor inspections) by groups as diverse as NGOs or commercial auditing firms are a relatively recent phenomenon, and the "social" monitoring industry is still in the early stages of evolution. This is reflected in the diversity of current approaches to monitoring, particularly in the apparel and footwear industries.

Almost all major apparel and footwear brands now outsource production entirely to extensive networks of suppliers, contractors, subcontractors, and sub-subcontractors. The supply chain is so extensive that some companies claim ignorance of the exact makeup of their supply chain. These chains are even more enigmatic in the apparel industry, given the potential mobility of production sites and wide range of producers.

As a result, the challenges to monitoring are great. The question is who, how, what, and where to monitor along the supply chain? Monitoring initiatives have chosen various avenues for meeting these challenges, with some focusing on systematically monitoring and certifying factories, others on monitoring entire supply chains, and still others on conducting independent investigations and verification on a case-by-case basis.

Beyond these differences in approaches to monitoring, there are substantial methodology questions involved, such as: Who should do the monitoring? Are for-profit auditing firms appropriate inspectors of social conditions? How can more nonprofit and local groups be empowered to independently monitor factory conditions? What should be monitored? Is the code of conduct enough? How much should monitoring also verify compliance with local labor law and ILO conventions? How regularly should monitors visit factories? How many announced and unannounced visits to a factory are appropriate? How should monitors establish their independence? When should monitoring reports be confidential for the workers, unions, management, and companies, and when should they be made public? What should the relationship between a monitor, unions, management, and workers consist of? There remains a long list of important and still unanswered questions on this topic.

In the absence of any standardized monitoring protocols, there are four crucial characteristics that monitoring procedures should incorporate in order to be credible:

- Applying measurable, meaningful standards
- Independence of monitors
- Transparency in reporting
- Incorporation of a local NGO and union dimension

With the incorporation of these four components, monitoring can potentially be an effective tool for building the visibility of labor rights and increasing corporate accountability.

Measurable, Meaningful Standards

A major challenge to the credibility of private monitoring initiatives is applying a consistent and credible standard both to ensure consistency in what is being monitored and to the monitoring procedures themselves. Without at least an industrywide standard, monitors assessing a factory where a number of brands are producing are often challenged to monitor a variety of codes simultaneously along with assessing compliance with local labor laws and international conventions. In the absence of universally accepted standards, what often results is a haphazard composite of standards a monitor chooses to verify that will change depending on the preferences of the company and the country in which the manufacturing takes place.

Arguably, at a minimum ILO's (1998) Declaration on Fundamental Principles and Rights at Work should form the basis against which conditions are measured. The Declaration proclaims four basic principles drawn from core ILO conventions as applicable to all nations, regardless of their level of economic development:

- freedom of association and the effective right of collective bargaining;
- the prohibition of forced or compulsory labor;
- the effective abolition of child labor; and
- the elimination of discrimination with respect to employment or occupation.

The declaration is applicable to all members of the ILO, regardless of whether or not they have ratified the "seven fundamental ILO conventions"[17] that correspond to these principles. These seven treaties reflect merely the most basic principles of labor rights—a number of other conventions cover issues such as health and safety in the workplace. However, while applicable to member states these standards do not directly obligate the activities of corporations. In addition these conventions are fairly broadly expressed and often need further clarification in relation to specific labor conditions on the ground. The Declaration and conventions per se are not presented in language that allows them to be readily measured in quantifiable and objective terms; thus they are interpreted in codes that may vary in the manner in which they present them.

Without standardized monitoring methodology, it is particularly difficult to assess the credibility and accuracy of monitor findings in the absence of a recognized procedure for monitoring different aspects of codes. The vagueness of codes often means that they are open to interpretation and verified according to that monitor's specific methodology. As a result, there are few meaningful measures that can be compared to other brands and monitor findings.[18] A significant challenge in the next few years is to transform the vague standards of disparate corporate codes into industry standards that can be used to specifically measure performance on a comparable basis across products, companies, and countries. One recent example of the increased demand for this type of standardized measurement (in this case on a country by country basis rather than company specific) is the action taken by the California Public Employees' Retirement System (CalPERS) to restrict its investments in emerging markets. One major factor in the CalPERS analysis was countries' performance on workers rights issues. This involved comparing twenty-seven countries based on factors such as their ratification of ILO conventions, strength of domestic labor laws, institutional capabilities to enforce those laws, and effectiveness in practice in addressing workers rights.[19]

Independence

Independence of monitors from the companies and facilities that they are inspecting is vital. The difficulty in monitoring recently experienced by some groups raises questions about the accuracy of their findings and strengthened the case for independent monitors whose allegiances are not with the company but rather with the workers.[20] The ideal independent monitors may, in many situations, be local nonprofit groups who are familiar with local dynamics of the country or locale of the factory, who speak the languages of workers and management, and who are able to monitor factories on a more consistent and regular basis. However codes can be complicated instruments that cover a diverse range of subjects, and an organization that is adept at interviewing and gaining the trust of workers may not have the requisite experience to audit a factory's health and safety performance.

Furthermore, independence of monitors is not solely independence from companies but also from other important players, particularly government, unions, and advocacy groups. Independent monitors have the unique task of actively defining their work as distinct and different from the work of unions, their local labor ministries or departments, and activists. If they fail to do this, they risk impeding the work of these other agents or becoming substitutes for them. If anything, monitoring must be an additive and be complementary to and reinforce the work of these agents.

Independence in monitoring has also played into questions about how the monitors should be paid. Should companies pay the monitors directly? If so, does it reflect on their independence? While there is little question about the fact that companies have an obligation to fully pay for the service monitors provide, the question may be more one of perception, and thus in some cases payments for monitoring are channeled through a third-party intermediary or paid into a general trust as per the Rugmark model.[21]

Additional issues concerning independence include questions about how monitors should be chosen. The FLA, for example, has been criticized for a lack of independence in monitoring. Recently, however, the FLA adopted substantial changes in its monitoring system. Whereas previously the companies were able to select their inspector from a list of FLA accredited monitors (which entail both international and local nonprofit groups), it is now established that the FLA, as an independent third party, will be responsible for selecting and paying the monitor.[22]

Transparency

Information is key to advancing workers' rights worldwide. But information about factory locations and working conditions is scarce. A decade ago, companies generally refused to disclose any information about their supply chain practices and would not open the factory doors to external observers. Gradually this is changing, albeit on a very limited basis and still largely by brand-focused companies, as companies responding to immense public and consumer pressure begin to recognize that increased transparency is a required part of business.[23]

Now, as many companies adopt code certification procedures and some engage in multistakeholder monitoring initiatives, some companies have not only begun to open their doors to external scrutiny but also have succumbed to public reporting on their conditions and a few on disclosure of factory locations. While these are important advances, it is so far only a drop in the bucket to building transparency on labor conditions. Absent from these advances are many of the largest retail companies that control a significant portion of the industry's profits in apparel but are lagging far behind on transparency advances or participation in multistakeholder initiatives.

The nature of an unregulated, mobile supply chain, operating worldwide in areas with weak labor enforcement and trade-union activity, makes the pursuit of information particularly challenging. Information is the engine behind the corporate accountability movement. By making labor conditions publicly visible, greater transparency has the dynamic ability to pressure companies to remedy their actions and in turn, build a common floor for labor standards.

In light of this, the credibility of external monitoring today is in many respects contingent on transparency in reporting. While advances in transparency must come from the top by pushing for corporate disclosure, they must also come from the bottom. In Guatemala, the independent monitoring group COVERCO[24] has set an important precedent in setting the terms for transparency in their monitoring contracts with Liz Claiborne, Gap, and, recently, the FLA. COVERCO considers it essential to set the terms of any monitoring effort they undertake to ensure their ownership of the information collected and their right to publish pertinent information from monitoring reports.[25] The next logical step in transparency could come from companies themselves, with businesses that have already undertaken systematic monitoring programs disclosing the results of those programs directly to the public.[26] The key element to watch for will be disclosure as a matter of business routine, rather than only in response to a crisis or specific criticism.

Incorporating a Local NGO and Union Dimension

Meaningful engagement with local unions and NGOs—whether they be community-based organizations, legal services organizations, women's groups, labor rights groups, religious groups—with a real interest in bettering working conditions is essential to ensuring the credibility of monitoring procedures. The right and ability of workers to organize is necessarily one of the most fundamental issues that need to be focused on in advancing the workers rights debate. The active involvement of unions and NGOs in all aspects of workplace issues and improvements is absolutely essential to advancing this right in real ways on the ground. These are the actors who are intimately familiar with local dynamics and working conditions and who are capable of ensuring that codes and monitoring bring real changes. To date, these actors have often been left out of the code monitoring equation—largely because codes and monitoring procedures have been conceived in the North—but their inclusion is essential in order to democratize regulation and enforcement.

The first important piece is by empowering more local NGOs to become independent monitors. As it stands now, there are very few examples of groups working in this capacity. To do this will require increased information sharing, and assistance in building coalitions and increasing the capacity of groups to undertake these activities. The Central American experience of COVERCO in Guatemala, GMIES in El Salvador,[27] the Independent Monitoring Team (EMI) in Honduras, and the newly formed coalition of Central American and Dominican groups, the Regional Initiative for Social Responsibility and Jobs with Dignity, is illustrative of how this process can be set in motion in engaging new groups in monitoring.

Beyond becoming monitors themselves, there are various other important roles that local NGOs and unions can and should play in global monitoring initiatives. They can engage as local permanent watchdogs of ongoing labor conditions in nearby factories, and in a sense act as "monitors of the monitors." This is a valuable role to play given that at present most monitors are not locally based, but come in from the outside for brief interludes a couple of times a year. Conditions change so frequently that it is crucial there are constant eyes on the ground monitoring these developments and able to assess the validity of monitor inspections.

Similarly, local groups have a valuable role to play in publicizing information to the outside world about problems in factories as they arise. Many code certification initiatives include provisions for third-party complaints, which are complaints lodged by anyone other than workers or companies. Workers in these factories rarely have proper, confidential channels for making complaints about their working conditions. Similarly, there are few channels for the communication of complaints of labor problems among key parties, such as unions, NGOs, companies, monitors, factory management and retailers, and so forth. Third-party complaint systems can potentially serve as a useful tool for creating these kinds of channels so that problems can be identified and addressed.

Advocacy also continues to be key. Beyond engagement in corporate code initiatives, it is crucial that local governments are pressured to improve their labor laws and enforcement capabilities. Local groups can use codes of conduct and monitoring reports as leverage over inactive governments and to challenge their commitment to enforcing labor standards when companies may be doing more. National governments retain fundamental responsibility for advancing labor rights, and if codes or any other commitments undertaken by companies can be used to facilitate this it should be encouraged. Reform at a regulatory level for the enforcement of workers rights is a long term goal—at regional, national, and international levels—and should be complementary to any efforts focusing on specific corporate practices.

Finally, local NGOs and unions can also play a role in building the capacity and knowledge of workers and management to ensure greater respect for labor rights. Improving conditions inside factories first requires that management and workers understand the legal and regulatory parameters within which they work. NGOs and unions can conduct "know your rights" training programs for workers and management under corporate codes, national law, and international conventions.

Potential Interplay between Private Procedures and International, Regional, and Governmental Procedures

Codes of conduct and monitoring schemes have developed in large part as a response to the void in international and national enforcement of labor standards. Yet activists cannot press for change in every industry and at all times, and it follows that as a long-term proposition, all the relevant actors— industry, NGOs, and unions, along with government and international institutions, have to combine their efforts to work toward effective national and international strategies to enforce labor standards.

Multinational intergovernmental institutions—notably the United Nations, the World Trade Organization, the International Labor Organization—need to work to strengthen their relationships, to coordinate and focus their efforts and strategies for this purpose. However, the discussion about the most effective approach to this issue is far from being settled, and the seemingly inevitable reform of the major intergovernmental institutions will take years to effect. The current political feasibility of establishing international legally binding norms governing corporate conduct with respect to human rights is doubtful. In the meantime new mechanisms of private governance and certification can exist alongside and within national and international efforts both binding and nonbinding, such as the North American

Free Trade Agreement or the OECD Guidelines Codes of conduct; their certification procedures can provide an additional level of scrutiny to draw attention to uneven standards and highlight inadequate national and international enforcement mechanisms. They can be used to highlight the disparity of standards between countries and act as an impetus for the debate about the applicability of universality of human rights, particularly workers rights.

With the rise of private governance initiatives, companies, unions, and NGOs have acquired invaluable expertise with respect to the actual enforcement of labor rights. There is an opportunity for government and intergovernmental initiatives to build on and draw from that experience or even foster such initiatives. The example of the development of the Apparel Industry Partnership, now the Fair Labor Association in the apparel and footwear industries, is indicative of the useful role government can play in encouraging such efforts. It is also encouraging to note some recent initiatives involving the ILO of how partnerships between local government or government agencies, industry, union leaders, and the ILO can provide a strong framework for tackling endemic labor problems. Its efforts to address the problem of child labor in the soccer ball industry in Pakistan and workers' rights abuses in the apparel industry in Cambodia are indicative of how public/private efforts can merge to create a stronger rights enforcement regime.

Case Study of the Apparel Industry: AIP/FLA

In recent years, consumers, human rights groups, and labor organizations have been at the forefront of demands for corporate accountability, pressing U.S. multinational companies to take responsibility for the conditions in which their contracted workers manufacture their products. Many of these efforts, oriented toward individual companies, demand stricter self-regulation by companies and monitoring of workplace conditions by independent experts. Sometimes consumer boycott campaigns are launched. While this movement has served as a catalyst for the proliferation of new voluntary workplace codes of conduct, as noted above, these codes vary widely in the degree of enforcement and monitoring and, ultimately, meaningful protection for the workers themselves.

Apparel and footwear companies first began introducing internal codes of conduct and accompanying internal compliance monitoring plans over a decade ago, starting with Levis in 1991, and followed by other high-profile brands such as Nike, Reebok, Gap, and Liz Claiborne shortly thereafter. In the mid-1990s in the United States, the profile of "sweatshop practices" employed by U.S. companies was on the rise. Accusations of the use of child labor in Honduras and enslaved workers in El Monte, California, fueled the debate. In 1996 the Clinton administration brought together an informal group of apparel and footwear companies, labor unions, and human rights, consumer, and religious organizations called the Apparel Industry Partnership (AIP). Through the AIP, these disparate groups developed a code of conduct and monitoring principles aimed at establishing a common industry standard to enforce labor rights. The AIP then began to plan for a successor organization that would implement and monitor the code of conduct.

In November 1998, a number of the AIP partners formed a new nonprofit entity, the Fair Labor Association (FLA). Key provisions of the FLA agreement and its Workplace Code of Conduct call for elimination in the workplace of forced and child labor, harassment, abuse, and discrimination. The code also enforces health and safety standards, recognizes the right of employees to freedom of association and collective bargaining, sets wage standards, imposes limitations on work hours, and establishes requirements regarding overtime compensation. The FLA accredits monitors (including nongovernmental organizations) to conduct independent inspections of factories. Over time, it will assess companies for compliance with its standards and serve as a source of information for the public about working conditions.

The FLA represents a new model involving business, government, U.S. universities (and their licensed companies), and nongovernmental organizations. The U.S. government has also played an important role in initiating and supporting the efforts of these groups. While the FLA is continuing to evolve, it is an important example of how disparate groups can come together, and it harnesses the combined power of government, business, and nongovernmental organizations to enforce labor rights.

Efforts to Eliminate Child Labor in the Soccer Ball Industry in Pakistan

International organizations also have a valuable role to play in instituting reforms where national governments may be less willing to take action. This example of action taken in Pakistan of a consortium of organizations illustrates the value of establishing multistakeholder partnerships to address seemingly intractable labor problems.

In 1997, the ILO, UNICEF, and the Sialkot Chamber of Commerce and Industry (SCCI) signed a Partners' Agreement on a joint project to prevent and eliminate child labor under the age of fourteen in the football manufacturing industry in Sialkot, Pakistan.[28] At that time, Sialkot was the center of Pakistan's football-producing industry, producing nearly 75 percent of the world's hand-stitched soccer balls. At the time of the Agreement's signing, almost 20 percent of the workforce was made up of children.

The Sialkot Partners' Agreement followed a campaign by the International Confederation of Free Trade Unions and the World Federation of Sporting Goods, which includes more than fifty brand names, to highlight the use of child labor in the production of soccer balls by the International Federation of Football Associations.

The Agreement provides for soccer ball manufacturers to establish a comprehensive internal monitoring system, including training programs for this purpose; to agree to independent monitors to verify compliance; and to work closely together with the ILO and other organizations in a "Social Protection Program," to remove children from conditions of child labor with the effort to provide such children with educational and other opportunities. The Social Protection Program provides educational opportunities and other support services to children and their families, including nonformal education, vocational training, and facilities microcredit. This aspect is handled by an NGO. The Agreement has since formed the basis for similar efforts in the carpet industry in Pakistan and in the football-stitching industry in India.

While the project still has a long way to go in eliminating child labor,[29] it is also illustrative of how public/private efforts can be combined to address abuses in the workforce. The efforts undertaken by the ILO in Pakistan to initiate these measures were a step up from the more traditional role it had often assumed in the past as an observer and reporter of labor problems. Likewise, the role it has recently assumed in Cambodia in monitoring apparel factories expands this role even further and provides much needed support for both corporations and the Cambodian government in addressing labor abuses in the local apparel industry.

Tackling Problems in Cambodia's Apparel Factories

A constant criticism of the ILO since its inception has been its limited ability to enforce compliance with its standards and its reluctance to tackle hands-on monitoring at a corporate or factory-specific level. In Cambodia it has recently begun to explore an expansion of its more traditional roles, by agreeing to monitor the U.S.-Cambodia Textile Quota Agreement.[30] This agreement, established in 1999 for a three-year period and recently renewed, sets an export quota for garments from Cambodia to the United States and provides for reduced tariff rates on U.S. exports to Cambodia. Renewal of the agreement was conditioned on the improved enforcement of labor standards in Cambodia's garment sector, promising a possible 14 percent annual increase in Cambodia's export entitlements to the United States.

The agreement referred to the implementation of a program to improve working conditions in the apparel industry, in accordance with international labor standards as well as the Cambodian labor law.[31] The U.S.-Cambodia Agreement has been credited with creating a large increase in exports to, and imports from, Cambodia. The value of textile and apparel imports increased by almost 200 percent in the first two years of the Agreement. Furthermore, the labor incentives clause in the Agreement has, at least in part, caused the growth in U.S. purchasing from Cambodia to be accompanied by improvements in working conditions for Cambodians.[32]

The ILO played a key role in designing this project, in consultation with the Cambodian Labor Ministry, the Garment Manufacturers Association, and the Cambodian trade union movement.[33] The ILO also assumed a groundbreaking role as a factory-labor monitor of the trade agreement. The establishment of both the initial agreement and the monitoring program is also reflective of the strength and voice of civil society in Cambodia. Labor abuses have long been rampant in its apparel industry, and there was a steady push for efforts to address them by harnessing the power of unions, NGOs, employers, government, and the ILO. The results of the ILO's monitoring efforts are reflected in the First and Second Synthesis Reports on the Working Conditions Situation in Cambodia's Garment Sector, published in November 2001 and April 2002, respectively.[34] Both reports indicate that there continue to be a multiplicity of labor problems in Cambodia's garment industry, particularly with respect to overtime hours and payment of wages, but the transparency of the findings and broad involvement of factories in this monitoring effort continues to be encouraging.

Conclusion

The strength and influence of voluntary codes of conduct are on the rise but are still very dependent on significant investment being undertaken in their monitoring and enforcement procedures. Codes are useful in highlighting standards to be met, but there must start to be greater consistency in the principles they espouse and a stronger movement to develop them in concert with a variety of stakeholders on an industry basis rather than continuing the proliferation of internal company specific codes. The adoption of codes and involvement in multistakeholder monitoring mechanisms must also be taken up on a broader basis throughout a range of industries and not just left to the lead of the brand-focused companies.

Codes of conduct and monitoring mechanisms alone cannot adequately address the abuses rampant in many of these industries, but they do have a role to play in linking together diverse stakeholders from the local, national, and international scene to promote greater respect for labor rights. While they should never detract from the responsibility of national governments and international agencies to address these issues, they are proving to be a useful advocacy tool for monitoring corporate performance by maintaining pressure on companies to protect workers' rights. The challenge is for all stakeholders to combine forces to continue this momentum so that the progress built up through the development of codes and certification procedures can pave the way for the development of eventual international legally binding norms to govern the behavior of corporations and human rights.

Notes

1. Lance Compa, "Wary Allies," *American Prospect* 12, no. 12 (July 2–16, 2001): 8–12.

2. Nike is now estimated to spend approximately $1 billion per year to market their brand image; O'Rourke, Dara. Power-point presentation "Codes and Monitoring in Global Supply Chains." Feb. 7, 2002. Puebla, Mexico.

3. Paul Redmond, "Sanctioning Corporate Responsibility for Human Rights," *Alternative Law Journal* 27, no. 1 (Feb. 2002): 23–28.

4. K. Gordon and M. Miyake, "Deciphering Codes of Corporate Conduct: A Review of Their Contents," Working Papers on International Investment, Number 1999/2. Organisation for Economic Co-operation and Development. Nov. 1999. This OECD study was the result of an investigation of 246 voluntary codes collected "from business and non-business contacts which OECD Member governments helped identify" (p. 8). Out of this set of codes, they found that 118, or 49 percent, of them were issued by individual companies (mostly multinationals), while 34 percent were industry and trade association codes, 2 percent issued by an international organization, and 15 percent by partnership of stakeholders (mainly NGOs and unions) (p. 9). See also Gary Gereffi et al., "The NGO-Industrial Complex," *Foreign Policy*, no. 127 (July–Aug.): 56–65, which states: "Global Reporting Initiative estimates that more than 2,000 companies voluntarily report their social, environmental, and economic practice and performance" (p. 57).

5. L. Compa and T. Hinchcliffe-Darricarrere, "Enforcing International Labor Rights through Corporate Codes of Conduct," *Columbia Journal of Transnational Law* 33 (1995): 663 at 686.

6. See Gereffi et al., "The NGO-Industrial Complex," pp. 56–65, which refers to first (internal), second (industry), third (external, i.e. NGO), and fourth (government or multilateral) party certification methods.

7. The Body Shop's Trading Charter (1994) specifically refers to their commitment to respect human rights "as set out in the Universal Declaration of Human Rights."

8. Gordon and Miyake, "Deciphering Codes of Corporate Conduct." This study of 246 voluntary codes found that "41.2 percent of the codes dealing with labor issues mention obligations on sub-contractors or other business partners" (p. 14). In twelve cases the codes "threaten" to terminate the contract with the supplier or contractor if their standard is not met throughout their supply chain (p. 26).

9. World Monitors; http://www.worldmonitors.com/showarticle.cfm?Key=1639 for information regarding the establishment of a new international monitoring body for child labor in Sialkot, Pakistan.

10. http://www.wrapapparel.org/infosite2/index.htm.

11. www.fairlabor.org.

12. http://www.cepaa.org.

13. http://www.workersrights.org.

14. http://www.ethicaltrade.org.

15. Guidelines for Multinational Enterprises, in Organisation for Economic Co-

operation and Development, "Declaration on International Investment and Multi-national Enterprises." The Guidelines were first adopted in 1976. They are most easily accessed at http://www.itcilo.it/english/actrav/telearn/global/ilo/guide/oecd.htm#text. Some background on the guidelines is provided at http://www.oecdobserver.org/news/fullstory.php/aid/446/The_trust_business.html. The OECD guidelines may be appreciated as a comprehensive instrument for corporate behavior that enjoys the broad endorsement of governments as well as social partners. However, the language is often too broad and lacks details. For instance, the Guidelines merely "encourage" the disclosure of ethical standards, which is subject to "due regard . . . of costs, busi-ness confidentiality and other competitive concerns." Moreover, there is no effective mechanism to ensure enforcement of the standards.

16. www.unglobalcompact.org.

17. The seven are: Forced Labor Convention (No. 29); Freedom of Association and Protection of the Right to Organize Convention (No. 87); Right to Organize and Collective Bargaining Convention (No. 98); Equal Remuneration Convention (No. 100); Abolition of Forced Labor Convention (No. 105); Discrimination (Employ-ment and Occupation) Convention (No. 111); and Minimum Age Convention (No. 138).

18. Dara O'Rourke, Charles Sabel, and Archon Fung, "Ratcheting Labor Stan-dards: Regulation for Continuous Improvement in the Global Workplace." May 2, 2000. http://web.mit.edu/dorourke/www/PDF/RLS21.pdf.

19. http://www.calpers.ca.gov/invest/emergingmkt/verite.pdf (accessed Mar. 29, 2002).

20. An illustrative example is provided by the recent experience of auditing firm PriceWaterhouse Coopers, which recently bowed out of the "social monitoring" in-dustry after being subject to intense criticism about their approach.

21. http://www.rugmark.org.

22. See http://www.fairlabor.org/html/FLA_PR_Apr._2002.html for a summary of the changes established by the FLA in Apr. 2002. Major changes are focused on in-creasing the effectiveness, independence, and transparency of the monitoring proc-ess. All monitoring by independent external monitors will be unannounced, and the FLA will select the facilities to be monitored and contract with and pay accredited monitors to conduct these audits. The FLA also committed to publicly disclose facil-ity-specific information on each facility that is independently externally monitored. Information to be disclosed on its website will include the name of the company, the nature, size, and country/region of the facility, the identity of the monitor, the date and length of the monitoring visit, summaries of compliance found and noncompli-ance found, a summary of remediation instituted, and the status of the remediation.

23. See, for example, the factory disclosure database of the Workers' Rights Consortium at http://www.workersrights.org/fdd.asp and that of the Fair Labor Association at http://www.fairlabor.org/html/disclosure_db.asp.

24. The Commission for the Verification of Corporate Codes of Conduct; www.coverco.org.

25. Maquila Solidarity Network. "Memo: Codes Update Number 9," Nov. 2001. www.maquilasolidarity.org.

26. This has occurred in only a few very limited cases so far. One example is the 1999 report released by Reebok International—Peduli Hak ("Caring for Rights"), examining conditions for workers in two Indonesian factories producing Reebok brand footwear. See http://www.reebok.com/Reebok/US/HumanRights/text-only/history.

27. Grupo de Monitoreo Independiente de El Salvador, GMIES; www.gmies.org.sv.

28. The Agreement is available at http://www.itcilo.it/english/actrav/telearn/global/ilo/guide/ilosoc.htm.

29. The Pakistan Newswire reported Mar. 15, 2002, that while violations of labor regulations in the manufacturing center of Sialkot have been on the increase, "officers and functionaries of labor department appear to be silent spectators and quite indifferent to the situation." World Monitors; http://www.worldmonitors.com/showarticle.cfm?Key=1958 (accessed Mar. 28, 2002).

30. See, for instance, the press release of Jan. 7, 2002, by the office of the U.S. Trade Representative and also http://www.lchr.org/labor_new/fr.htm.

31. Article 10B of the U.S.-Cambodia Textile Agreement.

32. In his testimony to the U.S. Senate Committee on Finance on June 26, 2001, Mark Levinson, Director of Policy and Research at UNITE (Union of Needletrades, Industrial and Textile Employees), stated that "labor activists in Cambodia report that the Agreement is responsible for opening some space for workers and unions to assert their rights."

33. The project aimed to provide assistance in the drafting of new laws and regulations; increase awareness of workers' rights among both workers and employers; support and strengthen workers and employers, and their organizations, to realize these rights; and support and strengthen government's enforcement capacity.

34. A copy of the reports can be found at http://www.ilo.org/public/english/dialogue/index.htm and http://www.ilo.org/public/english/dialogue/cambodia.htm under the chapter "Featured sites." See also the ILO press release at http://www.ilo.org/public/english/bureau/inf/pr/2001/50.htm#note1.

Free Trade and Labor Relations in México

ENRIQUE DE LA GARZA TOLEDO

Introduction

Over the past twenty years, several developments in economic conditions and economic policy have challenged traditional labor market conditions and arrangements in Mexico. Of these changes, the effect of the North American Free Trade Agreement (NAFTA) on labor market outcomes and institutions is of particular interest. This essay examines changes in labor conditions (including worktime, wages, bonuses, work qualification), labor relations (labor flexibility and collective bargaining), and pressures to transform domestic labor law since the beginning of NAFTA. The paper accords particular attention to the influence of NAFTA's labor side accord and the transformation of corporatist unionism in Mexico during the 1990s. It develops the viewpoint that labor conditions, labor relations, and unionism are impacted by both open markets and old and new institutions.

Background

NAFTA did not initiate the opening of Mexico to trade. Trade liberalization policies had been in place since the mid-1980s, and by 1986 Mexico had already joined GATT. In addition, a trend toward privatization, a substantial decline in government investment spending, and an emphasis on inflation control over and above economic growth, all were part of the background to NAFTA. The signing of NAFTA was simply the peak of this process (NAALC, 1998a). In June 1990, the Mexican and U.S. presidents declared that they would sign a Free Trade Agreement. That same year, the Mexican government formally asked the U.S. government to start negotiations.

In 1991 the U.S. Congress approved fast track negotiations, and the United States, Mexico, and Canada initiated formal proceedings (Vega, 1991). These negotiations concluded in August 1992. In February 1993, the three governments initiated discussions of NAFTA's so-called labor and environmental side agreements. By the end of 1993, the congresses of all three countries had approved NAFTA, which came into force on January 1, 1994 (Arroyo, 1993; Grinspun, 1993). NAFTA is a free trade agreement and has no other juridical implications for the three signatory countries, such as a single currency, migratory unification, free labor mobility, or compensatory funds. Exceptions to the above are the labor and ecological side agreements, of which we will analyze only the former (Blanco, 1994).

NAFTA eliminates barriers to the movement of goods, services, and capital between Mexico, the United States, and Canada with the following exceptions. First, in order to enjoy reduced or eliminated tariffs, goods must qualify under NAFTA's rules of origin. Second, while most goods were exempted from tariffs immediately, in some cases tariffs or quotas would be phased out over a period of five, ten, or fifteen years. Third, there are special rules for textiles, cars, energy and basic petrochemicals, agriculture, land transport, telecommunications, and financial services. With regard to investment, NAFTA countries must give investors from all three countries national treatment and most-favored nation treatment. Capital from the three countries has no export or national content requirements, and public sector purchases are open to foreign investment from NAFTA countries (Fernández, 1993). Lastly, there are special rules regarding intellectual property (Kessel, 1994; Holter, 1993).

NAFTA's Labor Side Agreement, the North American Agreement on Labor Cooperation (NAALC), was created to watch over effective enforcement of labor laws in the three countries. NAALC was also signed with commitments to exchange information, publications, statistics, and research; to promote better working conditions and standards of living; and to establish eleven labor principles to protect, improve, and validate workers' rights, which will be analyzed below in Section 5 (Commission for Labor Cooperation, 1996; Fernández, 1993).

1. NAFTA, Productive Restructuring and Work Conditions

NAFTA has had two important immediate effects on Mexico. It helped to increase both the flow of foreign direct investment and manufactured goods
exports, which after the 1995 crisis became the main source of financing balance of payments deficits. NAFTA has also helped to increase input and fixed
asset imports for industry as well as consumption goods imports, which has
unbalanced the trade balance. Mexico had a severe financial and production
crisis at the end of 1994 and into 1995, followed by a strong recovery in gross
domestic product (particularly manufacturing) and finances from 1996. At
the end of 2000, a new productive crisis began. During the decade of the
1990s, the annual growth rates of gross domestic product (GDP) and per
capita GDP were 3.7 percent and 1.7 percent, respectively.

NAFTA probably has had an unequal effect on industrial firms in Mexico
(Ruiz Durán, 1998). The international competitiveness of firms already varied widely when the treaty came into effect, and industrial exports continue
to be the privilege of a limited number of firms in Mexico. This situation has
not changed since the great devaluation in 1995 that lowered the price of
Mexican products in other countries. Mexican exports are heavily concentrated in a few branches of industry and among a relatively small proportion
of firms. Since 1996, when exports shot up, 67.3 percent of all exported goods
belonged to three sectors: the auto and auto part industry, the electric and
electronic industry, and machinery and special equipment. Seven hundred
firms export 80 percent of the total, representing only 2 percent of the export-oriented firms. (In 1996 there were 27,924 export firms in Mexico out of
a total of 2,186,655 establishments of any type.)

Even before NAFTA, the industrial structure in Mexico was already extremely polarized. The socio-technical distance (technology, organization,
labor relations, and labor force profile) existing between industrial poles may
nevertheless have increased with the agreement (De la Garza, 1998).[1] Close to
10 percent of large-scale manufacturing establishments (with more than 250
workers) were restructured in 1994 (De la Garza and Melgoza, 1994). This
situation had not changed much toward the end of the 1990s, when the
manufacturing sector remained polarized. In Pole 1 we find NAFTA-favored
firms: firms with high or medium technology, where total quality and just-

in-time are only partially applied. These firms tend to have medium flexibility and low bilateral levels with labor unions, but they lack important links with the local area. Toyotaist work organization had been introduced into 2.7 percent of the establishments, but the combination of Toyotaism and Taylorism occurred more often (5.1 percent) and Taylorism prevailed followed by the traditional form of work organization (De la Garza, Salas and Torres, 2000).[2] In this Pole there are two types of labor force participants: the "restructured labor force," which is mainly male, middle-aged, with higher wages, qualifications, and job stability, and the "new labor force," characterized by a strong presence of young, female, low-wage workers with limited qualifications and high turnover. The socio-technical configurations that were not restructured are, on the one hand, medium and large industries with Taylorist-Fordist processes, and, on the other, micro, small and some medium firms with nonscientific administration of work.

With regard to the socio-demographic profile of manufacturing workers, in the 1990s they were mainly young men (although the number of men was already dropping) with some education who were heads of families (the women tended to be daughters of the family). According to ENESTYC (Encuesta Nacional de Empleo, Salarios, Tecnología y Capacitación)[3] the average worktime per week in the manufacturing sector in 1998 was forty-seven hours, irrespective of establishment size. This is consistent with data from the National Employment Survey that found that in 2000, 73.9 percent of those employed in manufacturing worked more than forty hours per week. Labor force burnout in the manufacturing industry does not come only from increased labor intensity but also from long hours (Table 1).

The population that does not work or that works less than fifteen hours per week, both in manufacturing and in the total employed population, is not very significant, nor has it varied substantially in the last nine years. A more severe problem relates to the surplus of working hours per week. In the year 2000, 25 percent of workers in manufacturing worked more than forty-eight hours, and in 91.8 percent of the cases this schedule was considered to be a normal worktime. In the last nine years, the worktimes per week that increased most in the manufacturing industry were those of workers working over forty-eight hours through overtime or double employment.

TABLE 1
Worktime per Week in the Manufacturing
Industry in the Year 2000

Workweek	Percentage of population employed
Does not work	2.7%
Less than 15 hours	4.8
Between 15 and 40 hours	18.6
More than 40 hours	73.9

SOURCE: INEGI (2001) Encuesta Nacional de Empleo, Aguas Calientes.

With regard to the wage profile, income levels in manufacturing are between one and two times the minimum wage, regardless of establishment
size. This data corresponds to the National Employment Survey (1998):
manufacturing workers received between one and two times the minimum
wage, the same as all wage workers. This survey also shows that the most frequent wage level does not change with the workers' qualification level
(except for unschooled workers and top professionals, all the other qualification levels have wage modes of between one and two times the minimum
wage, even though many studies consider five times the minimum wage to
be the poverty line in Mexico). Although social benefits averaged 24 percent
of total remuneration in the manufacturing industry, 42 percent of the employees in this sector did not have economic benefits in the year 2000.

The year 1994 saw the beginning of a broad policy of firms signing productivity agreements with labor unions. The Department of Labor (De la
Garza, 1997) promoted this policy as part of a campaign to promote the approval of NAFTA to such an extent that in 1994, productivity agreements
were included in 50.7 percent of all wage negotiations at the federal level
(equivalent to 78 percent of all hired workers at the federal level) (De la
Garza, 1995). In more recent years, however, the number of new agreements
has hardly grown (Samaniego, 1997). Global results related to workers' income were nevertheless discouraging. Some 90 percent of the agreements
signed in 1994 granted only a 2 percent increase for productivity, the same
percentage granted to minimum wages, with very limited effects on wages
(Ruiz Durán, 1998). Since 1995, the policy to recover real wages through productivity bonuses became neutralized in the face of 51.9 percent inflation,
and an average of only 1.2 percent productivity bonuses were granted

TABLE 2

Percentage of Manufacturing Workers According to
Qualification Level (1992)

Size	Qualified workers	General workers
Micro	22.7%	77.3%
Small	32.2	67.8
Medium	36.9	63.1
Large	36.8	63.2
TOTAL	33.4	66.6

SOURCE: INEGI (1992) ENESTYC.

(NAALC, 1998). Freer trade has not produced a positive correlation between the growth of real wages and productivity in the manufacturing industry. Negative real wage evolution cannot be attributed to low productivity in the manufacturing firms in Mexico.

With regard to the labor profiles, unskilled workers prevail in all strata of establishments of all sizes. The larger the firm, however, the higher the qualification level (Table 2). In 1999, 40.1 percent of the workers in the total manufacturing industry were skilled, and 59.8 percent of all workers were unskilled. In other words, although there was an increase in the number of skilled workers, unskilled workers continue to prevail.

To sum up, in the 1990s, the socio-demographic profile of the manufacturing labor force is young male workers with secondary school education who are the heads of families. In labor terms, unqualified workers with long work weeks and extremely low wages prevail. A high proportion of workers work in micro businesses (firms with fifteen workers or fewer). In the year 2000, 18.8 percent of the workers employed in manufacturing worked in micro businesses, and 19.7 percent worked in establishments without premises. The percentage of the total employed labor force working outside a shop or factory setting went from 8.2 percent in 1988 to 19.7 percent in the year 2000. Some 23 percent of the total wage and piecework workers in this branch worked off-site last year, and 33 percent of all wage earners in manufacturing had no written contract, whether individual or collective.

From previous research, we have also concluded that the Mexican productive apparatus is polarized between businesses that have modernized their

TABLE 3

Percentage of Women, Qualified Workers, Worktime per
Week in Hours among Manufacturing Workers

	Total manufacturing industry		Large establishments	
	1991	1999	1991	1999
Women	27.2	27.6	24.9	26.8
Training	32.9	6.46	39.3	7.9
Workweek	47	47	47	47

SOURCE: INEGI (1992, 1999) ENESTYC.

technology, work organization, or labor relations, and the vast majority of businesses that have not made important changes in the last ten years (De la Garza, 1993a). The labor force is more homogeneous with respect to labor and wages, but not in socio-demographic terms vis-à-vis business heterogeneity (Alarcón, 1994; Boltvitnik, 1998). We could refer to an old working class constituted by mature and relatively stable middle-aged, male, machine-specialized workers located in traditional production (who nevertheless have suffered personnel cutbacks because of privatizations and firm rationalization), and a new, young and unqualified working class with a high female presence and low employment stability, some of whom are employed in precarious jobs and others of whom are employed in vigorous modernized firms. This new working class is clearly the majority in the manufacturing industry, especially if you consider its presence in the maquila.

In general, the opening of markets, particularly in the wake of NAFTA, had important economic effects for Mexico before the present productive crisis started in November of 2000. Foreign investment inflows and manufacturing exports grew, but labor conditions (including worktime, wages and work qualifications) generally did not improve. The next section will analyze developments in the foreign capital and export firms and provide contrasts with the manufacturing sector in general.

2. Foreign Capital, Export Firms, and Labor Force

With regard to the differences between export and nonexport firms, as well as between national and foreign capital, we can state that:

1. Foreign firms have an important intra-firm exchange of commodities and a high content of foreign inputs (De la Garza, 1998).

2. With regard to technological levels, neither NAFTA nor opening to trade in general have translated into an expansion of the high technological level, although foreign firms had a slight advantage over national firms.

3. With regard to work organization, it would seem that the division of work in foreign firms tends to follow stricter Taylorist and Fordist schemes than national firms, perhaps because there is a greater presence of non-scientific administration in the latter, whereas foreign firms tend to formalize work in a Taylorist sense (De la Garza, Salas and Torres, 2000).

4. As far as flexibility levels are concerned, there do not seem to be differences between types of firms (De la Garza and Bouzas, 1998; Hernández Laos and Aboites, 1990).

5. With regard to wages, income is low in all types (De la Garza, 1998).

6. With regard to labor force, the only difference relates to the fact that workers in foreign firms are younger, with less seniority, and with a schooling level on the increase (De la Garza, 2001).

With regard to the variables related to the socio-technical bases of the productive processes that were considered, the condition of being a foreign or national firm was more significant than whether it was an export or nonexport firm. This situation is important when we consider that the firms with foreign capital in the manufacturing industry represent 22.4 percent of the employment in this sector. In this sense, NAFTA may be triggering changes in firms, but it is strongly adapting to the Mexican system of industrial relations, which is hardly protective of labor. Foreign firms in Mexico seem to arrive with Taylorist and Fordist organization schemes mixed in with partial applications of Total Quality and Just-in-Time, but which ultimately continue allocating low qualification tasks to the workers as opposed to the technicians and engineers. In this sense, the important change the labor force has experienced globally is not due to the creation of an important stratum of requalified workers, but to the inclusion of a young female labor force with a large external turnover, low wages, and low qualification levels.

All this is likely to help maintain a loop that can hardly be considered virtuous for industrial development. Large firms that are mainly export-oriented increasingly import their inputs and do not employ domestic out-

TABLE 4

Average Real Daily Wages per Employed Person,
1994 Baseline (in pesos)

Year	Average manu-facturing wages	Average contractual wages	Average wages in the maquila
1994	46.44	196.9	26.20
1995	39.05	102.2	23.6
1996	35.9	101.3	21.8
1997	36.6	83.9	22.95
1998	37.9	73.15	23.4
1999	39.12	64.8	23.3
2000	41.7	60.5	24.5
2001 Jan.–June	42.2	59.6	25.8

SOURCE: STyPS (2001) Labor Statistics (Estadísticas Laborales).

sourcing. The small and medium-size firms are thus not encouraged to modernize, change technology and organization, or work just-in-time or with acceptable quality levels. Nor does the loop close from the dissemination of the industrial districts and clusters. The maquila in the north is a clear example that productive chains and client and supplier chains in the country are not linked. In spite of the maquila's official discourse favoring clusters, domestic inputs have remained a very low proportion since the beginning of the current economic model in 1982.

NAFTA, however, has had a small positive effect on the growth of real wages and employment, particularly with regard to the latter. There have been positive correlation coefficients between real wages and exports to the United States and Canada in export-oriented industry. The global effect on the economy as a whole has nevertheless been small because of export specialization in a few branches and the disarticulation of productive chains in both wages and employment. Employment in the maquila grew, but it decreased in other manufacturing branches; the result was zero net employment growth. Although NAFTA's effect on wages has been positive in the branches that export more to the United States and Canada, the differences in wage levels are not so significant. Besides, NAFTA has not been an effective mechanism to increase manufacturing wages in a sustainable way. The economy's cyclical behavior manifests itself with very short periodicities: wages increased in real terms after large drops in 1995 and 1996, but did not reach the same level as in 1994 until the year 2001. Macroeconomic policies, as well as monetary policies to prevent inflation, have traditionally affected wage evolution in Mexico.

In the next section we will discuss some aspects of changes in labor relations in Mexico in these years. The discussion will focus on labor flexibility—that is, the ability of management to hire or lay off workers depending on conditions in the product market; multitasking and internal turnover; and linking part of workers' income to productivity. The decision to increase labor flexibility in the firms can be jointly decided by management and labor unions (bilateral) or decided only by management (unilateral).

3. Labor Relations

Under the new neoliberal economic model, characterized by deregulation of markets, privatization, and reduced importance of the state in productive investments (since 1982), labor and industrial relations have been through three different stages in Mexico (De la Garza, 2001):

1. *Unilateral flexibilization.* Between 1985 and 1992 there was a general trend toward flexibilizing labor relations, and the labor unions have lost power and play a diminished role in the development of labor and economic policies. During this period, some of the most important collective contracts were flexibilized (in aviation, oil, iron and steel, telephone, auto industry, for example), and flexibilization implied management's unilateralism in production-related decision-making. There was mainly numerical and functional flexibility, but not wage flexibility (De la Garza, 1990; Covarrubias, 1992; Contreras and Ramírez, 1992; Pozas, 1992; Montiel, 1991; De la O and Quintero, 1992; Rueda, 1993; Arteaga and Carrillo, 1990).

2. *Reaching agreements.* The second stage comprised the period from 1992 to 1994, when the government promoted productivity agreements including the bonus scheme as a way of recovering wages and a new notion of variable wages. During this stage, there was talk of a crisis in state corporatism, of the need for a new unionism allied with both the state and firms in the battle for competitiveness. This process officially started with the signature of the National Agreement for an Increase in Productivity and Quality (1992), through which, at least in discourse, it is recognized that labor unions should dialogue with management about modernizing their firms. This agreement de-

tails the government's proposal of carrying out a productivity agreement that takes ownership of the most current concepts of Total Quality, establishes a framework of bilaterality between firms and labor unions, and tries to design a whole model of industrialization (Quintero, 1993; De la Garza, 1993; Covarrubias and Lara, 1993).

The scope and impact of productivity agreements might differ according to the restructuring strategy the employers follow to carry out changes in technology, organization, or labor relations. When human resources management (HRM) is not understood as a core factor to increase productivity, it is likely that management will show little interest in bilateral agreements. Even when HRM is considered relevant, management may choose to sign agreements with little cooperation with unions, preferring to deal directly with the workers.

Productivity agreements can be classified into two types: active and passive agreements. In the former, the labor union fully participates in developing, implementing, and evaluating these plans. In relation to the productivity program, the labor union can participate in decision-making about aspects related to technology, organization, training, work conditions, work environment, measurement of productivity, and the determination of criteria to distribute economic benefits. Passive productivity agreements limit labor union action to merely accepting employer projects in exchange for preserving certain work conditions, and particularly incentives for productivity. In this case, the labor union does not participate in developing the corresponding plans or in defining productivity indicators. It is an instrumental agreement that does not actually modify labor relations between the firm and the union. In a few words, it sanctions employer "laissez faire" in exchange for supplementary income for the workers. Passive agreements prevail so far and are actually turning into agreements on bonuses for certain results in production, although many of them do not go beyond punctuality and attendance premiums.

3. *Limits of the "new labor culture."* The third stage of change in labor relations, from the middle of 1995 up to the present, first shows a buffering of the productivity agreement and bonuses strategy. This was caused by the economic crisis of December 1994 that considerably depressed real wages and neutralized the effects bonuses have on workers' income. However, to-

ward mid-1995, the Mexican Workers' Confederation (CTM) and one employers' confederation (COPARMEX) started negotiating a "new labor culture." These negotiations concluded in August 1996 and established that new relations between unions and employers must be no longer confrontational, but based on cooperation to win the fight for competitiveness. The resulting document incorporates the best-known doctrines of total quality and just-in-time. This may become an agreement of principles signed by both worker and employer organizations to change the Labor Law, something the Department of Labor has tried to take up under the Fox administration.

However, in the face of deteriorating work conditions, toward the end of 1997, some of the largest official labor unions (industrial, telephone, social security, and aviation workers) decided to break away from the Labor Congress and together with other independent unions, such as the National University Union and the Authentic Labor Front (FAT), created the National Workers' Union (Unión Nacional de Trabajadores/UNT). Since then, the UNT has been disputing the hegemony of what used to be known as official unionism. The other more radical current of independent unionism that created the First of May Coordination (Coordinadora Nacional Primero de Mayo) in 1995 initially managed to carry out a certain level of activity, but disputes among leftist groups led to its dissolution. Although the UNT has played an important role in public dialogue with the authorities during a period of growth shortly after its foundation, it has not managed to replace Labor Congress unions, particularly in the industrial sector, and essentially remains a confederation of modern service workers.

The most important change in labor relations in Mexico in the 1990s can be summarized by the trend toward work flexibility in large firms. This trend began in the mid-1980s and although it has not yet affected the Labor Law, NAFTA is likely to intensify it (Rodríguez, 1992). Productivity agreements with bonuses are more widely used. Most of them are not significant and constitute a sort of precarious Toyotaism imposed from the top, from the state, employer, and union leadership elites.

Collective contracts and labor law are the more important formal regulations of labor relations in Mexico. Collective contracts are changing in the direction of greater flexibility. Since NAFTA, there has also been pressure from business and government to increase the flexibility permitted in national labor laws. The argument is that businesses require higher productivity to compete in open markets, and the rigidities in present labor law inhibit productivity growth. The next section discusses proposed reforms in labor relations legislation in Mexico.

4. NAFTA and Labor Legislation

Although there is a current debate about the possible flexibility of the Mexican Federal Labor Law, it has not changed at all since 1970, as we shall see later on (De Buen, 1989). Before NAFTA, legislation and labor contracts in the three North American countries showed important differences (Cavazos, 1993). In contrast to the American and Canadian constitutions, the Mexican Constitution recognizes the right of both workers and employers to strike as well as to associate. Labor law in both Mexico and the United States has a federal jurisdiction, whereas in Canada there are eleven different legislative labor-related systems. With regard to union registration, a minimum of twenty workers is required in Mexico, but a union does not need to have the majority of the workers of a firm. Mexican unions do not have to go through certification before registration, nor is a secret ballot required. In union representation elections in Canada and the United States, unions must win a majority of the votes cast. In contrast to Canada and the United States, closed shops are frequently established in Mexican collective contracts and have been used as an instrument to intimidate opposition to union leadership.

In the United States, Canada, and Mexico, firms are not obliged to sign a labor agreement with a certified union. With regard to labor conflicts, most of the Canadian provinces have obligatory arbitration, whereas the United States and Mexico do not. In the United States and Canada, collective bargaining contracts are usually negotiated at the firm level. Although this is common in Mexico, some contracts may be signed at the industry level. In Canada and the United States, strikes during the term of a collective agreement may be prohibited by contractual language, whereas in Mexico they are not. During economic strikes in the United States and Canada, it is possible for employers to replace the strikers with nonunion workers, whereas replacement workers are not permitted in Mexico (NAALC, 1996).

With regard to working conditions, the Mexican law is more protective of employment stability, regardless of whether there is a verbal or written individual or collective contract. The law thus considers unjustified dismissal as a legal figure that may lead to reinstating or compensating the worker. In Canada and the United States, the employer is free to dismiss nonunionized workers, but workers can protest in court; arbitration measures including reinstatement with back pay are established only in collective contracts. In the United States, depending on the number of employees, a worker may be laid off without notice or compensation, unless these clauses are included in the collective contract. The work week in Canada varies according to province. The United States does not establish a maximum length for the work week. Mexico does: forty-eight hours per week. There are no minimum wages in Canada. Mexico and the United States do have minimum wages, although Mexico is way behind in relation to a survival income, which many estimate would be five times the minimum wage.

The most important differences between the contents of collective contracts in Mexico and those in the United States and Canada are that in Mexico the economic benefits, social security, and dispute resolution mechanisms are established in federal laws, whereas in the United States and Canada, they are sometimes contained in contracts (De la Garza, 1992).

Up to now, the labor laws in Mexico have not been modified. However, a debate on the need to flexibilize the labor law was started in 1988. Not only does it continue, but it has also intensified since NAFTA came into force. The first proposals to modify the law came from business organizations CONCANACO (trade businessmen) and COPARMEX (employers' union). The core point was labor flexibility, justified by the new context of market and production globalization, productive process modernization, the need to increase investor trust, and above all to increase productivity and quality (Bensunsan, 1995; De Buen, 1989).

The initial proposals, apart from limiting worker-employer conflicts, included the three classical aspects of work flexibility. With regard to *numerical* flexibility, they proposed reviewing the concepts of "lost wages" (days paid after a strike) and lay-off compensation, simplifying worker retirement, as well as a reformulation of the process of rescinding a contract. In relation to *functional* flexibility, they proposed flexibilizing the work week and establishing multiskilled qualification and productivity commissions. As far as *wage* flexibility is concerned, they suggested rethinking the concept of remunerative wages and redefining wages according to each firm's productivity and economic conditions. They propose reformulating the idea of economic benefits so that they depend on each firm's capacities, as well as introducing hourly wages. In relation to employer-employee disputes, they requested that solidarity strikes be banned, establishing the unions' responsibility if strikes were declared without merit and greater restrictions to strikes in public services.

In 1989, the worker caucus of the Partido Revolucionario Institutional (PRI) managed to get the Mexican Congress to carry out a popular consultation regarding possible modifications to the Federal Labor Law. The Labor Secretariat created a tripartite commission to develop a modification project, which did not issue any public results. Since then, employers have been demanding a new Labor Law, and labor unions have been divided into those opposed to any modification and those who accept modifications that do not affect the rights they have already gained, especially those that call for a new chapter on modernization and productivity (the Telephone Workers' Union and the Authentic Labor Front).

The employers' systematic proposal is contained in a document the employer organizations COPARMEX, CONCANACO, and CANACINTRA (industrial employers) presented to former president Ernesto Zedillo, then the PRI elected presidential candidate. The economic policy guidelines in this document include a section on labor. This document argues that in order to achieve higher competitiveness, it is necessary to change labor legislation. According to the employers, the main points to be modified would be:

1. Functional and geographic multiskilled mobility.
2. Temporary contracts per hour or with a reduced workday.
3. Rationalizing reasons to rescind a contract.
4. Limitations regarding responsibilities in labor lawsuits for the payment of lost wages.
5. Payment per hour.
6. Democratizing strikes: certifying through secret ballot that most of the workers agree to go on strike. The same procedure should be followed to call a strike off.
7. Disappearance of conciliation and arbitration councils.

8. Disappearance of law contracts that rule over a whole branch.

9. Establishing training contracts without implying a labor relation.

10. Putting an end to the blind wage scale and changing it for a capacity-based wage scale.

11. Establishing labor and union benefits according to each firm's conditions (thus challenging the way social security works in Mexico).

12. Eliminating the exclusion clause (closed shop) for union membership.

13. Freedom of unionization.

14. Apolitical unionism, putting an end to the relationship with political parties.

In this context, during the previous administration the National Action Party (PAN) presented its bill to reform the labor laws. The PAN project, developed by well-known lawyer Nestor de Buen, has two main innovative components. First, it considers labor flexibility in various aspects, essentially coinciding with COPARMEX's and CONCANACO's proposals. Second, it includes the democratization of worker organizations, which moves away from the proposals made by the government and the employer and worker elites.

With regard to labor flexibility, the PAN project changes basic labor rights principles that had prevailed in Mexico. It denounces the state's patronizing attitude toward the weakest part of the labor relationship and gives the state the new role of guarding the balance between production factors. In this framework, the goal of promoting employment and productivity replaces the goal of social justice as the primary guiding principle. In this sense, the bill introduces the notion of an apprentice contract with a trial period. It also reduces the costs of terminating employment and regulates outsourcing. With regard to inner flexibility, it specifies that work conditions can change upward or downward. It increases a firm's capacity to move its workers from one post to another, geographically and in their workdays and schedules. It particularly flexibilizes the distribution of time throughout the work week (which it suggests should be forty hours long) to the employer's convenience according to production needs. It stipulates that the worker is obliged to work overtime and on holidays if production so requires. This obligation, however, is not applicable to the weekly days of rest. In the wage scale, it privileges capacity over seniority. With regard to wage flexibility (wages according to productivity or quality), it does not propose one single form of wages, such as hourly wages, but rather opens possibilities for many different forms of payment in a clearer way than does the current law.

To sum up, the main flexibility characteristic the PAN bill proposes is employer unilaterality. In other words, except for the two cases that follow, it is a form of flexibility that does not imply coming to an agreement with the workers. The two exceptions where the workers must be taken into account are when technological or organizational changes affect employment. The technological or organizational changes that do not imply reducing the labor force remain within the realm of employer discretion. The other aspect subject to bilateralism relates to productivity and training programs that follow the current productivity agreement model promoted by the Labor Secretariat. This model notes that the employer must specify the goals and actions of these programs, as well as the productivity indicators, the type of information to be provided to the workers, and the amounts of the bonuses and training.

The other great innovation in the PAN project relates to the representativeness of worker organizations and their democratization. This theme has two core aspects: eliminating the registration of worker organizations at the Labor Secretariat with the workers being free to unionize or not, eliminating the exclusion clauses (closed shop), making it possible for collective contracts to coexist with individual contracts and opening channels for unionizing confidential workers (employees who carry out leadership and organization tasks); and eliminating the obligation to ratify work agreements at conciliation boards, which are replaced by social courts that are part of the judiciary branch.

The other important aspect of the democratization of worker organizations is the appearance of the category of Company Council as a body that is different from the unions and that in the project actually replaces the unions as signatories and supervisors of work agreements, and calls a strike if need be. In other words, unions are reduced to a sort of political current of free affiliation that can participate in the ballot lists at the Company Council elections, but do not represent the workers as such in collective bargaining. It is true that there is one exception, since the bill foresees negotiations articulated as an umbrella from branch to firm. At the branch level, the majority union would represent the workers.

The bill takes up the European experience of creating Company Councils that would represent all workers who are not managers, whether they are unionized or not. These committees would be expressing representative democracy through delegates with intense participation of the rank and file in assemblies and very strict surveillance of the electoral process. Besides, they democratize calling a strike by making the workers' assembly obligatory as a decision-making body. Conciliation is considered strictly voluntary. The Company Council calls a strike and can desist at any given moment. After a month on strike, either party can request a strike assessment. In the case of community service workers, a time deadline would be established. The principle that strikers cannot be replaced or that a minority continue working during a strike is preserved.

In August of 2001, under Vicente Fox's new administration, the Department of Labor created a commission (the Central Table on Decision-making) to develop a Labor Law bill. This commission includes the Labor Congress (CT) and employer organizations as well as UNT representatives. From the beginning of 2002 negotiations in the Central Table of Decision-making accelerated. The main points in discussion are: (1) For management and government, introduction in labor law of the concepts of multitasks and internal turnover, the contracts for training; the hourly pay; the flexibility in weekly worktime; prohibition of collective contracts for the economic branch; a pay scale based on abilitiy rather than seniority. (2) For independent unions, to take government out of the process of certification of unions; to establish the secret ballot for the election of union leaders; to change tripartite boards of conciliation for labor courts, to guarantee by law the right of the workers to know their collective contracts and the internal rules of their unions. On the other side, management pushes for the end of the union closed shop and the requirement that union members vote on whether or not to strike.

Mexico has not yet changed its labor laws. Pressure from employers and the government to flexibilize the labor laws has increased since NAFTA was signed. The main argument in favor of flexibilization is related to the need to gain competitiveness in order to export more and draw foreign direct investment.

ILO conventions ratified by the Mexican government have had a very slight influence in labor relations in Mexico, in part because union representatives are from the main corporatist confederation of workers and because ILO recommendations are only that. But NAFTA's Labor Side Agreement includes potential mechanisms of enforcement if there are violations in labor standards. In the next section, we discuss if this side accord helped to improve labor conditions in Mexico.

5. The Labor Side Agreement

As we pointed out in the introduction, in 1993 the U.S. government promoted the Labor Side Agreement (NAALC) (Smith, 1997). For different reasons, NAALC faced opposition from the large union organizations in Mexico and criticism from U.S. and Canadian union organizations. The Mexican unions argued that NAALC violated Mexican sovereignty. The U.S. and Canadian unions argued that it was not coercive enough, with the firms or countries infringing labor norms (Campbell, 1997; Ranney, 1997; Moncayo and Trejo, 1993; Puga, 1993). Through NAALC, the governments of the three countries are committed to promoting the following eleven principles, as well as to improving workers' work conditions and their standard of living:

1. Freedom of association and workers' rights to associate.
2. The right to collective bargaining.
3. The right to strike.
4. A ban on forced labor.
5. Restrictions on child labor.
6. Minimum work conditions.
7. Elimination of discrimination at work.
8. Equal wages for equal work among men and women.
9. Prevention of occupational injuries and diseases.
10. Compensation in case of occupational injuries and diseases.
11. Protection for migrant workers.

Organizationally, NAALC has the following structure: it is headed by the Side Labor Agreement Commission constituted by the labor ministers of the three countries, followed by the Secretariat with headquarters in Dallas, Texas, with a Director plus fifteen additional posts distributed trinationally. The Secretariat's role is to research, analyze, and inform. It is supported by

expert evaluation committees and, in case of complaints, by arbitration pan-
els. Finally, the agreement foresees the creation of a National Administrative
Office (NAO) for each country where NAALC-related complaints can be
lodged. Although complaints can be filed for violating any of these eleven
principles, sanctions are possible only in three cases: when there are systematic violations that affect the production of tradable goods and services
among the parties in terms of health and safety norms, child labor, and violation of minimum wage norms, according to standards established by each
country. Regarding the other cases, NAALC's job is to carry out studies,
seminars, and exhortations to the parties in the event of a complaint. In the
three areas deserving sanctions, the process starts at the Labor Ministers'
Council. If the Council does not reach a solution, a panel of experts is created to come up with a solution plan in sixty days' time. If this plan is not
possible, the defendant is requested to present a plan for action, and the
country where the violation was produced may be fined instead of the company. Should the country refuse to pay the fine, NAFTA benefits, up to a
maximum of $20 million per year, may be suspended (Commission for La-
bor Cooperation, 1996; Robinson, 1995).

So far, there have not been cases to go into or initiate the sanctioning
process. Complaints have focused on violation of the right to join a union
(70 percent of the twenty-four cases presented until 2001) in companies established in Mexico and in the United States. The small number of complaints should be noted. Most of them have implied alliances between independent unions in Mexico and the U.S. AFL-CIO. The violations that have
been reported have mainly fallen on companies in Mexico or Mexicans who
work in the United States (Steinberg and Vicario, 1997). In general, these alliances have been effective in protecting the freedom to unionize, not because of NAALC's coercive capacity, but because of the coalescence of civic
campaigns pressuring governments and companies, especially in the United
States (NAALC, 1997). Up to now, NAALC has not influenced Mexico from
a labor legislation perspective, nor can this be expected to happen. The public projects developed by PAN, PRD, the CT unions, or the new federal government do not include any international juridical dimension related to
NAALC in the contents of the new labor code.

Finally, we will discuss possible relationships between open markets and changes in unionism. For many decades, the dominant form of collective representation of Mexican workers has been the corporatist union, subordinated to government with an important function in political and labor control of workers. Many analysts consider these unions unrepresentative, undemocratic, and not interested in the productivity and quality of the companies. With the more open economy since NAFTA, some representatives of business organizations and the government proposed to transform the old corporatism into a new unionism that will be in alliance with management in the struggle for competitiveness, and may be more democratic and representative of workers to involve them in the goals of the companies.

6. Unions, Corporatism, and the New Administration

In 1978, Zazueta (1984) reported that there were 2,667,000 unionized workers in Mexico. In 1998 it was estimated there were 3,853,939 actively unionized workers—that is, workers who actually review their collective contracts. Another segment of the workers never change their collective contract and can be considered to belong to protection unions (i.e., fake unions). In 1998 the active unionization rate was 32.6 percent. The active unionization rate is estimated as the number of workers whose collective contracts are reviewed, divided by the total potentially unionizable waged workers (over fourteen years old and in companies with more than twenty workers). In 1995, according to ENESTYC, the INEGI survey,[4] an estimated 42.2 percent of the workers in the manufacturing industry were actively or passively unionized. If the unionization rate is measured in relation to the economically active population, this rate was 10.46 percent in 1978 and 11.68 percent in 1997. If the unionization rate has not dropped in Mexico, except with the great crisis of 1995, it is perhaps related to the role labor unions play in labor relations and in policies for the state.

In Mexico, close relations between labor unions and the state can be traced back to the end of the Mexican Revolution. They were strengthened with the official incorporation of the Confederations into the Party of the Mexican Revolution (the PRI antecedent) in 1938. The network of corporate relations in the good times (the 1960s were the golden years of union corporatism) implied that labor union leaders would occupy quotas of popular election and government posts; unions would intervene in tripartite bodies related to social security; unions would influence the government's labor policy; an expansion of collective bargaining and of the benefit system would be included in contracts; and there would be clientelistic relations with workers at a company level. Since the mid-1980s, spaces of labor union action have been reduced and have lost strength. They nevertheless continue supporting open economy and structural adjustment policies.

With the PRI having lost federal presidential elections, various alternatives opened up to the Fox administration regarding relations with the unions. The first alternative is to favor labor union freedom as set forth in Fox's campaign discourse, which would allow him to take action against "protection contracts" and state support to corporatism, as well as to promote a democratic reform to the Labor Law (secret ballot to elect leaders, banning closed shops, less governmental control over union registration, collective bargaining, and the right to strike). The second alternative, which is more moderate than the first one, favors respect for the existing legal framework with honest officers on the Conciliation Boards (where work conflicts are aired, including collective bargaining) and on the Register of Associations (which grants legal registration to unions). The third alternative is not to make great changes, which is what has happened with the PAN in states with PAN governors, such as Northern Baja California, where the PAN has gone into a modus vivendi with the corporate confederations, playing them off against one another, fighting against independent unions, and resorting to legal and extralegal mechanisms to create a sort of PAN corporatism interested in pleasing investors in the maquila.

Various options are also open to the CT unions. The first option is to continue blindly following the PRI, supporting PRI electoral and parliamentary campaigns, and expecting to win new elections. The second option is already being implemented by some large unions, such as the oil workers' and the teachers' unions: to create fronts with independent unions in an attempt to place themselves in a better position with regard to not losing union privileges and eventually dialoging with the new government. The third option is to join the UNT.

The UNT has already started to implement its only option: to show the new administration that they are the foundation of a new democratic and proactive unionism that takes into account the economy and company interests, and is concerned about productivity. The UNT's strategy moves from drawing CT unions to its field, to being in the center of a new social agreement based on productivity, legality, and democracy.

The large-scale employers that control most employer organizations may criticize corporatism for its corruption, lack of representativeness, and minimal interest in productivity. Nevertheless, that same corporatism permits them to pressure the government so that nothing changes except flexibility at the level of the labor law. They can even settle accounts with unions and workers by openly promoting antiunion and antilabor policies.

Not all these options are equally likely. Besides, the different options intertwine and come up with joint probabilities. The most likely joint probabilities can be reduced to two:

1. The Fox administration chooses to respect the legal framework more closely with regard to union registration, collective bargaining, and leader replacement, which will mainly favor the UNT and, should labor conflicts continue, they will create trouble for the Labor Congress and upset employers (the way the Department of Labor acted in a recent conflict in the Lázaro Cárdenas steel complex created this kind of reaction).

2. The government responds to complaints made by employers that feel threatened by both union democracy and attacks on corporatism, and would prefer these organizations remained roughly the same. The idea is for the government to play around with the Confederations and in part with the UNT without disturbing the power structure. This policy would favor the Labor Congress instead of the UNT (recent conflicts in maquilas in the north are examples of this strategy).

The policy choice provides the option of turning the Agreement for a New Labor Culture into the axis of the new administration's labor strategy. Abascal, the current Mexican Labor Secretary, was one of the initiators of this elitist corporate-style Agreement for a New Labor Culture, together with the CTM. Decisions are taken at the top, and once they have been approved, the rank and file is informed about them. Its impact on workers or company productivity has hardly been relevant because of the antidemocratic way in which it was subscribed, without involving the mass of workers or employers, and because of the lack of representation in the signature organizations. In other words, the alternative that the Abascal faction represents would imply reinstating corporate relations with official unions that would ensure control over the workers in exchange for dialoging and certain protections by the Department of Labor. Foxist corporatism would be a continuation of the old regime in the labor sphere, supported by employer organizations with little interest in union democracy and fearful of the danger of workers going beyond the limits of worker organizations.

Apart from ensuring the continuity of the labor issue, the Abascal faction can provide a new discourse: the re-emergence of the Christian right-wing discourse related to labor (that was suspended in the 1920s with the defeat of the "Cristeros"). It is a discourse that places the concept of an immutable human essence before the existence of workers and employers with differentiated interests. This discourse places human dignity, essence, and spiritual nature before conflicts of interests. The social sciences left behind this concept of human essence over a century ago, replacing it with the notion of the socially and culturally constructed subject. The concept of a constructed subject and not a subject given by the spirit or by nature is followed by the notion of the existence of multiple subjects that may have contradictory interests regardless of their reaching different agreements. The right-wing Christian concept opposes Marxist, socialist, and laborist currents, as well as business unionism, owing to which the contradiction of interests between capital and work cannot be solved in a definitive way. In this sense, the workers must not be understood as a cost to be minimized, but as individuals with dignity. This ideology, however, fails when faced by the reality principle Foxism has established, since the struggle against inflation and the attraction of foreign direct investments will require contained wage increases as in neoliberal times. The conservative Christian doctrine regarding labor relations thus veils the work crisis in Mexico (crisis in the capacity to survive by selling one's labor, which is increasingly labor-intensive, a disaffection reflected in high voluntary labor turnover). Its effectiveness in the Mexican context is expected to be limited.

What is certain is that discussion on the new Federal Labor Law has been resumed. It is now based on Christian principles, such as those aforementioned: the UNT is in favor of its democratizing and anticorporate reform with chapters on flexibility and productivity. The CT unions and some independent unions, such as the Mexican Electric Workers' Union (SME, which in spite of belonging to the CT, behaves as an independent union), see dangers in reviewing the Labor Law. The former see dangers for corporatism and the latter see dangers regarding their possible flexibilization. The independent unions that used to belong to what was known as the First of May Coordination would be against any changes to the Law. Yellow unions (i.e., unions directly controlled by the employers) in keeping with their tradition of not getting involved in politics would hardly participate. The Fox administration might favor flexibilizing the law and some democratizing reforms. Faced by the threat of union democratization, employers would only bet on flexibilization. Although the PAN would support Foxist reforms, it would not necessarily support the bill Fox presented at the Chamber of Senators two years ago. The PRD would be divided between a minority that accepts the reforms of the PRD bill, which was not approved, and a majority reluctant to accept any reform. The PRI could work with the corporate unions.

However, these are not all the actors that might emerge. There are also the ordinary workers who have personally suffered the Labor Crisis and might prefer alternatives to the options the leaders have offered. To what extent will the impression of a state that no longer controls worker organizations, unions without support from the state, a weakened PRI, and divided official leaders instil trust in the workers or initiate a period of conflict?

Conclusions

Throughout its short life, NAFTA has constantly influenced the behavior of the economy and labor and industrial relations in Mexico (Morris, 1997; Morales, 1998). The opening of the economy not only has helped increase exports but also has increased difficulties in the balance of payments current account balance. Although exports have increased for several years, import growth has been larger, producing growth with a current account deficit. In 1994 foreign direct investment (FDI) started to flow in larger amounts than portfolio investments but following the crisis in December 1994 dropped considerably until 1996. In other words, although NAFTA has favored the entry of foreign productive capital, it is affected by other macroeconomic factors, such as the demand for manufactured goods in the United States, the overvaluation of the peso, and the political crises—to such an extent that this agreement on its own is not enough to ensure massive capital inflow. On an immediate level, the opening of the economy has not generated employment in a significant way, nor has it had positive global effects on wages. It is likely that the companies' rationalization policies to gain competitiveness, as well as the state's policies that consider wages as a macroeconomic adjustment variable, and the kind of exchange that takes place between the state and the labor unions, continue being important factors influencing wages and employment (Littleheale, 1995).

On the other hand, the Mexican productive apparatus has always been extremely heterogeneous, and since the deregulation and opening of the economy, particularly the signature of NAFTA, most companies have not been in condition to export, to such an extent that this capacity is still concentrated in a few hands (around seven hundred firms in the industrial sector). Besides, there have not been important productive links to draw small and medium firms to the larger companies via outsourcing. The fact that these companies are export firms does not imply that Mexican labor standards are leveling with standards in the United States and Canada, although the most dynamic branches, such as the auto industry, do tend to equalize productivity and quality levels. We should also take into account that foreign companies that set up in Mexico or Mexican companies that have become export-oriented may not have labor relations strategies that imply bilaterality with the unions, but are instead based on unilateral flexibilities and low wages (Henk, 1995) and that the political system still overdetermines industrial relations, which inhibits other types of transformation on the shop floor. If flexibility adopts a diversity of forms and contents in Mexico, this is mainly due to the different employer modernization strategies (leaving aside the flexibility forms existing before the current productive restructuring). Although there may be different strategies of this sort, we can summarize them in two main strategies:

1. To gain competitiveness and productivity through new work organization, goals that somehow imply flexibility and cultural change. This strategy, however, currently faces the confirmation that flexibility is established and

the workers are asked to get involved in and identify with the company's aims. But training is lacking, decision-making power has not been delegated to the workers, wages are low, and labor is high-intensity.

2. The second strategy assimilates the notion of flexibility as unilateral deregulation favoring the firm with low wages.

The two forms of flexibility prevailing in Mexico face important contradictions, potential tensions, and a gap between one discourse and another, particularly the Toyotaist discourse and reality (Buroway, 1985; Wood, 1991, 1993).

The trends toward flexibilization are real, but the unilateral employer form still prevails and the possibility of reaching agreements with the unions in the workplace is more rhetoric than real (with a few exceptions) (Tolliday, 1992). In fact, export firm modernization has not been as dramatic as could have been expected, perhaps because low wages are still a comparative advantage in many of these firms. Export firms with low wages, a poorly qualified labor force, and a relatively good schooling level with intermediate technologies and partial application of total quality and just-in-time, particularly low worker participation with productivity bonus plans the workers consider unattractive, and low bilaterality with unions would seem to be based on low wages and intensive work rationalization, rather than on the creation of a sort of post-Fordism or lean production. Productive restructuring in Mexico is real, but follows its own path, dependent on employer strategies, a specific institutional context, public policies and labor markets, labor relations, unions and cultures of all these actors with their own specific characteristics (Hernández, 1998). Taylorism-Fordism with partial aspects of total quality and just-in-time, all this with a work division that continues segmenting the operative tasks on the floor from conceptual tasks. That is why restructuring in general is not accompanied by higher qualifications or training levels among workers, but changes the labor force profile from the old working class with low schooling levels, empirical qualification in the use of machinery, middle-aged males with seniority and low wages to a new labor force that is young, female, with high external turnover, low qualifications, and also low wages.

The years under NAFTA in Mexico have proven that labor standards do not simply depend on increasing marginal productivity, since it has grown more in the Mexican manufacturing industry than in the United States. In Mexico, it is still essential for the state to be present in the definition of labor relations. The new Fox administration has made attempts to reconstruct the old-style corporate agreement based on employer, union, and government elites. It has tried to make this agreement on productivity, flexibility, and a so-called new labor culture without insisting on freedom and democracy in the unions. Particularly in relation to wages, it is the state that has placed parameters on wage increases through minimum wages. Although contracted wages have gone up more than inflation since 1999, in real terms they continue to be lower than wages in 1994. On the other hand, the unions have not been capable and perhaps have not been truly interested in modernizing company organization or in dialogues about productivity. It is true that union participation has increased, but we are far from witnessing a widespread change in union policies. Labor union corporatism seems more interested in reaching a new agreement at the top than in becoming an authentic representative of the workers. The impact of the new UNT unionism has been very limited so far, and this organization has not managed to penetrate the maquila's central sector. To summarize, neither the employers nor the state, and far less the unions, seem to be setting out to democratize labor relations in Mexico. It is likely that we will have to wait for the political system to go through greater transformation first, before we can impact labor relations at the firm level.

State corporatism of course has not died. It manifests itself in very old themes, such as the support by government's economic policies, particularly wage limits, and the network of commitments among employers, union leaders, and government officials at a middle and micro level to ensure labor peace with low wages. If we could say there are innovations in corporate unionism, they would be the agreement for a new labor culture, which gave continuity to the Salinista new unionism. In cultural terms, this corporatism has not changed. It is still characterized by vertical structure, lack of democracy, the rank and file delegating decisions and their lack of participation in decision-making, clientelism (although it has been curbed because there are fewer resources to share), and paradoxically the subordination to the policies of a state that is no longer controlled by the PRI. On the other hand, although all the large confederations hold different currents of opinion, they negotiate productivity with the firms without confronting the stagnated national leadership. Only a minority participates in these currents of opinion, and they have had an extremely low repercussion on workers' incomes. Besides, the union elites have levels of authoritarianism nobody dares challenge.

The deepest labor reality, that which comes from the way work is carried out, has nonetheless been transforming. The 1990s gave rise to a new working class as such. It is younger, female, with low wages and low qualification levels, high turnover, without a union tradition although it is clustered in protection unions, particularly, with a labor and union culture that differs from that of the working class during times of stabilizing development. This class with fewer corporate traditions has hardly made its collective presence felt. In any case, it has filed individual complaints or left work, migrated, thus adopting new forms of sociability, clothing styles, music, ways of seeing the country, and perhaps hardly participating in unions, although a large proportion is actually unionized.

The UNT, on whom so much hope had been placed, has only walked paart of the way. The unions that gave birth to the UNT have a very important social and union capital: the telephone workers' capacity to negotiate productivity and restructure firms, the Social Security Union's defense of social security, the FAT's experience in international relations of a new type, the experience of the Sindicato de Trabajadores de la Universida Nacional Autómo de México (STUNAM) in union independence. This wealth of experience summed up in the UNT's programs has nevertheless not translated into concrete struggle tactics.

The situation the UNT is experiencing is, in part, due to its real or imagined relations with the state. Undoubtedly, the government was not pleased to see the foundation of the UNT, but the UNT has been trying not to confront the state too bluntly. This is due not only to the personalities and ambitions of the UNT leaders but also to the fact that the Mexican state continues to be highly centralized in union decisions. A part of the UNT would thus seem to be constantly flirting with the state so as to be seen as an alternative favored from the top, as happened during the Salinas administration. Considering not only the centralized role of wage and economic policies but also the governmental control over union registration, the right to strike and collective bargaining, this flirtation has a cost.

The UNT unions have established new international relations, there are new social movements, and the influence of NGOs related to human and labor rights is spreading. In other words, this sort of neo-Lombardism (Lombardo was a Mexican Marxist leader who justified the CTM's alliance with the state in the 1930s), which looks for the state's approval in order to know what to do and with whom to ally, implies a limitation on UNT possibilities. In this sense, the disciplinary role played by economic policy and wage limits also applies to the UNT unions and thus leaves workers with a choice between keeping their source of work and employment and going for wage increases.

On the other hand, competition between the leadership of the three largest UNT unions: STUNAM (university workers), STIMSS (social security workers), and STRM (telephone workers) has led the more proactive parts to put aside their insistence on a new union strategy. The UNT has thus taken up the most basic aspect of independent unionism: denunciation as the core aspect of practice during the last year. This reduction of union strategy to its most rudimentary aspect partly demonstrates that the union cultures that come from official unionism have not been repaired within the UNT. Elite decisions regarding tactics and strategy, delegating power to leaders without counterweights, and clientelism are part of the life of a large number of unions. Besides, there is the influence of the struggle for power within the UNT, not so much because there are different projects, although the large unions do express differentiated strategic practices, but because the different unions of which it is composed are after leadership hegemony. Added to this, there is the temptation of making alliances with parties at the level of the political system, which divide the UNT unions between the PRD and the PRI. Lastly, the interesting initiative to create the Social Workers Movement (MST in Spanish), as a political association in search of nonlabor allies and union hegemony in the masses with the aim of creating a different national project has remained on paper, with no practical outcomes whatsoever (in spite of the fact that the MST supported the PRD during the last elections). This situation can be explained by the need to find a balance within the UNT itself: If one of the unions stands out more than the others, this upsets the correlation of forces and endangers the organization's integrity. It also challenges the UNT alliance policy, which implies that political opportunities and alternatives for the country become more important than the unions' priorities. National politics and the labor sphere continue overlapping intimately. The UNT unions that dared break away from the Labor Congress and state their stance in relation to the Coordination have not done the same in relation to the government and the political parties or have not done so with clarity.

Notes

1. Here production is considered high technology level when central labor processes in an establishment use automatic and/or microelectronic reprogramming technology; medium level when the productive process is mechanized but not automated; and low when it is based on the use of tools.

2. Taylorism, Fordism and Toyotaism are forms of work organization. Taylorism is characterized by a division between conception and operation in the labor process, standardization, simplification, and measuring the operations of the workers in each task. Fordism adds the assembly line to Taylorist principles. Toyotaism, inspired by Japanese experiences, considers multitasking, involvement and participation of workers in decision-making, and supposedly a new labor culture and identification with work and company.

3. National Survey of Employment, Wages, Technology and Training, with a sample of five thousand establishments, representative by size and sector.

4. INEGI = Instituto Nacional de Estadística Geografía e Informática (National Institute of Statistics, Geography and Informatics).

Bibliography

Alarcón, D. 1994. *Changes in the Distribution of Income in Mexico and Trade Liberalization*. Tijuana: El Colegio de la Frontera Norte.

Arroyo, A. 1993. *Impactos regionales de la apertura comercial*. Guadalajara: UdeG–UCLA.

Arteaga, A., and V. J. Carrillo. 1990. "Automóvil: hacia la flexibilidad productiva." *El Cotidiano* 21: 25–38.

Bensunsan, G. 1995. "La propuesta panista de un nuevo modelo de regulación laboral." *La Jornada,* 28.

Blanco, H. 1994. *Las negociaciones comerciales de México con el mundo*. México: FCE.

Boltvitnik, J. 1998. "Pauperización." *La Jornada,* Oct. 16.

Buroway, M. 1985. *The Politics of Production*. London: Verso.

Campbell, B. 1997. "NAFTA and the Canadian Labor Market." *Momento Económico* 92 (July–Aug.): 25–30.

Carrillo, J. 1993. *Condiciones de empleo y capacitación en las maquiladoras de exportación en México*. Tijuana: México Secretaria del Trabajo y Previsión Social y El Colegio de la Frontera Norte.

Cavazos, B., et al. 1993. *Estudio comparativo entre las legislaciones laborales de Estados Unidos y Canadá y el derecho del trabajo mexicano*. México: Trillas.

Commission for Labor Cooperation. 1996. *Annual Report*. Dallas: NAALC.

Contreras, O., and M. A. Ramírez Sánchez. 1992. "Mercado de trabajo y relaciones laborales en cananea, la disputa en torno a la flexibilidad." *Trabajo* 8: 20–36.

Covarrubias, A. 1992. *La flexibilidad laboral en Sonora*. Hermosillo: El Colegio de Sonora.

Covarrubias, A., and B. Lara. 1993. *Relaciones industriales y productividad en el norte de México: tendencias y problemas*. México: Fundación Friedrich Ebert.

De Buen, N. 1989. *La flexibilidad en el derecho del trabajo*. México: Fundación Ebert.

De la Garza, E. 1990. "Reconversión industrial y cambios en el patrón de relaciones laborales en México." In Anguiano A., comp., *La modernización de México*. México: UAM-X.

———. 1992. "El tratado de libre comercio y sus consecuencias en la contratación colectiva." *El Cotidiano* 48: 15–20.

———. 1993. "Reestructuración productiva y respuesta sindical en América Latina." *Sociología del Trabajo* 19: 1–20.

———. 1993a. *Reestructuración productiva y respuesta sindical en México*. México: IIEc.-UNAM.

———. 1993b. "Reestructuración del corporativismo en México: Siete Tesis." *El Cotidiano* 50: 10–20.

———. 1995. "Cogestión, calidad total y sistema de relaciones industriales." In *Competitividad vs democracia industrial*. México: Fundación Ebert.

———. 1997. "La flexibilidad del trabajo en América Latina." *Revista Latinoamericana de Estudios del Trabajo* 5: 80–92.

———, coord. 1998. *Modelos de industrialización en México*. México: UAM-I.

———. 2001. *La formación socioeconómica neoliberal*. México: UAM.

De la Garza, E., and A. Bouzas. 1998. *Contratación colectiva y flexibilidad del trabajo en méxico*. México: IIEc.

De la Garza, E., and J. Melgoza. 1994. "Estrategias sindicales y productividad en México." Paper presented at the meeting "Inequalities and New Forms of Popular Representation in Latin America." New York: Columbia University.

De la Garza, E., C. Salas, and J. Torres. 2000. *La organación laboral flexible*. Mexico, D.F.: Secretaría del Trabajo.

De la O Martínez, M. E., and C. Quintero. 1992. "Sindicalismo y contratación colectiva en las maquiladoras fronterizas: los casos de Tijuana, Ciudad Juárez y Matamoros." *Frontera Norte* 8 (El Colegio de la Frontera Norte, July): 1–35.

Fernández, R., ed. 1993. *Sectorial Labor Effect of North American Free Trade.* México: ITAM.

Grinspun, R., ed. 1993. *The Political Economy of North American Free Trade.* New York: St. Martin's.

Henk, T. 1995. *Globalization.* London: Zed.

Hernández Laos, E., and J. Aboites. 1990. *Identificación de los factores que obstaculizan la movilidad de la mano de obra en el sector industrial mexicana.* México: STyPS.

Hernández, T. 1998. "La Organización 6 de Octubre en la Maquiladora Hang Young de Tijuana, Baja California." Paper presented at the II Congreso Nacional de la AMET, Jalapa, Ver., Oct. 28.

Holter, D., ed. 1993. *Beyond the Free Trade Debate: Labor's Future in California and Mexico.* Los Angeles: UCLA.

Kessel, G., comp. 1994. *Lo negociado del TLC.* México: McGraw Hill.

Littleheale, J. S. 1995. "National Trade Union Federations, Labor Standards and Social Clauses: The Political Economy of North American Integration." University of North Carolina at Chapel Hill: Mimeo.

Middlebrook, K. Y. C. Quintero. 1998. "Las juntas de conciliación y arbitraje en México: registro sindical y solución de conflictos en los noventa." *Estudios Sociológicos* 16, no. 47 (May–Aug.): 1–40.

Moncayo, P. P., and R. Trejo. 1993. *Los sindicatos mexicanos ante el TLC.* México: SNTE.

Montiel, Y. 1991. *Organización del trabajo y relaciones laborales en VW.* México: Cuadernos de la Casa Chata.

Morales, J. C. 1998. "Cadenas productivas y empresas del vestido en Ciudad Juárez, Chihuahua." Paper presented at the II Congreso de la AMET, Jalapa, Ver., Oct. 28–30.

Morris, J. T. 1997. "The Strategic Terrain for Independent Union Organizing in Mexico's Autoparts Sector." Twentieth International Congress of LASA. Guadalajara, April 17.

NAALC. 1996. *La legislación laboral de México: canadá y estados unidos.* Dallas: ACLAN.

———. 1997. *Cierre de empresas y derechos laborales.* Dallas: ACLAN.

———. 1997a. *Los mercados de trabajo en América del Norte.* Dallas: ACLAN.

———. 1998. *Ingresos y productividad en América del Norte.* Dallas: ACLAN.

———. 1998a. *Los mercados de trabajo en América del Norte: un análisis comparativo.* Dallas: ACLAN.

Pozas, M. de los A. 1992. *Reestructuración industrial en Monterrey*. México: Fundación Ebert.

Puga, C. 1993. *Organizaciones empresariales y tratado de libre comercio*. Facultad de Ciencias Políticas y Sociales: UNAM.

Quintero, C. 1993. "Tendencias sindicales en la frontera norte de México." *El Cotidiano* 56: 25–30.

Ranney, D. 1997. "NAFTA and Devalorization of Labor Power: A U.S. Perspective." *Momento Económico* 92 (July–Aug.): 30–40.

Red Mexicana de Acción Frente al Libre Comercio. 1997. *Espejismos y realidades: el TLC tres años después*. México: RMAFLC.

Robinson, I. 1995. "The NAFTA Labor Accord in Canada: Experience, Prospects, and Alternatives." *Connecticut Journal of International Law* 10, no. 2 (spring): 475.

Rodríguez, E. 1992. "Crisis, reestructuración y flexibilidad." *Estudios Sociales, Revista de investigación del noroeste* 4, no. 6 (July–Dec.): 60–72.

Rueda, I., et al. 1993. *Tras las huellas de la privatización, el caso de Altos Hornos de México*. México: Siglo XXI.

Ruiz Duran, C. 1998. "Empleo, productividad y salarios dentro del TLC: el caso de México, un análisis multisectorial." In NAALC (1988) Seminario sobre Ingresos y Productividad en América del Norte. Dallas: Feb. 26–27.

Samaniego, N. 1997. "Cambio tecnológico, competencia comercial y transformación en el entorno de la empresa en México." In NAALC Seminario sobre Ingresos y Productividad en América del Norte. Dallas: NAALC, Feb. 26–27.

Smith, R. 1997. "An Early Assessment of the NAFTA Labor Side Accord." Meeting of IRRA, New Orleans, Jan. 4–7.

Steinberg, J., and E. Vicario. 1997. "A Discussion Paper Based on the Report: North America Labor Markets." *Momento Económico* 91 (May–June): 18–30.

Tolliday, S. 1992. *Between Fordism and Flexibility*. London: Berg.

Vega, G. 1991. *México ante el libre comercio con América del Norte*. México: El Colegio de México.

Wood, S. 1991. "Japonization and or Toyotaism." *Work Employment and Society* 5, no. 4.

———. 1993. "The Japonization of Fordism." *Economic and Industrial Relations* 14.

Zazueta, C. 1984. *La estructura del congreso del trabajo*. México: Fondo de Cultura Económica.

Index

International Labor Education and Research Fund v. Bush, 128
International Labor Organization (ILO): codes of conduct and workers' rights, 207–14, 218, 221; conventions, 17–25, 29–30, 32, 35–36, 38–39, 45–48; decent work and developing world, 61–63, 64–67, 72–75; form follows function, 179–205; international competitive advantage, 15, 17–39, 45–49, 52–55; introduction, 2–9, 12, 129–78; labor law for a global economy, 84–85, 91, 93, 95, 99–103, 108–9, 113, 118–20, 123–24, 126; limitation of ILO approach to current world working conditions, 187–88; need for international labor standards, 130–36; new initiatives, 180–87
International labor standards: case for, 136; formulations of, 179–205; need for, 129–78; seven fundamental ILO conventions, 13; uneasy case for, 81–128; *see also specific standards*
International Longshoreman's Association, 98
International migration, 2
International Monetary Fund (IMF), 6, 55, 66, 68, 86, 133
International Trade Organization (ITO), 148
Intracompany loans, 55
Investments, 16, 90, 94
IPEC, *see* ILO Program on the Elimination of Child Labor
Iran, 50
Iraq, 50
Ireland, 50
Irian Jaya, 142
Israel, 50
Italy, 50, 83, 86
ITO, *see* International Trade Organization

Jacksonville Bulk Terminals, Inc. v. International Longshoremen's Association, 122

Jamaica, 50, 70, 93
Japan, 50, 84, 86, 94, 97, 134
JCPenney, 110
Jewish countries, 25
John Doe v. Unocal, 116
Jordan, 50, 72, 106, 132
Just-in-Time, 234

Kenya, 30, 50, 53, 70, 88
"Know your rights" training, 218
Korea, 50, 88–89, 98, 134
Kuwait, 50, 119

Labor conditions: determinants, 26–29; international competitive advantage, 19–26; ratification, 19–26. *See also specific conditions*
Labor Congress (Mexico), 11, 244, 246, 248–49, 251
Labor cost (compensation) analysis, 29–35
Labor costs, 16, 20, 29, 39, 45–46
Labor force quality and price, 42–6
Labor law, for a global economy, 81–128. *See also specific aspects of labor law and specific cases*
Labor market outcomes, 2, 5
Labor Side Agreement, NAFTA, 12, 245–47
Labor Union of Pico, Korea, Ltd. v. Pico Products, 98, 121, 128
Labor unions, 67–68
Lack of jobs, 88
Latin America, 12, 70
Law, *see specific aspects of law and specific cases*
"Law-making," 183
Lázaro Cárdenas steel complex, 249
League of Nations, 17, 84
Leary, Virginia A.: biography, vii, 1; introduction, 8–10; text, 179–205
Lesotho, 50
"Let-Them-Eat-Cakers," 106
Levi-Strauss, 110, 135, 146
Levin, Sander, 107, 109
Liberia, 50

Lightning Source UK Ltd.
Milton Keynes UK
UKHW042133180219
337468UK00007B/326/P